Praise for
The Authentic Heart: An Eightfold Path to Midlife Love
by John Amodeo, Ph.D.

"*The Authentic Heart* is a groundbreaking, insightful, warmly written book that I highly recommend to anyone wanting more loving, joyful relationships. John Amodeo is a thoughtful and heartfelt writer who addresses with great clarity, wisdom, and practicality the key steps that are necessary for building authentic, mature, loving connections—not only with others, but also with oneself."

—John Bradshaw, author of *Healing the Shame That Binds You*
and *Bradshaw on the Family*

"Just what millions want to know—not only how to make love last, but how to make lasting love new again and again. This warmhearted and clear-headed book is full of practical wisdom."

—Gay Hendricks, Ph.D., and Kathlyn Hendricks, Ph.D.,
authors of *Conscious Loving* and *The Conscious Heart*

"*The Authentic Heart* offers practical, wise, and compassionate guidance for midlife love."

—Jack Kornfield, author of *A Path with Heart*
and *After the Ecstasy, the Laundry*

"John Amodeo is a master guide for the relationship path. His knowledge and love pour through this book on every page. With the aid of this book's grounded wisdom, we can untangle the knots of our own making and find our way clear in any relationship of significance, no matter how challenging it might be."

—Jacquelyn Small, author of *Awakening in Time*
and Director of Eupsychia Institute

"If you ever have a thought of wishing you were younger, run, don't walk, to pick up this book. Open to any page and you will find the life-affirming wisdom that will allow you to celebrate yourself."

—Jordan Paul, Ph.D., coauthor of *Do I Have to Give Up Me
to Be Loved by You?*

"*The Authentic Heart* is a beautifully written, hope-filled celebration of spiritually rich intimacy. If that's what you are seeking, you must read this book."
—Judith Sherven, Ph.D., and James Sniechowski, Ph.D.,
authors of *The New Intimacy* and
Opening to Love 365 Days a Year

"John Amodeo is a brilliant writer. With breathtaking clarity and simplicity, he makes the enduring truths of conscious relationships fully accessible to contemporary readers. His penetrating insights illuminate the path to deep love and intimacy."
—William Collinge, Ph.D., cofounder of The Intimacy
& Healing Project and author
of *The American Holistic Health Association Complete
Guide to Alternative Medicine*

"Full of warmth and wisdom, this book inspires us to let go of the illusions of youth, learn from the lessons life has taught us thus far and begin again with a renewed sense of humility and compassion."
—Susan Campbell, Ph.D., author of *The Couple's Journey*,
Getting Real, and *From Chaos to Confidence*

"John Amodeo is the most thoughtful writer on relationships that I know. I recommend this book to anyone seeking insight and solutions to relationship issues."
—Dr. Jim Dreaver, author of *The Ultimate Cure* and *The Way of Harmony*

The Authentic Heart

An Eightfold Path
to Midlife Love

John Amodeo, Ph.D.

John Wiley & Sons, Inc.

New York • Chichester • Weinheim • Brisbane • Singapore • Toronto

Published by John Wiley & Sons, Inc.
Published simultaneously in Canada

Grateful acknowledgement is made to the following:

"To the Tune 'Glittering Sword Hilts'" by Lui Yu Hsi from *One Hundred More Poems from the Chinese* by Kenneth Rexroth. Copyright © 1970 by Kenneth Rexroth. Reprinted by permission of New Directions Publishing Corporation.

From *Letters to a Young Poet* by Rainer Maria Rilke. Copyright © 1934, 1954 by W. W. Norton & Co. Inc, renewed © 1962, 1982 by M. D. Herter Norton. Reprinted by permission of W. W. Norton.

From *The Collected Poems of W. B. Yeats, Revised Second Edition*, edited by Richard J. Finneran. Copyright © 1934 by Macmillan Publishing Company, copyright renewed © 1962 by Bertha Georgie Yeats. Reprinted by permission of Simon & Schuster.

From *Tao Te Ching* by Lao Tzu, translated by Stephen Mitchell. Translation copyright © 1988 by Stephen Mitchell. Reprinted by permission of Harper-Collins Publishers.

From *The Prophet* by Kahlil Gibran. Reprinted by permission of Alfred A Knopf, a division of Random House.

ISBN 0-471-38757-6

Printed in the United States of America

10 9 8 7 6 5 4 3 2 1

This book is dedicated to

Steven Ruddell, a man with a wise, kind heart, whose love, caring, and encouragement over the past twenty-five years have taught me the meaning and value of true friendship.

My dear mother, whose warm and loving presence blessed me with a good start in life.

Awakening the heart of each reader.

Contents

❦

The Fifth Step: Practice Self-Soothing and Self-Connection

The Sixth Step: Respect Others through Kind Conversation

The Seventh Step: Build Trust through a Process Commitment

The Eighth Step: Deepen Your Understanding of Love and Sexuality

Acknowledgments

❦

My deepest appreciation to friends and colleagues who gave valuable feedback and encouragement.

Special thanks to Maggie Kline, Louise Robinson, Soretta Rodack, and Fred Zarro for their caring, detailed attention to the manuscript.

I also appreciate the valuable help with different parts of the manuscript given by Sue Amodeo, Lynn Bergman, Anata Carney, Ann Weiser Cornell, Linda Cunningham, Deborah Hill, Robert Leverant, Peter Levine, Malcolm Miller, Steven Ruddell, and Ernie Sherman.

Many thanks to my literary agent, Stephanie Tade at the Jane Rotrosen Agency, who recognized the value of my work.

My deep gratitude to Tom Miller, my caring and attentive editor at John Wiley & Sons, who made the birth of this book possible.

I want to express heartfelt appreciation to the many other friends, mentors, and teachers who have supported and inspired me over the years. Prominent among them are Bob Altheim, Shepherd Bliss, Eileen Campbell, Peter Campbell, Ken Cohen, William Collinge, Jim Dreaver, George Feldman, Eugene Gendlin, Lee Glickstein, Joseph Goldstein, Robert Hall, Robert Kantor, Jack Kornfield, Loren Krane, Bob Marcus, Edwin McMahon, Brad Parks, Janis Paulsen, Nick Rudin, Maxine Scharf, Don Schwartz, Neil Selden, Jacquelyn Small, William Staniger, John Tarrant, Ray Vespe, Chris Wentworth, Kris Wentworth, John White, Charles Whitfield, Gloria Wilcox, Cheryl Woodruff, and Aaron Zerah.

Introduction

I realize today that nothing in the world is more distasteful
to a man than to take the path that leads to himself.
                                                —Hermann Hesse

∾○∾

To be human is to long for love. We want to feel close, connected, and cared about. But sadly, love relationships often
leave us disheartened, cynical, or angry. Is our quest for love
just a wild ride toward nowhere, or is there some awareness we're
missing in order to find it?

Much pain and confusion stem from unrealistic attitudes and
expectations about love and romance. We don't understand what it
really takes to love and be loved. Distorted dreams of our youth sway
us to fit the round dream of romance into the square peg of authentic love.

Young images of romance are destined to disappoint us. But as
with any art, it takes time to become an adept lover; our early attempts
often fail. Not knowing how to make sense of our pain, disillusionment, or despair, we may give up the search, or settle for very little.
We may also give up on ourselves—and on life.

Satisfying relationships don't just happen. It's not merely a matter of finding the right person and then living happily ever after, as
in a fairy tale. Loving partnerships and friendships are created and
maintained through a commitment to a certain path of growth. The
search for love is simultaneously a search for ourselves.

This book assembles and synthesizes the main pieces of the
orchestra so you may savor a full and resounding symphony of love
that touches, delights, and expands your heart. It moves beyond
amiable companionship or marital contentment, and invites you to

1

explore the further reaches of what's possible in relationships. This book is based on the premise that growth is a lifelong process, and it offers a path toward actualizing love on ever deeper levels as you harvest your life experience.

An Extraordinary Opportunity

Many couples love each other and consider themselves happily married but have difficulty showing their love and allowing its fullest unfolding. Others hesitate to acknowledge that they're dissatisfied because they fear losing what they have. Still others have hurt each other deeply, which has created distance; they're wary and mistrustful and have settled for an uneasy truce or they bicker constantly.

If you're currently in a partnership, you may want to bring greater depth, delight, and dynamism to it. You may want more moments of *feeling* the love that's there. Or you may be wondering if there's enough love and connection to stay together now that the kids are grown. Or perhaps you feel this might be your last chance to create a rich relationship.

Midlife holds the extraordinary potential of becoming more fully awake and alive—more wholeheartedly available to give and receive love. By being committed to relationships of equality and respect, you have a precious opportunity to unearth rare treasures. Something new explodes into birth through the cross-pollination of two hearts who feel safe and enlivened being together.

If you're currently single, you're blessed in a different way. Periods of being single offer opportunities to understand relationships from a new perspective. Perhaps you need time to heal before opening yourself to someone new—and time to understand what happened from a distant perch safely removed from the confusion of partnered life. Being single can be a time to strengthen yourself and become more insightful before launching anew into the sacred struggle and sacred joy of authentic relating.

Whether or not you're in a partnership, friendships are an underrated source of depth and satisfaction in life. This book is also about availing yourself of the rich connections possible through close friendships.

The Gift of Midlife

Never before have we humans lived so long. Life expectancy was thirty-five years when our country was founded; it jumped to forty-seven years in 1900. Thanks to advances in health care and self-care, that figure has rocketed to seventy-three years for men and seventy-nine years for women! By age fifty, life expectancy for men becomes seventy-eight years and for women eighty-two years. These are exceptional times.

Life expectancy is likely to increase even further with advances in medicine. And with research on hormone therapy to slow aging, along with products that promote vitality, our later years can be robust ones.

But despite what science has done for us lately, our main hope lies in what we can do for ourselves. As poet and essayist Diane Ackerman puts it, "I don't want to get to the end of my life and find that I lived just the length of it. I want to have lived the width of it as well." A long life might be a curse, not a blessing, if we're lonely and unhappy.

Thanks to discoveries about our biochemical nature, we have an opportunity to live long and prosper. But unless we use our gift of time to understand our human nature, true happiness will elude us. The crucial question this book addresses is, what will we *do* with the gift of life we've been granted? What will it take to fulfill the deepest longings of our heart?

This book explores an aspiration that deepens as we mature—to love and be loved. It offers a sound, soulful, and research-supported pathway toward the depth and delight that are possible through loving partnerships and friendships.

When Is Midlife?

Defining when midlife begins is tricky. Most authors on the subject reckon midlife as beginning at around forty or forty-five and continuing into our early or mid-sixties. I encourage people to get an early start on discovering the richness of midlife. Why wait any longer than necessary to acknowledge that you've entered your middle years? No one can know for sure how long he or she will live. You probably hope you'll live well into your eighties, nineties, or beyond. But time is precious and the sooner you tackle the developmental tasks of midlife, the sooner you'll awaken to your fullest potential. It's easy to succumb to denial and the delusion that you'll live forever and to postpone getting on with your life.

I saw my thirty-fifth birthday as a halfway point, assuming I'd live to be seventy. Although thirty-five seems quite young now, it was a wake-up call. There was no denying I was closing in on forty. Gail Sheehy, author of the classic book *Passages*, reinforces my experience: "The first glimpses of a midlife perspective usually begin to startle us in the middle of our thirties. Time starts to pinch." If I had to be nailed down, I'd say that early midlife begins roughly at thirty-five, median middle age occurs between forty-five and fifty-five, and later midlife is fifty-five to sixty-five. But these labels don't really matter. The important thing is to find and create meaning in your life as soon as you realize that time is precious and caring relationships are your top priority. Most people discover this during their middle years, as they become aware of their mortality and physical limitations.

Recent discoveries of planets rotating around other suns were the product of eight years of painstaking research. Similarly, the authentic love of midlife is not designed for those who luxuriate in a culture of fast food and instant gratification. The McLovers who seek simple formulas to have it all now will never create the foundation that love requires.

The good news for people in midlife is that true love isn't dead. It's just further away than we imagined. It awaits discovery by those who find the will and wisdom to move forward despite treacherous terrain. But instead of searching further outside yourself, you must gently turn your sight inward toward your own heart and mind—looking more deeply into yourself to ripen your readiness for love. The prospect of loving relationships grows as you prepare a sacred place within your heart for special connections.

Finding and nurturing love requires growing discernment, patience—and yes, work. Like learning to play a musical instrument, the art of giving and receiving love is a creative venture leading to deepening meaning and exquisite pleasure.

Midlife love is attainable for people who persevere despite setbacks, like those who succeed in business after bankruptcy. The disillusionment of your early romances or first marriage may have overwhelmed you with anger, sorrow, and/or humiliation. Being hurt or feeling like a failure, you may have abandoned the search for love—or settled for something that made you wonder, "Is love really possible?" As one middle-aged woman told me, "I've given up! I've had enough pain and disappointment. I'll stick with my cats!"

My previous work, *Love & Betrayal: Broken Trust in Intimate Relationships*, was an attempt to help people heal relationship wounds so they wouldn't give up on love. This current book ventures beyond betrayal and broken trust into a world where authentic love becomes possible.

Learning what it takes to love means developing both awareness and skills. The eightfold path to love is a distillation of nearly twenty-five years of experience practicing psychotherapy. This book has been over twelve years in the making.

Rather than bemoan past mistakes or others' transgressions, take the opportunity midlife offers to reenvision your priorities so that you may actualize your longing for love. Through your tears and triumphs, you've earned your credentials to enter this new stage of life. Like fulfilling the prerequisites for college, you've laid the groundwork necessary to move toward authentic love.

For many of us, entering midlife means we've known the hurts of rejection and the heartache of betrayal. We've delighted in the joys of being in love and connecting deeply. We've lived enough years to be on both sides of various relationship issues, thereby making it possible to develop the sensitivity necessary for true love. Perhaps we were the betrayer in one relationship and the betrayed in another, or the one who was rejecting and then the one who was rejected, or the one who longed for more intimacy and then the one who felt trapped by the other's needs and demands. By midlife, we become more familiar with the terrain of love and more ready to do the inner work necessary to avoid the land mines.

By knowing how it feels to be on either side of various relationship dynamics, you're better positioned to nurture compassion and understanding for yourself and others. Over time, humility and wisdom have an opportunity to germinate in your weather-beaten heart, creating a fertile climate for love to thrive.

Having danced in the light and wrestled with the darkness, you can now take time to integrate what you've learned throughout your life. Perhaps you carry baggage and scars from romantic misadventures, with their legacy of multiple wounds, a divided family, and opportunities lost. But rather than abandon love and retreat to a world that's safe but sterile, you can make the most of midlife as a time to open your heart and free your imagination while planting your feet firmly on the ground. It's a time to recapture your innocence, yet integrate it with the compassion born of sorrow and the wisdom born of mistakes. It's a time to complete whatever grieving remains from jagged partings of the past. It's a time to value yourself as you are rather than shape yourself according to others' expectations. And it's a time to move toward a wise innocence—authentic love for grown-ups.

Some people have felt so beaten in the courtyard of love that they just want a sabbatical from relationships. Others prefer to commit themselves to spiritual pursuits apart from relationships, although the path of love is inherently a spiritual one. Still others have a need to make their career a priority for a time.

Pursuing love is dangerous. You can get hurt. It's reserved for the adventurous—those willing to risk getting hurt again to reap the rewards of authentic love. Yet as you grow toward midlife and beyond, your heart can be increasingly fortified by the wisdom and discernment that come with experience.

Courageous people in midlife hold a mature vision of possibilities. They're willing to take intelligent risks. Perhaps they long for the shimmering delight of searching into their partner's eyes, or the experience of gently holding each other while gazing at the night sky, or lovemaking electrified by connecting from the heart. These brave souls have tasted the heartbreak of rejection and separation—perhaps knowing more than their share of adversity. Yet these wounded warriors of love are willing to learn from their pain and misfortune rather than diminish themselves by retreating from others or concluding that love isn't for them.

This book is for people who want to reconsider possibilities they may have abandoned or overlooked, or for those who simply want more joy in their relationships. We often find true love once we've abandoned unreal hopes and begin to replace them with what it really takes to love. This book offers a pathway for attracting, creating, and deepening vibrant partnerships and friendships.

The Journey Begins

Our journey toward authentic midlife loving begins by distinguishing the dreamy romance of young love from the depth of mature love. Step two along the path involves uncovering the subtle shame and self-criticism you carry and realizing how this dynamic duo has prompted you to manufacture an inauthentic self that will never bring you love. Step three is the realization that authenticity forms the basis for true love, and the discussion here explores what it really means to be authentic. The fourth step is to develop appropriate boundaries that protect and support your authentic self so that it may thrive, despite how you're viewed or treated by others. Step five invites you to learn the skills of self-soothing and self-connection so that you may cultivate a safe refuge within yourself when there's conflict or when things don't go your way. Step six involves expressing your feelings in a gentle way so that communication becomes less critical and more kind and effective. Step seven is to revise what it means to be committed so that you may build trust and connect deeply without losing yourself. Finally, step eight involves deepening your understanding of authentic love and discovering how sexuality flows from a deep connection with your lover. In conclusion, we'll explore how a mature spirituality evolves naturally by practicing these steps.

Throughout the book I've drawn upon the experience of friends, acquaintances, and clients, as well as my own experience. I've changed names and altered identifying characteristics to protect people's identities. I have often combined vignettes from several people to better illustrate key points and further protect confidentiality. After reading my previous books, people have often told me that they think I'm writing about them! This is only because our human experience is surprisingly similar. Also, although my examples are from heterosexual relationships, the growth necessary for midlife love is relevant to gay and lesbian relationships as well.

I've tried to be thorough in giving proper credit to others. Please let me know if you think I've omitted referencing anyone. As the poet T. S. Eliot recognized, "Originality is the ability to conceal one's sources." I'm happy to acknowledge the writings of others, as I'm grateful for the chance to build upon their creative work.

The path of growth that leads to midlife love opens your heart and strengthens your spirit. It opens you to life, even if no partner comes right away—or ever. The risk of closing yourself to love is that you close your heart to life. The courage to pursue the path of love simultaneously opens you to the mystery and magic of being alive.

∽∾∽

Prepare Your Understanding: From Young Love to Mature Love

One reason why we have so much trouble with relationship today may be out of neglect of its study. We expect to find intimacy naturally, without education or initiation.

—THOMAS MOORE

1

New Beginnings

Since love is the most delicate and total act of a soul, it will reflect the state and nature of the soul. . . . If the individual is not sensitive, how can his love be sentient? If he is not profound, how can his love be deep? As one is, so is his love. For this reason, we can find in love the most decisive symptom of what a person is.

—José Ortega y Gasset

∽⚬∾

If anthropologists from another planet observed a young human couple in love, they'd be bewildered. When meeting, these humans seem so kind and thoughtful. They say sweet things: "You're great! I'm crazy about you! I can't live without you." They declare their devotion, make passionate love, and eventually marry—vowing to honor and cherish each other forever.

Then things somehow change. Six months—or five years—later the scene is very different. Bewildered, our foreign observers now notice that the same couple who seemed so "in love" are now at each other's throats, followed by a jagged parting of the ways and a sad parting of hearts.

Lisa, a young model, and Mark, an illustrator, epitomize this radical shift of sentiments. When she was newly married, Lisa had stated buoyantly, "I will follow Mark anywhere and anytime." But after they separated, she remarked, "I have no idea where he is and I could care less!"

Why did Lisa's romantic hopes fade? Why did Mark's once kind words turn critical and accusatory? Why did their warm intimacy lapse into glacial distance and their sexual passion become sexual boredom? Are love relationships always destined to disappoint us? Or is there something we're lacking—something that rarely graces the young?

As we age, a wistful regret may haunt us: that we weren't wiser during our youth. "I wish I knew then what I know now!" is a recurring mantra as we move through life. Yet, no doubt, we did our best according to what we knew at the time.

Like many people in midlife who are married or partnered, you may feel that you're doing okay but sense that something is missing. Maybe you're not as close to your family or friends as you'd like to feel. Or you may be lacking the joy, depth, and delight that you clearly envision but can't seem to manifest in your relationships. Rather than let yourself sink into apathy and cynicism, you can use midlife as a time to apply yourself with renewed devotion to create satisfying relationships.

One unlikely gift of midlife is a sobering truth: we won't be around forever! This realization hits home gradually as one birthday follows another with increasing rapidity. Or our mortality may strike suddenly after some adversity: a frightening illness, the death of a parent or friend, or just seeing our children leave the nest. The sudden deaths of young celebrities such as Princess Diana and JFK Jr. serve as sober reminders of our mortality and the need to "seize the day."

Wisdom rarely comes during the innocent days of youth, when life seems endless and we have an inflated view of our powers. The wisdom necessary to achieve meaningful partnerships and friendships often doesn't dawn until we reach some crisis point that prompts us to become more serious about life and love. We might hit this wall during midlife—the proverbial "midlife crisis," when we realize that our long-held dream of "making it" isn't panning out. Failed expectations, romantic disillusionment, the drudgery of work or family life, the emptiness of materialistic values, and a nagging meaninglessness make us wonder, "Is this all there is? Is this the fruit of all my labors?"

The Advantages of Losing Hope

The good news is that disillusionment is often the beginning of wisdom. The philosopher Nietzsche, acclaimed by Freud as having a more penetrating knowledge of himself than anyone who ever lived, put it starkly: "Not a day passes when I haven't rid myself of another comfortable illusion."

Is your heart sometimes heavy, your mind restless, and your soul searching? Or are you simply wanting more love and joy in your life? Then you're ready to ask these crucial questions:

1. What's really important in life?
2. Do I need new priorities?
3. What's getting in the way of the deeper connections I want with people?
4. Am I doing something that's pushing people away?
5. Are my expectations too high in some ways and too low in others?
6. What can relationships provide for me, and what do I need to do for myself?

Allowing these questions to incubate in your heart and mind can bring realizations that lead to a new era of loving. As you practice the eightfold path that I'll outline, you'll be able to respond to these questions more clearly.

Midlife is a time to fulfill the deeper longings of your soul. The sacred salve of disappointed love can be an impetus to listen to what life is trying to tell you. Perhaps you first needed to chase the romantic fantasy of having a partner and two kids before you could realize that you had fallen into an alluring trap. Perhaps you needed to climb the corporate ladder before you could discover, as one forty-five-year-old executive put it, "Business achievements didn't do it for me. I have money and status. I'm the American dream of success. I've made it, but I'm unhappy. There's no love in my heart. During the next half of my life I want a new kind of success—fulfilling relationships."

Men often lag behind women in forming friendships and strong social ties, which are important not only for happiness but also for health and longevity. During the middle years, many men are eager to move from "competing to connecting." They want to "finally get love right," as one man expressed it. Many women in midlife also want deeper relationships, though without being defined and delimited by them.

When I was younger, I thought I had only to find the perfect woman and I'd be happy. I was so picky that I found myself alone much of the time. I didn't grasp the concept that love is something that grows by sharing our imperfect selves.

The possibility of deep, authentic loving can dawn only as you lose hope in the innocent romantic views that masqueraded as true love. You must lose faith not in love itself but in true love's alluring cousin: naive, romantic love. You must peer through the subtle veils that obstruct true connection with both your inner self and your partner before you can graduate to a more fulfilling, lasting love.

As one woman entering midlife realized, "I had to go through a period of giving up. But I was actually giving up the fantasy of being rescued—the dream of being taken care of by someone else. I gave up relationships so I could stop giving up myself! Now that I have more of *me*, I'm ready for a partnership, but in a new way." This wise woman used her past disappointments as an impetus to listen to what life was trying to tell her.

The essence of Buddhism and many spiritual paths is to discover and express your true nature—to find your essence beneath the mask of your everyday personality. You can begin this process at any age, but midlife is an especially ripe time to discover who you really are. As you come to know and show yourself, you create the foundation for authentic love.

Old views must sometimes die in order to make way for the new. As you move beyond young views of love based on merging and blended identities, you are ready to learn what it takes to share your authentic heart and live in a way that is deep, joyful, and workable. You are ready for mature, midlife love.

Young love is the stuff of fairy tales and Hollywood. It's the romance of your childhood dreams. Society promotes naive romance through myriad movies and love songs that drip with the excruciating pain and pleasure of our longing. Young love is responsible for deep disappointment when you discover that the captivating romantic myth fails to match the reality of your life.

Prince Charles and Princess Diana were such a storybook couple. They seemed so in love as they trotted around the globe, smiling into television cameras. When their marriage dissolved, the bitter salt of reality was a shocking disappointment to many. Sadly, Diana's tragic death cut short her own quest for love, although it serves as a vivid reminder for us to pursue our heart's desire while we're blessed with the gift of life.

Young love contains seeds of something deeper. This riper love retains the sparkle of its younger cousin, yet it embodies an added quality of depth and substance. Searching for a word to describe this rare elixir is challenging. Dare we call it "mature love"? Oh no, not that! Mature? Has it come to that?

For some people the word "mature" rankles a bit. It can have the ring of being old—and in our youth-crazed society we certainly don't want to be accused of that! For others, "mature" sounds stiff and stuffy—nothing too exciting. However, the Old French word *maturus* evolved into the word *mur* meaning "ripe." Maturing involves ripening. Immature is green and tart. Mature implies the full glow— sweet, full of flavor, and ready to be enjoyed. A Latin derivative is "Matuta," the name of the Roman goddess of the dawn. Midlife is a passage to a new, more mature beginning.

EXERCISE:

Here are some questions to consider before delving into mature love.

- What does love mean to you apart from sex and romance?
- What does being in love mean to you?
- What are you looking for in a partnership?

The Passion of Mature Love

Mature love is thoroughly enlivening and passionate, but you're being more intelligent about it. You're beginning to know what you're doing and why you're doing it. You have an interest and excitement in knowing your partner more deeply—and in understanding more about *yourself* through the relationship. You appreciate the delicacy of love and you're learning to nurture trust and intimacy rather than sabotage it. You feel the sparkle and pleasure of giving and receiving love—and opening to life. And if a relationship fails, you know that you have a refuge within yourself, and therefore know how to soft-land rather than crash-land into a wasteland of bitterness and despair.

Midlife is a time to move toward a love that is more stable and less hazardous to your health. And, perhaps more difficult to recognize, it's a time when *you* become less hazardous to others. Maturing beyond the narcissism of youth brings greater awareness of the effects you have on people.

As you learn to create conditions for love to ripen, you ride the tiger of your longings without being thrown around so wildly. You take responsibility for how you're contributing to not getting what you want. You learn to deal with conflict and differences in ways that bring closeness rather than disconnection. By allowing passion to be seasoned by wisdom and exuberance to be grounded in sobriety, you open the door to a more authentic and satisfying love. Far from boring, mature love is exhilarating. But the source of aliveness is within yourself; it does not originate from the other person.

When I refer to young or naive love, I'm referring more to emotional development than chronological age. Many people cling to naive notions of love well into their later years, while some younger people are blessed with a smoother transition to mature love. Although personal experience provides the raw material to create a more refined love, what is most crucial is what we learn from that experience. Some twenty-year-olds pursue love in a more mature manner than some fifty-year-olds.

But generally speaking, most people aren't prepared for mature love until they've had sufficient life experience—including ample failures—to gain the humility and wisdom that forge the foundation for maturity. The poet Rilke said it well: "Young people, who are beginners in everything, cannot yet know love: they have to learn it. With their whole being, with all their forces, gathered close about their lonely, timid upward beating heart, they must learn to love." Few people embody mature love in our culture, and therefore we have few role models to guide us forward.

My hope is that you will acknowledge—even honor—the young views of love that brought you where you are today. These experiences, however painful, have qualified you for a journey into love's deepest chamber. Each failed romance can be a preparation for mature love—if you learn from your setbacks. Failures and reversals are a necessary rite of passage toward the joy of midlife love.

2

Comparative Love 101

Can I see another's woe,
And not be in sorrow too?
Can I see another's grief.
And not seek for kind relief?
—William Blake

∽◦∾

Some people just aren't interested in understanding the intricacies of love. They insist that love is a mystery, not a subject for mortal minds to comprehend. Certainly, love contains more riddles than answers. When asked, "Why do you love him?" or "What do you love about her?" we're often stymied by the question. "I don't know why, I just do!"

Love is too large to be captured by narrow definitions; it participates in a much larger mystery than what your mind can ever grasp. Happily, this sublime mystery adds wonder, awe, and possibilities to life.

Yet if you never understand what it takes to support and nurture love, you'll be tossed around wildly by love's awesome currents. Consequently, you'll keep creating messes in your life—often the same ones over and over again. You may complain, "I have no idea what happened! I can't figure out this love thing!" Rather than become love's victim, you can explore your history of successes and failures to learn more about yourself—and more about what it takes to love and be loved.

Comparing young love with mature love provides a grid to allow a greater understanding of love. As you mix wisdom with the poetry of love, you can navigate treacherous territory with greater awareness and skill. As you add insight to the art of loving, you can enjoy love's nectar without choking on its alluring sweetness. As you add self-awareness to the ecstasy of love, you can delight in love's joy without falling off the cliff when differences and conflicts arise. By familiarizing yourself with love's ways, you can respond to love's call with your eyes open to what's really happening.

As you read the following contrasts between young love and mature love, see how many apply to you—and notice how far you've come in your journey toward mature love. You might also discover your own distinctions.

YOUNG LOVE: I long for you so I must love you.

MATURE LOVE: Longing isn't the same as love.

The alluring beliefs and images that weave young views of love and romance are deeply embedded in our collective psyche. In Western culture, romantic love came into full bloom during the twelfth century in France. "Troubadours" were skilled poets and musicians who idealized sexual passion or platonic union with their beloved. Romantic epics and poetry venerated women as a source of spiritual bliss while idealizing torment as a noble sign of frustrated longing. One rule of romantic love insisted, "A true love is continually and without interruption obsessed by the image of his beloved." Another rule destined to confuse future generations declared, "Love easily obtained is of little value; difficulty in obtaining it makes it precious." The romantic quest for the inaccessible woman—and proving oneself worthy of her affection—became the very reason for one's existence.

Sadly, society hasn't progressed much beyond the misguided views of love promulgated centuries ago. Modern-day trumpeters of naive romance, such as Hollywood producers and the entertainment media, profit from our appetite for amour. However, the repackaged message for prime time is the same: "If I love you, I'll be tormented by your absence."

Turn on your radio and on any music station you'll hear popular love songs declaring some version of "I can't make it without you," or "Life was nothing till I found you." These messages confuse dependency with passion and lust with love. Fortunately, midlife is a time to give a proper burial to images of love that generate torment and misery. It's a time to rethink your understanding of what love is and how to attract it into your life. As one person in midlife put it, "I'm glad I'm almost fifty. I'd never turn back the clock to when I was looking to my partner for salvation. I don't miss the gigantic highs and lows of my twenties and thirties. I know what I'm looking for now—what's possible and not possible."

As a young romantic, we were massively confused about what love is, but we didn't know it! We thought it was love because we felt it so strongly. At least we felt something—and it must be this thing called love. After all, we thought about this person all the time, wanted to be together constantly, and couldn't imagine living without him or her. So we were obviously in love, right? Sadly, this confusion of love with longing and obsession may endure well into our later years.

Are You Loving or Needing?

Being human, we're endowed with a restless longing to be connected, loved, and wanted. This yearning is a rich, wonderful feeling; welcome it, do not obliterate it. Gently embracing your longing is like plowing a frozen field of lost dreams and betrayed hopes. As the hardened ground of your being softens, you're prepared to welcome new seeds of love during midlife.

A hardened heart is not porous enough to receive love. Connecting with your longing delivers you to a vulnerable edge of being ready for love. But if you confuse this longing with love itself, you're setting yourself up for a relationship based on dependency, not love. As a fifty-five-year-old lawyer, Dennis, put it, "I used to confuse love with need. When I said, 'I love you,' I was really saying 'I need you.' I was pulling on people with my longing—for sex, acceptance, love— but I wasn't aware of what *they* wanted. My needs were so strong that I wasn't extending myself to them." Dennis felt sad, yet relieved, when he came to the realization that his longing for love through sex, which had alienated one partner after another, was blinding him to other ways of connecting.

Misidentifying love and longing, you may pursue people who are emotionally unavailable. You may insist that you're still in love with someone who repeatedly mistreats you. Romanticized longing keeps you addicted to a person you don't really know and can't really trust.

Many people who claim to be "in love" are actually "in need." They give to get. They say "I love you" in order to wrest the reassuring reply, "I love you too."

It's a rare and special moment when the words "I love you" spring from the experience of pure caring and closeness. Is there a warm glow in your heart as you speak those precious words? Are you *feeling* love as you voice it tenderly? Are your words prompted by a spontaneous feeling of affection or gratitude? The habit of "giving to get" can be difficult to see.

Meeting someone you find attractive may spark interest in what you can *get* from a relationship. But mature love is about the mutual sharing of tenderness and caring. It's not just about the supplies you can extract from your partner. It's also about what you can give— your nonjudgmental acceptance, empathy, and understanding—the very things you also want. *Sharing* love is the deepest human longing. It means finding a balance between extending attention and caring, while being open to receiving, and knowing you're worthy to receive.

YOUNG LOVE: Blinded by the light.

MATURE LOVE: Dancing in the light and the darkness.

In young love, we lose perspective in a dizzying whirlwind of sexual longing and passion. We want the other person, no matter what the cost to our own soul. In our eagerness to melt into an ocean of sensual rapture, we leave our common sense behind. Good judgment is supplanted by youthful, romantic images and bountiful hormones. Despite the other person's signals of disinterest or unavailability, we may still pursue love. Possessed by passion, we may even overlook dangers such as sexually transmitted diseases or unwanted pregnancy—to our later dismay.

Blinded by the light of your heart's desire, have you ever magnified your beloved's alluring traits, ignored his or her flaws, and projected qualities that didn't exist? Did you see what you wanted to see (selective perception) and conveniently ignore the rest (selective inattention) until the reality of who you were dealing with could no longer be denied? Did the confidence and self-assurance that attracted you turn out to be arrogance and narcissism? Did the kindness and caring that touched your heart turn out to be tainted by codependency? Did you become bored as your partner constantly deferred to you instead of meeting you with a strong self? Were you left feeling perplexed or discouraged?

In mature love, there is attraction and delight, with allowable doses of infatuation and idealization, but we realize that whatever light is present will produce a shadow. When we discover that our partner is not everything we imagined—that he or she doesn't bind every wound, satisfy every desire, read our mind, and understand each nuance of our feelings—we reach an impasse that can be either a death knell or a turning point in our lives.

Embrace Conflict

Approaching true maturity, we realize that some expectations will be disappointed, some wants unfulfilled. There will be times of anger and frustration, heartache and sadness, fear and disappointment. We accept that relationships have joys *and* limits. Rather than throw a temper tantrum or make a quick exit, we embrace and express our feelings in ways that don't destroy the good things we share.

Young love expects perpetual harmony; we believed in our youth that love transcends conflict. Role models like Ozzie and Harriet and the Cleaver family bolstered our expectations of eternal, uncomplicated bliss.

In midlife, we need to realize that love must be large enough to embrace inevitable conflicts. We need to be able to talk about our difficulties, not just to get through them but to understand each other so we can grow closer. If we're dating, why stick around once it's clear that this person isn't interested in working through conflicts? Mature partners recognize the need to agree on a way to deal with discord before committing to sharing their hearts and silverware.

In young love, we believe that we have only to find the right part-ner—then we can merrily ride off into the sunset. As a mature per-son seeking love, we must come to realize that a climate for love must be *created* between two people who know themselves fairly well and are willing to do the personal and interpersonal work that produces the grounding for a satisfying, lasting relationship.

Journey into the Underworld

Before you can create a truly satisfying relationship, you must embark on your own private odyssey—a journey into the underworld of your self, to confront old hurts, fears, and other emotional baggage that block your path to true maturity and continuing growth. Embrac-ing the dark and light sides of love and life is necessary for cutting through romantic illusions and dysfunctional values and moving you toward greater fulfillment.

If we spent as much time developing the awareness and skills nec-essary to love as we do watching sitcoms and ball games, or surfing the Internet, we'd improve our chances of finding love. If we don't get our priorities straight during midlife, our opportunity to create a mature partnership will vanish.

Believing that you will magically meet the perfect mate without doing the inner work necessary to have a satisfying relationship is the wishful thinking of youth. No matter how many people you meet through personal ads or social gatherings, you won't attract—and keep—a mature partner if your understanding about relationships hasn't matured.

YOUNG LOVE: I can't live without you.

MATURE LOVE: Life is richer with you.

When love is based on dependency, you look to the other for your source of well-being. That person becomes the holder of the life energy that you are reluctant to hold within yourself. You look to him or her as the source of all that is soothing and good.

Mature love is based on our connection with ourselves and with life itself. The spark for life glows quietly within our own heart. When we come together with a partner, that light glows brighter;

life becomes richer. A partner augments the life and love that already exist within us.

Perhaps young romantic adventures disappointed you because they were based on the misguided mind-set of *needing* a partner to survive rather than *wanting* a partner because he or she would enhance the quality of your life. Young romance is often rooted in an under-lying sense of deprivation and desperation—seeking a relationship with a partner before having one with yourself.

In youth, we often have only a tentative connection with our-selves. We look to the other person for our strength, well-being, and identity. Attraction is usually based on the image we hold of an ideal partner, whether based on looks, status, or personality traits embod-ied by a role model or parent. Or we seek someone totally opposite from our parents in an attempt to differentiate ourselves from them. In either case, the attractions of youth often aren't based on the trust and intimacy of seeing and understanding each other; more often they are driven by a potent brew of biology, social conditioning, and outmoded patterns. They are propelled by our hormones and history, not our heart and wisdom. Consequently, we might feel compelled to remain in a painful or even abusive relationship. When asked why we stuck it out, we innocently reply that love made us do it.

Is It Love or Dependency?

Even in abusive relationships there may be some strands of love, but what's usually more pronounced is dependency. "I can't live with him/her and I can't live without him/her." From the viewpoint of Jungian psychology, we're desperately seeking the lost parts of our-selves through a relationship. When we say, "I must have you," we're really saying, "I want to find and integrate the lost parts of myself; I need to embody some of the qualities that shine in this person." Fatal attractions can be based on elements that are missing in our lives. They might include a fear of living alone or difficulty taking care of ourselves financially.

The bottom line in dependent relationships isn't so much that we love, but that we fear abandonment. We don't want to face failure and aloneness. We're not confident that we have the inner resources to live life on our own.

Moving toward mature love means learning the difference between truly loving someone and clinging to a person based on a fear of being abandoned and alone. Midlife is a time to learn this crucial difference between mature love and your need for acceptance and approval. There's certainly nothing shameful about the human need for acceptance and belonging, but you're deluding yourself if you mistake this longing to be loved with love itself.

To move toward mature love, you need to develop the resiliency to reach out and connect while staying close to yourself. Being connected with your depths, you'll no longer use relationships to try to fill an emptiness that no human being can fill for you. In mature love, a connection with another person *enhances*, rather than *provides*, your well-being. Others cannot furnish happiness, they can only amplify it.

Salvation Within or Without?

When I was younger, I believed that falling in love was the ultimate goal of life. But when partnerships didn't work out I felt devastated, bouncing between outrage and resignation. What I didn't realize was that I needed to strengthen my own sense of self. I needed to have a self to bring to the relationship and a self to return to if the relationship failed. Even if the relationship didn't succeed, *I* could still succeed! I could still have a relationship with myself, with cherished friends, and with life.

By nurturing a connection with yourself, you'll find that separation is less devastating if someone leaves you, or if you need to part from an unworkable situation. If you don't trust that you have a self to return to, then parting becomes a life and death struggle. As *The Dhammapada*, a popular Buddhist text, advises, the wise person would rather be alone than with people who are destructive for him or her.

The experience of falling in love awakens a wonderful sense of possibilities. You see how rich and beautiful your life could be. The common delusion is to become attached to your partner as the source of this wonderful feeling. This attachment creates huge anxiety or jealousy at the slightest hint that your bond may be disrupted.

As mature lovers, we use relationships as an inspiration and impetus to nurture resources within ourselves. Mature love is a dance between connecting with our partner and connecting with an ever broader sense of ourselves. Connecting with your quiet depths, you're prepared to commune with those similarly connected to their depths. When your longing to connect is balanced with the capacity to stay close to yourself, you're more emotionally and spiritually available for mature love.

> YOUNG LOVE: Love is enough.
> MATURE LOVE: Love is a good start.

As a young romantic, we were so smitten that we were certain we were in love. Whether we exuberantly announced it to the world or held it quietly in our heart, there was no doubt that Aphrodite had sprinkled love dust upon us.

The midlife lover also relishes this exquisite feeling; there's no greater high than being in love. But as a naive romantic we equate the feeling of love with the certainty that this is the right partner for us—the one we've been waiting for. If sex is great, we may become even more convinced that this is a marriage made in heaven!

As a young romantic, we didn't realize that it takes more than love and attraction to create a viable partnership. We didn't understand the dynamics of relationships, nor did we have the skills and savvy to convert the romantic dream into a living reality. We naively assumed that love and connection would—somehow—triumph over any conflict.

In young love, we believed that love was enough. In mature love, we appreciate that love is a good start. Our early sense of excitement and connection keeps us engaged in the process of learning and growing together. We're eager to move forward. But we don't allow enthusiasm to distort mature judgment. Our eyes and ears are open to who this person really is. Love and friendship may then grow by our relating to the actual person before us rather than insisting that our romantic fantasy prevail. A sexual relationship then deepens our connection rather than creating it.

Essential Trust

A foundation of trust is necessary to support love. Real trust is based on seeing who a person really is, apart from our imagination and wishful thinking. The blind faith of young love assumes that we know a person based upon early impressions or the way that person presents himself or herself. The genuine trust of mature love allows us to know a person based on a history of being together and communicating honestly and openly. This trust permits us to weather crises and difficulties that inevitably confront every partnership.

In my early twenties when I moved to California, I was so smitten by a beautiful woman I was dating that I overlooked some obvious red flags. She was angry at her neighbor and gleefully told me how she sought revenge. She discovered a supply of condoms in this woman's dresser and proceeded to put tiny pinholes in each one of them! I remember thinking this wasn't so cool, but I wasn't sufficiently horrified to question what her actions said about her character and whether I wanted to be with someone capable of such chicanery.

Building mature love and trust means being alert to early warning signs of trouble. We gently address matters that feel hurtful or not quite right—perhaps a disrespectful comment, a failure to return our phone call, the dismissal of our viewpoints, or a questionable behavior. Rather than allow our feelings or concerns to slip into a black hole of neglect, where they accumulate a charge that overwhelms us later, we communicate our hurt or concern. Love without nurturing communication is like planting a garden without watering it. Do you tend to:

- Ignore hurtful comments that leave you feeling distant?
- Not address behaviors that create anger or hurt?
- Hope that by avoiding issues they'll somehow go away?
- Believe that love is enough and conflicts will just work themselves out?

If the answer to any of the above is yes, you may have a pattern of avoiding conflicts and issues that must be faced to allow love to deepen.

When you were smitten by young love, you might have dismissed your partner's cutting words or made excuses for questionable behaviors. Watching your partner humiliating you or drinking too heavily, you might have concluded: "He didn't mean anything by it," or, "That's just how she deals with stress."

As a young romantic, we often accepted destructive behaviors without realizing the distance that was created. We didn't have clear boundaries. In mature love, we address our concerns until we're satisfied that no disrespect is intended, or that the problem is due to a simple misunderstanding, or that our partner is committed to altering behaviors that are hurting us. Of course, we must also be committed to hearing how we may be hurting our partner. In short, we must keep communicating our changing panorama of feelings, wants, and viewpoints to create a foundation of trust and compatibility to support the deepening of midlife love.

YOUNG LOVE: Seeking the perfect partner.

MATURE LOVE: Choosing acceptable limits.

The wide-eyed romantic in us projects qualities of goodness and perfection onto our beloved—akin to the way a child idealizes a parent. "You are my everything!" Grown-up love involves accepting that in addition to our beloved's wonderful traits, he or she may have attributes that aren't on our "A list." He or she may possess qualities that are undesirable and have habits that annoy us. In addition, we might see a dark side that we didn't bargain for.

As we grow wiser, we realize that being human means having flaws, limits, and traits that don't match our adolescent model of perfection. An adult lover knows that it takes time to become familiar with how another's personality traits show up. Our partner may have needs and rhythms that don't correspond to our own—or habits that downright irritate us—just as we may have idiosyncrasies that irritate our partner.

When we were younger, we were more innocent about people; we were more likely to glimpse their goodness. Then, as one or more romances disintegrated, we began to glimpse people's self-centeredness, pettiness, hostility, and perhaps real meanness at times. Consequently, some of us have swung to the opposite conclusion about people: they can't be trusted.

Many people in midlife become cynical after being wounded in love. I've often heard complaints that "men are emotionally immature and incapable of loving," and "women are too self-centered and hostile to care about a man." Such generalizations push people away. But they do contain the seed of a sobering realization: all humans have a shadow side. The evolved lover knows that everyone—including himself or herself—has a dark and light side. Balanced relationships require gently holding both sides rather than fixating on either cynicism or idealization.

When you were younger, you may have ended relationships when you encountered someone's dark side or noticed traits that made you uncomfortable. A major challenge of love is to become clear about what imperfections you can live with and what you absolutely cannot accept. If you're clear that you can never accept something about your partner or potential mate, then do both of yourselves a favor and get out while the getting is good.

It's helpful to be aware early in a relationship of what you can and cannot tolerate. You can develop this discernment through the wisdom that comes with experience. As you perceive things more soberly, you may not enter into partnerships so casually anymore. In fact, you run the risk of seeing things too darn clearly! As one man explained to me, "I just can't do superficial dating anymore. I'd rather be alone than spend time with someone I'm not really into."

By being unwilling to jump into something that may turn out to be unsatisfying, you may find yourself more alone. Taken to an extreme, you may become totally afraid of risk, keeping yourself isolated by developing zero tolerance for any possible disappointment.

Being invested in seeing yourself as all good, you may overlook how your own shadow side plays itself out in a partnership. Perhaps you withdraw self-protectively when you're hurt or develop strategies of controlling your partner that stem from a fear of abandonment. Or you may become punishing when you don't get your way.

Knowing that everyone is a mix of generosity and self-centeredness—beauty and the beast—the mature lover isn't so shocked when witnessing his or her partner's shadow side emerging. The important questions then become:

- Am I willing to deal with this?
- How do I deal with differences and annoyances?
- Am I able to accept and deal with my own limits and imperfections?

Later, I'll talk about how communication must be based on knowing ourselves.

Men and Women Are from Earth

Midlife is a time to give up the search for the rescuing prince or princess—the man or woman without a shadow. Perfect people don't exist on planet Earth. Midlife is a time to create a partnership with someone whose dark side is acceptable to us—not too noxious, not terribly destructive—and someone who, we hope, is committed to self-development. As one fifty-year-old woman put it when speaking of her imperfect partner, "He doesn't clean up after himself very well, he eats too many desserts, and he sometimes forgets our anniversary. But he's a kind man, I feel loved by him, we have fun together, and he's always been good to the children—those are the things that really matter. And lately he's been making an effort to share the household work."

This isn't to say that you should hold no expectations or requirements. If you feel inadequate or undeserving, you may put up with too much and expect precious little. You may lament, "Oh well, I guess this is as good as it gets." As nothing gets talked about and the relationship deteriorates, you get depressed. If you expect very little, you will get just that—very little!

However, by midlife you've probably realized that you're not going to get *everything* you want. Life presents limits. The popular New Age notion that we can have everything promotes narcissism, not love. "Having it all" is the wish of the naive romantic—the eternal child who refuses to grow up, despite life's attempts to provide the disillusionment that leads to maturity.

Authentic love can thrive only once you see and embrace your partner's limits and accept limitations to the relationship. As the saying goes, "You can't always get what you want, but you can get what you need."

For example, you may be the quiet type, while your partner enjoys lively conversation. You like to dress casually, while he likes to dress up. You love art shows and concerts, while she is a homebody. Can you accept these limits and differences in light of the good things you share? Can you meet your different needs through other relationships or through solitary pursuits? Can you live without it? Or would your soul truly shrivel if you couldn't share 100 percent of your wants and interests with your beloved?

Even deeper differences may surface. You're a spender and he's a saver. You have two kids from a previous marriage; she has two cats and a dog and she wants you to accept them. If you want to live together, will you expect her to give up her condo near the beach or will you ask her to gather up her kids and pets and relocate to your town? Are you both willing to deal with these challenges and stretch yourselves in ways that feel uncomfortable at first?

The Challenge of Freedom

Each partnership comes with a different set of limitations—the fine print you ignored in your youthful leap into love. Moving toward mature love means discovering the limits you overlooked in your days of premature bonding. It means knowing what you absolutely need in a partnership—your basic minimum requirements—and what you can give up without feeling deprived or resentful.

The major challenge of freedom is knowing what you have to give up in order to get what you want. A hard-earned lesson of maturity is realizing that by exercising your freedom to choose one thing, you might forgo another option. By choosing one partner, you eliminate others who have appealing qualities. You can't have a love 'em and leave 'em outlook if you want a rich, monogamous partnership. The trick is to understand yourself well enough to know what combination of limits you're willing to embrace in order to nurture the love and intimacy you want.

As you grow older and wiser, you're better positioned to know what you absolutely want—perhaps a partner who can communicate and work through conflict with a minimum of blame and defensiveness—and what you might like but can still thrive without, such as someone with the perfect body or one who owns property in Hawaii.

Admit Your Own Flaws

Accepting others' limitations comes easier as you develop the humility to admit your own flaws. Liberating yourself from the burden of perfection, you can bring your authentic self to your partner. You can relish the freedom and empowerment that come with accepting yourself and being yourself. As one mature woman who entered a midlife partnership put it: "I know I'm not perfect and I don't expect him to be perfect. If he can accept *my* flaws, I'm willing to accept his." Being honest with yourself about your limitations—acknowledging them unashamedly—can help you relax and feel closer to people.

There's an old Sufi tale of Nasruddin, the wise fool, sipping tea in a café with a friend. Their conversation turned to love.

"How come you never got married, Nasruddin?" asked his friend.

"Well," replied Nasruddin, "to tell you the truth, I spent my youth looking for the perfect woman. In Cairo, I met a beautiful and intelligent woman, with eyes like dark olives, but she was unkind. Then in Baghdad, I met a woman who was a wonderful and generous soul, but we had no interests in common. One woman after another would seem just right, but there would always be something missing. Then one day, I met her. She was beautiful, intelligent, generous, and kind. We had everything in common. In fact, she was perfect."

"Well," said Nasruddin's friend, "what happened? Why didn't you marry her?"

Nasruddin sipped his tea reflectively. "Well," he replied, "It's a sad thing. Seems like she was looking for the perfect man."

Looking for a person with no limitations disregards the fact that we have an ample supply of our own. As people in midlife, we're more likely to have experienced rejection, perhaps many times. Knowing life's heartbreaks can sensitize us to others' pain and teach us to handle people with care and respect. Sorrow forges humility and sensitivity, which provides grounding for mature love.

YOUNG LOVE: Chasing an ideal.

MATURE LOVE: Embracing what's real.

During your days as a young romantic, you may have fixated on an ideal and used it as a standard to measure your partner's love and loyalty. Perhaps you insisted on fitting your partner into your pet model of how he or she should behave. As one woman told me, "I used to believe that if my husband loved me, he'd always be under-standing, never angry, and always attentive to my feelings and wants. I pushed people away because this was mission impossible. I was so self-centered!" The demands and expectations that come from romantic ideals create untold havoc.

As we'll see, young love is disappointing because it's based on creating a false self and relating to the other's false self. Mature love and connection are only possible when you're being genuine—and when you create a safe climate in which others can be authentic. By being real with people, you can discover the aliveness and presence that are hallmarks of mature love and attraction.

When love is based on a rigid model of how your ideal partner should look and act, you'll inevitably judge and belittle a prospec-tive or current partner because that person will never measure up to your perfectionistic standards. You'll either dump that partner or want to adjust him or her to match your idealized image. Trying to change people—a common strategy when romance goes awry—cre-ates power struggles that can blow up in your face and cause emo-tional damage to both parties.

The midlife lover realizes that people come "as is." Who you see is who you get. Love implies accepting who this person is right now. Falling in love with someone's potential is a hallmark of the young lover. As one woman put it, "My boyfriend was a man with great potential; I could see it so clearly. I knew he drank too much, but he promised me that he'd give it up. He never did. He was so tender and loving at times—that really touched me. But I couldn't take his verbal abuse anymore; it was too hurtful and was damaging my self-esteem. I couldn't accept the whole package."

Of course, your potential companion needs to accept whatever baggage *you* bring to the relationship as well. By having the courage to reveal yourself, you allow your partner to decide whether he or she wants the real *you*. You may find yourself withholding aspects of yourself, fearful that people will reject the very parts of yourself that you find distasteful. What you think is baggage, such as old hurts or fears, can actually be pathways to the beauty of who you are—if you learn how to open yourself to them.

Inevitably, your real self will come out in a relationship, espe-cially those parts of yourself that you perceive as vulnerable or embarrassing, such as feelings of unworthiness. You devalue yourself by attempting to hide what you think is unacceptable. By courageously showing these vulnerable parts of yourself, you'll discover whether you'll be accepted. Rather than struggling to show an idealized self—highlighting your loveliness and hiding your limits (or what you think are limits)—you'll get to see whether you can relax into your authentic self with another person. It's an expansive, joyful feeling to find someone who can accept you as you are, someone you can trust.

Like most people in midlife, you're probably sick and tired of changing yourself to please people. It's time to acknowledge that you come with strengths and weaknesses. It's time to understand the paradox of accepting yourself as you are while being committed to working on those things you want to change.

Authentic love means relating to the actual person before you. It means relishing the intimacy that comes when two kindred souls are open and real. It means creating a climate of trust that derives from extending kindness and understanding. It also means becoming large enough to embrace conflict. When two worlds meet, they are bound to collide at times, however compatible they might be.

People sometimes ask me, "Is conflict really inevitable in a partnership?" It's inevitable because the other person is not *you*. That person comes from a different family and may have contrary models and rules for having a relationship. He or she has a different set of feelings, values, needs, wants, and wounds.

For example, Bob liked space and solitude because his parents were intrusive and invasive. They often told him what to do and rarely left him alone. In contrast, Mary needed contact and conversation. Her wound was one of neglect—her parents often ignored her.

During their days as impulsive romantics, Mary and Bob weren't interested in understanding how the other person's past was affecting them in the present. Mary deemed his need for space as "distancing and fearing intimacy" rather than as a legitimate need for solitude. Conversely, he judged her requests for contact as being "needy and demanding," not comprehending her legitimate need for intimacy. As they realized that their differing needs were based on diverse backgrounds and temperaments, they began to understand, accept, and respect each other. Deeper understanding led to mutual tenderness.

Celebrate Differences

In youthful love, we try to change the other person to be like us. In mature love, we respect differences or even celebrate them; they are often what attracted us in the first place! Perhaps our partner's slow pace, which sometimes infuriates us, also reflects a patience and equanimity that we might benefit from. Perhaps the assertiveness and self-confidence that sometimes rankles us reflects qualities of strength and self-worth that we need for our own personal growth. Through such differences, we learn about ourselves and become more whole. Life would become boring if everyone were just like us. Love thrives in a climate of accepting differences and learning about ourselves through them.

Your dissimilarities provide opportunities to develop deeper compassion and caring. One client, Beth, was upset because her husband, Hal, often expressed frustration with his job. As she put it, "I was angry because I wanted us to be happy. Finally, I realized that he needs me to listen and be there for him. I can't rescue him from his struggles—I can only love him. In a few more years, he'll get his pension and can retire. In the meantime, this is just one of the burdens we have to bear."

Beth realized that she needed to accept her husband in this situation rather than administer an attitude adjustment. This shift in perspective enabled her to tap a deeper source of caring and compassion within herself, which helped him feel more supported and understood.

Grow through Conflict

Experienced lovers realize there will always be some cross to bear in every partnership. It might be a nagging health issue or caring for children still troubled by a marital breakup. Financial struggles may predominate, or it may be dealing with aging parents or in-laws who need support. Or it may be learning to find a balance between the demands of work and the delights of being together. Midlife lovers know that relationships become more challenging as youthful light-heartedness is encroached upon by life's complexities.

Embrace life's struggles and imperfections, learn to love people as they are. By keeping your heart open amid struggle, you will learn to love with more depth and substance. Burdens will become teaching tools for you to discover more about real love and life.

Avoid Self-Betrayal

Although you may feel love, you may no longer be willing to tolerate a spouse who resorts to self-destructive habits or verbally or physically abuses you. You may have learned through bitter experience that such relationships create too much pain and are unworkable. You may realize that you need a mate who is willing to communicate respectfully and who respects himself or herself.

If we accept a partner who generates too much pain, we encounter the pain of self-betrayal, which eventually leaks out in ways such as attacking, withdrawing, or being constantly critical, which hurts others and destroys our relationships.

Accepting differences or difficulties doesn't mean you must stifle your feelings about them. Neither is it wise to blurt out feelings that might steamroll over your partner's sensibilities.

If you're less sexually attracted to a partner who, for example, is overweight or has bad breath, can you sensitively broach the topic without humiliating him or her? If your beloved doesn't verbalize his or her love as much as you'd like, can you gently share your sadness and your need for more reassurance? Tact, which means "skill and grace in dealing with others," rather than the brutal honesty that some "communication experts" recommend, preserves trust and love. The Buddhist teaching of "right speech" offers three parameters for mature self-expression:

- Is it true?
- Is it kind?
- Is it helpful?

YOUNG LOVE: Hole-filling

MATURE LOVE: Whole-making

Youthful love weaves the dream of being made whole by another person. We try to fill the hole in us through the other: "You fill my emptiness. You take away my loneliness. You complete me." This dependent attitude makes the loss of the relationship all the more shocking and disorienting.

Mature love isn't about being rescued. It's not about finding our "other half" so we can be whole. It's about two people *becoming* more and more whole through being together. Rather than lament, "I can't live without you," we declare, "Life is richer with you." Separation might be painful but not devastating. We experience the sorrow of losing our *partner* without the added havoc of losing *ourselves*. We grieve the loss of connection, but we maintain the inner resources of resiliency, adaptability, and self-regard to deal with our loss.

The predisposition to be filled by another person may be partly based on a sense of deprivation and neglect as a child. If you haven't enjoyed the strong presence of at least one loving parent, you may feel a persistent need to have someone there for you. Entering adulthood, you may look to a partner to compensate for a multitude of unmet needs. You may not realize that you hold the key to awakening a source of goodness, strength, and vitality that exists within yourself.

As you move toward mature love, you come to realize that your worth and value don't depend on your partnership. Therefore, no matter what happens in the relationship, you can return to yourself; you can affirm life even as you're delivered to a new shore.

Paradoxically, you're more likely to get what you want if you can live without it—if you can love and soothe yourself when you're alone and meet some of your needs through friendships and other connections. The less desperately you need love, the more readily you can invite it into your life.

YOUNG LOVE: Our relationship is forever.

MATURE LOVE: Our caring endures.

Young love and mature love are further distinguished by your attitude toward changes in partnerships. In youthful love, you lived with the innocent certitude that your partnership would last forevermore. Consequently, you're not equipped to negotiate rough waters or deal with endings. If the relationship doesn't work out, there may be a hostile turning against each other. Your idealized darling is now devalued and denigrated—once a hero, now a villain.

Midlife lovers are also guided by a quest for an enduring union. Yet there's a recognition that a relationship may go through changes that we can't anticipate. We may hope to stay together till death do us part and sincerely commit ourselves to fulfilling that sacred covenant. However, as we grow older and, we hope, wiser, we make ever diminishing claims to omniscience and omnipotence. We can't know with certainty whether unexpected forces will lead one or both of us to conclude that a partnership just isn't working. We can't know whether our changing personalities will remain compatible over time. Nor can we predict how our mate's dark side might play itself out during the course of being together—or how *our* dark side might sabotage our alliance. The more we know, the more we realize how much we don't know—and can't possibly know. Humility has always been a core value of spiritual traditions.

Relationships come with no guarantees. As we grow, we realize that we have less control over life than youthful idealism would concede. However, as mature people, we can apply ourselves to preserving the love that brought us together.

Mature love is guided by an abiding caring. When a true bond of love has been formed, love doesn't end when the partnership ends. Although you may need a break from a partner who has hurt you, or need to create a boundary of no contact, when authentic love has been present, it can persist in a new form. Even if you've been mistreated there may remain a tender spot inside you—one you may be reluctant to acknowledge to yourself or reveal to friends who can't understand why you still harbor love for a partner who treated you so badly.

Once there's a place in your heart for your beloved, if you try to rip that person out of your heart you may do so at great peril to your own well-being. As the nineteenth-century poet Thomas Moore knew, "the heart that has truly loved never forgets." In a triumph of love, you may work toward resolving your anger and hurt and come to honor your partner's well-being—seeing him or her as a person with hopes and aspirations, fear and confusion, beauty and blind spots, just like yourself. This compassionate attitude, even if from a prudent distance, creates a climate for healing. Achieving mutual respect is especially helpful if you have children, whose pain is eased when they see their parents being warm—or at least civil—with each other.

Buddhist and Christian teachings about love and compassion are easier to apply when life is going well. But when fortunes go awry, you face a deeper challenge to your capacity to love.

Reaching midlife, you may wonder wistfully, "What's happened to my love relationships? I've invested so much time and energy and have nothing to show for it." If you're feeling sadness or remorse for having parted too hastily and leaving jagged edges that jab you later, you may question yourself about how you approach relationships—and the sloppy ways you end them. Maybe you feel moved to contact an old lover, or wonder with a bittersweet feeling where that person is and how he or she is doing. You might regret how you've discarded people in your single-minded pursuit of the perfect mate; or perhaps you simply didn't have the awareness and skills to resolve impasses that occur in every partnership. Self-compassion and forgiveness are an essential foundation for extending compassion toward others.

Focus on Healing Your Hurt

The romantically inclined often make a quick getaway when their partner doesn't live up to their fanciful ideals. A mature lover is prone to honor and preserve the love that has united two hearts, even if the romance crashes. The young Romeo is opportunistic, seeking a steamy romance or nothing at all. The seasoned lover values love and friendship as a foundation for the relationship. Then, if a romantic liaison doesn't materialize, there's the prospect of relishing whatever closeness and support are still possible.

As romantic hopes yield to separation, do your best to maintain goodwill toward your former lover. Even if you feel angry that trust was broken, don't act out or seek revenge. Don't point fingers or assign blame. However brokenhearted you may be, try to realize that healing your hurt, not hurting your partner, is what will ultimately bring you peace.

Retribution is an irrational impulse, the knee-jerk reaction of a confused mind. Don't waste precious time on retaliation, such as by having an affair or becoming embroiled in legal power plays to destroy your partner. Such acts will only get in the way of any new growth you want to accomplish. Following is an exercise that can help you draw upon inner resources to maintain your dignity and part amicably, even if sorrowfully.

EXERCISE:

Think of a relationship that recently ended or one that you still have feelings about. Allow yourself to explore the full range of your emotions, including anger, sadness, fear, or humiliation. Know that these feelings are natural, normal, and human; they don't mean that anything is wrong with you (however, if you were abusive, you surely need help to overcome this). Know that you have the inner strength to deal with these feelings and that they will heal over time. Affirm the following to yourself:

I did my best in this relationship. It didn't work out for reasons beyond my control. I want to spend my time healing, not trashing my ex-partner. I forgive myself for any shortcomings that may have contributed to our difficulties. I want to take responsibility for any shortcomings I had in the relationship and learn whatever I can so I don't repeat mistakes. It's okay to feel sad that things didn't work out. I realize that my partner probably did his or her best. He or she wants to be happy just as I do. May we both learn and grow from our experience together.

Honor the Connection You've Had

When you've touched the heart and soul of another person, you may want to honor the depth of that precious connection, even if the nature of the relationship changes. By loving in this fashion, you triumph over the rage and anguish of losing the object of your desire. Be aware—this is no easy task. It will not happen without pain, struggle, and ample time. Beyond anger or retreat—or perhaps intermixed with these—is a love that's longing to be salvaged.

Sadly, maintaining a friendship is often not possible, especially if one or both people were particularly unkind or oblivious during the relationship or vengeful after parting. Oftentimes, it's just too painful to stay in touch because you become restimulated upon seeing or hearing a person who's been dear to you. If your longing gets painfully reactivated, you will need time apart to heal—possibly a year or more. Or you may need to wait until your needs are met through a new relationship before considering contacting a former partner.

Once a mature lover has worked through the feelings and appreciated the dynamics of a broken relationship, the realization comes that love between two hearts—even if from a distance or at a future time—could be possible. Maturity means balancing this consideration with a full honoring of your human limitations—knowing what you can and cannot handle.

In my own experience, I've been blessed to remain close friends with my former wife. Although there was a brief period of little contact, we've emerged with deep love and caring for each other. This has remained consistent for many years now and has felt very good to both of us.

Get Beyond Blame

As a mature, midlife lover, we're not interested just in what we can *get* from a relationship. Having had our hearts broken, we know the pain of separation. Having been hurt by rejection, we don't casually discard people because they've outlived their usefulness. A prerequisite for mature love is getting beyond our narcissism enough to value and respect people—respecting their right to make choices for themselves, even if those choices hurt us, while honoring ourselves enough to set the boundaries we need.

Although our heart can be broken at any age, the youthful heart is especially vulnerable. Until it is tempered by strength and resiliency, rejection is often met with resignation or indignation: "How could you do this to me? I won't let you get away with this!" The heart of the mature person—seasoned by loss and rejection—is more kind and gentle toward itself and others. A heart informed by wisdom understands that sorrowful things happen in life, often through no one's fault. We are then equipped to resist blaming ourselves or others when life doesn't go our way.

Obviously, there isn't enough time to remain friends with everyone whom you've dated or had a significant relationship with. Also, life can get complicated, such as when a new partner feels threatened by contact with a former lover, or if you're at risk of sabotaging a new relationship by keeping the flame alive for an old one. By remaining attached to someone or something you can't have, you distract yourself from pursuing what you really want. Still, mature love can enable special friendships to evolve when they truly pose no threat to a new partnership—and when they support the growth of both people.

Maturity helps us separate with respect and compassion, rather than self-righteous indignation and animosity, which is so painfully common. As philosopher Sam Keen puts it: "Even soul mates may come to a fork in the road where their paths diverge, and they must grant each other the hardest gift of fidelity—a loving divorce."

YOUNG LOVE: You and I against life: exclusive love.

MATURE LOVE: You and I engaged in life: inclusive love.

As young lovers, we hoard love. We hold tightly to each other and battle the world together.

Love based on ownership is driven by fear, deprivation, and a desire for power and control. It's a desperate clinging to a soul not yours to own. Sadly, this possessive attitude leads to failed marriages when your partner feels too constrained to spread his or her wings. Blind clinging is also a breeding ground for domestic violence. Uncontrolled rage is a reaction largely triggered by the fear of losing love and connection.

If you felt disconnected, lonely, and unsafe growing up, you're especially prone to latch on to someone who seems to extend warmth, kindness, and security. The vacuum in your soul may lead to a bonding that prompts you to tolerate the intolerable.

Open Yourself to Life

While the young lover builds a fortress in opposition to the world—viewing life as "us against them"—the evolved lover understands that love's healing opens us to life. The strength and inspiration of our pairing spurs us to engage in life, not protect ourselves from it. Rather than bond, we *connect*, which implies having a self that can also stand alone. This allows for a healthy sense of boundaries, which supports a natural rhythm between being together and being autonomous.

Mature love involves an orientation of openness and caring toward the world. Rather than gaze into each other's eyes and lose sight of the world, you're energized to offer to the world some measure of your gathered love.

Preparing for the Eight Steps

Young views of love brought us to where we are today. We need compassion toward ourselves for the inevitable oversights of our youth, especially in a culture that idealizes young love. Jungian analyst James Hollis says it plainly in *The Middle Passage:* "In retrospect, one is often chagrined, even humiliated, at the mistakes, the naivete, the projections. But such is the first adulthood: full of blunders, shyness, inhibitions, mistaken assumptions, and always the silent rolling of the tapes of childhood. . . . Reviewing one's life from the vantage-point of the second half requires understanding and forgiveness of the inevitable crime of unconsciousness. But not to become conscious in the second half is to commit an unforgivable crime."

As we become clearer about what love is and isn't, we're prepared to explore the next portions of the path that are essential for creating satisfying, midlife love. By understanding and practicing this eight-fold path, we can create a fertile ground for an ever-deepening love and intimacy.

Exploring Your Readiness for Love

Take a few deep breaths and allow your attention to settle into the center of your body. When you're ready, ask yourself the following questions.

1. What qualities or traits attracted you to a partner in the past? What were you looking for? What attracts you now? What are you looking for now in a partnership?
   (Notice whether your wants have evolved over the years.)

2. What do you absolutely need in a partner? What things would you like but can live without? What limits are you willing to accept? Are there ways in which your expectations are too high—or do you tend to limit yourself by expectancies that are too low?
   (Are you being too picky and persnickety in some ways? If so, can you let that go? Are you giving up on yourself in other ways? If so, would it feel right to take the risk to ask for what you want?)

3. Are there times when you look to your partner to supply something you must give to yourself—or receive in other ways?
   (A relationship can provide only so much for us. We also need to develop our life outside of the relationship.)

4. Are you willing to face conflict in your partnerships and friendships or do you tend to avoid it? Do you expect things to

always go easily? Are you attracted to conflict on the one hand and avoidance on the other?

(The fear of conflict throws a monkey wrench into the healthy working of a relationship. If you fear rejection and loss, or being the object of anger, you may need to strengthen yourself to deal with these feelings if they arise. Later, I'll explain how to develop skills for coping with stress, which will increase your tolerance for conflict.)

5. Are you willing to explore blind spots that may be contributing to relationship difficulties? Or do you tend to blame and accuse others when things don't go your way?

(It's always easy to think that the problem is the other person. We often resist looking at ourselves, or we just don't have the skills to do it. Courage and awareness are necessary to examine the stone in our own eye, rather than noticing the speck in the other person's eye.)

6. Have you remained in relationships due to a fear of being alone? Do you see a partnership as a life preserver or life enhancer?

(Relationships go better when we can relish periods of solitude. Unless we know how to be alone—at least to some extent—we'll tend to become too dependent on people, which may stifle our relationships.)

7. Do you accept your partner as is, or do you try to change that person into your image of who you'd like him or her to be? Do these control issues reflect ways you tend to control and judge yourself?

(Trying to change people usually creates power struggles and defensiveness. Acceptance creates a climate for open communication.)

8. Do you want a partnership to protect you from life or help you enter into life more fully? Are you willing to embrace joy and sorrow? Or do you shrink from life in an attempt to protect yourself?

(Relationships don't flourish when they serve as a mutual protection racket. We need to use the strength and support of the relationship to engage in life more fully, not escape it.)

∾•∾

Identify the Shame That Keeps Love Away

Psychologists, admittedly chagrined and a little embarrassed, are belatedly focusing on shame, a prevalent and powerful emotion, which somehow escaped rigorous scientific examination until now.

—DANIEL GOLEMAN

3

The Nature of Shame

If I feel humiliated, I can reduce this affect by blaming someone else. The blaming directly transfers shame to that other person, enabling me to feel better about myself.

—Gershen Kaufman

∽o∾

Young views of love wouldn't be so troublesome if we simply outgrew them as we age. But aging isn't synonymous with maturing. As the saying goes, "Growing old is inevitable; growing up is optional."

Unfortunately, the problem runs deeper. Our entire identity—who we think we are, how we relate to people, our perceived wants and needs—solidifies around mistaken ideas about what it takes to be accepted, loved, and happy.

Being human means having a core vulnerability: we need people. Humans are pack animals. We don't do well when we're alone and isolated. Research shows that people who don't feel loved and cared about may have three to five times the risk of premature death and disease from all causes. Emotionally, we get depressed, anxious, or angry when our longing to be accepted and loved is thwarted, which impairs our happiness and health. Physician Dean Ornish summarizes the abundant research in his book *Love & Survival:* "Anything that promotes a sense of isolation often leads to illness and suffering.

Anything that promotes a sense of love and intimacy, connection and community, is healing."

Clearly, we need people, but how can we pursue relationships that are truly a good match for us so that marriage doesn't become another name for loneliness? And if we're in a partnership or friendship, can we bring out the best in each other so that midlife becomes a passage to deeply satisfying relationships and a healthy lifestyle?

Self-Contortion versus Authenticity

Our authentic heart has been variously called our true self, real self, or genuine self (psychological terminology)—or our higher self, Buddha nature, God within, or Christ within (spiritual language). Both psychological and spiritual traditions recognize that something deep, powerful, and real exists within us, waiting to be discovered or born. This is our true nature.

Society has been structured around a core mistrust of our basic nature. The contortion of our true heart begins with the toxic message that we're not okay as we are. Especially for those currently in midlife, child-rearing had its gnarly roots in the heavy-handed belief that we have to whip the devil within us into shape. We have to suppress the selfish beast within our breast—the Mr. Hyde who'd randomly injure and abuse people if left unchecked. Only then will society be safe.

It is the distortion of who we really are that leads to problems for self and society. Destructive behavior reflects the rage of *not being allowed to be and become our authentic self*. The suppression and mistrust of our basic nature creates a cascade effect that generates violence and other social ills. Studies reveal that altruism is basic to human nature. We need to create conditions that foster the natural caring and cooperation that evolve from nonshaming, healthy human development.

Most of us grew up believing that we must be the well-behaved boy, the nice little girl, the child who never upsets anyone. If we break the rules, we'll be criticized, ridiculed, or worse. Big boys don't show fear or tears; big girls don't get angry. Being courteous means not disagreeing or speaking our mind in polite society.

Children are also hurt when parents are too permissive; they become spoiled brats when they're given no boundaries. The middle path is to set appropriate limits and provide guidance in a firm, non-shaming way.

Renowned family therapist Virginia Satir has estimated that only 4 percent of families are nurturing ones—that is, where children are given the message that "human life and human feelings are more important than anything else." That leaves 96 percent of families where degradation and dysfunctional treatment have left children questioning their worth and value. This statistic spells big trouble for future love relationships.

The prospect of being shamed and criticized sends jolts of fear through a child's vulnerable heart—the fear of being disrespected, rejected, and unloved. Being ridiculed is shatteringly painful, especially when the child is left to deal with his or her sense of shame and rejection in isolation. Therefore, adaptable children learn to shape up according to others' expectations rather than discover who they really are.

Another incubator of shame is the achievement ethic in society. Many parents and teachers reserved recognition and praise for when we were "doing well," which meant performing according to expectations. Our worth and value depended on what we did, not who we were. Even if our parents supported us unconditionally, we may have felt inadequate seeing schoolmates applauded for sports triumphs or exceptional grades. If we didn't get noticed and praised, we might have wondered, "What's wrong with me? Why don't I measure up?"

There's nothing wrong with achieving and doing your best. The point is to learn how to value your intrinsic worth as a human being whatever your social standing or level of accomplishment. If you come to believe that achievements and financial net worth are the *measure* of your self-worth, you'll feel shamed and devalued when you fall short. You'll feel a vague anxiety based on the fear of not measuring up. Lacking inner stability and peace of heart, you will lack the foundation for loving deeply and consistently.

The Anatomy of Failure

Susan Faludi, a feminist and a Pulitzer Prize–winning journalist, conducted in-depth interviews with a diverse group of American men.

She concluded that many men feel insignificant and powerless today (full of shame), largely due to a media-driven cultural shift toward the worship of celebrities and athletic heroes. As Faludi sees it, "We're becoming more and more of a commercially driven consumer culture that's all about celebrity and image and being a winner all by yourself. . . . So many of the men I talked to felt that there was no middle ground anymore. Either you were this winner who just dominated everything and was larger than life and had the biggest muscles and drove the biggest car, or you were a nobody, a loser."

Men aren't the only ones infected by a fear of being disrespected and demeaned if they don't compare well to those glorified by the mass media. Many girls and young women who pursue sports such as gymnastics are driven by the dream of being an Olympic superstar—a fantasy fueled by our collective worship of athletic celebrities.

Accolades and awards are especially appealing to those who haven't been shown that they're valuable just as they are. The desire to be accepted, loved, and special can become so compelling that it commonly leads to anorexia and bulimia. It's all part of a program to shape a body capable of bending and twisting in ways that bring cheers of approval and guard against the shame and fear of being inadequate.

A sad effect of this coronation of a class of superstars is that we overlook the everyday heroes around us. We fail to properly recognize and value the unpretentious contributors to our society's well-being. Teachers and day care workers, nurses who attend to us, farmworkers who feed us, people who sacrifice salary to serve others—these are among the true champions who deserve our respect and admiration.

Like a colorless, odorless gas, the social inculcation of shame is more insidious than you might realize. It foments a movement away from your authentic self in order to win approval and respect. Unless you understand the nature of shame and how it operates, you risk succumbing to a depression based on not feeling enough self-respect. You may give up on life or be propelled into a desperate search for love and recognition.

Whether you become depressed or driven (or both), shame poisons your psyche in ways that may lead to problems in the bedroom, even if triumph in the boardroom. It's no wonder that many people's love lives are a mess today and that the divorce rate in the United States is 50 percent.

How Shame Blocks Growth

The world of psychology has been undergoing a quiet revolution. It's based on a clearer recognition of how shame prevents our lives and relationships from maturing. By understanding the heartrending effects of shame, we can see how we unwittingly sow seeds of mistrust—and contribute to love's withering, despite our best intentions.

One day while browsing in a bookstore, a stern father started yelling at his son for harmlessly dropping a book. "What the hell's wrong with you!" he shouted. "Can't you do anything right!" I winced as I heard these sharp words violate the boy's self-worth and dignity. As he became sullen, I felt those degrading words penetrate my own soul—cold words that triggered old feelings of not being good, worthwhile, and valuable.

I felt sad to think that here was another child destined to grow up feeling small, self-conscious, and demeaned—inwardly bracing against the next accusation of being stupid or clumsy. Here was the training ground for an adult who won't trust his own feelings and impulses—and worse, his own value. Here was another person likely to remain self-protective, defensive, and hidden, holding back his natural self-expression to protect himself from anticipated judgments and assaults.

Shame Makes You Hide

Trusting relationships are problematic if you haven't internalized the message that you're precious and lovable—and that people want to know your real feelings, thoughts, and wants. Intimacy will not be forthcoming if you've decided that people aren't safe and that you must stay small and hidden to protect yourself from embarrassment and hurt.

Shame is that sinking feeling in the pit of your stomach that bespeaks a sense of feeling defective. It's the pained recognition that you're being perceived in a degraded, contemptuous way by another person. It's a feeling of not being likable and lovable, not being wanted on the team—or the humiliation of always being the last one chosen.

Webster's Dictionary defines shame as "a painful feeling of having lost the respect of others." Repeatedly losing respect makes you resentful, depressed, or mistrustful. Even worse, shame leads to doubting and hating yourself.

Therapists Marilyn Mason and Merle Fossum define shame as: "an inner sense of being completely diminished or insufficient as a person. . . . It is the ongoing premise that one is fundamentally bad, inadequate, defective, unworthy, or not fully valid as a human being."

Dr. Joan Borysenko describes it as the "sudden vulnerability and threatening feelings we experience whenever the bridge of trust and acceptance between us and others is suddenly broken." Intimate connections are possible only when you trustingly open yourself to people. By keeping you small and hidden, shame disconnects you from life.

Philosopher Jean-Paul Sartre saw shame as a pained recognition that you're being seen as an object, that you're being held in a degraded or fixed way by another's gaze. Shame—that "immediate shudder which runs through me from head to foot"—may arise when you believe you're being perceived in a narrow, negative light, like the boy in the bookstore. Sartre believed that the effects of this shaming are so powerful that he made his now famous declaration, "Hell is other people!"

EXERCISE:

> Write down three embarrassing or degrading experiences you had as a child—ones where you felt painfully shamed or criticized, whether at home, in school, or on the playground. Who disparaged you? Do you remember how you felt? Did you have anyone to talk to about it? Did you experience the shame or burden of holding destructive secrets?
>
> (Understanding some of the roots of your current shame can help you realize how a sense of inadequacy was conditioned in you; it's not who you really are. This awareness can serve to put some distance between you and your shame. You may experience embarrassment or humiliation, but you are *not* your shame.)

Shame Numbs You Out

Developmental psychologists have learned that we develop much of our sense of self from how we're perceived and treated by others.

Unless we're affirmed as an individual—as a "thou" instead of an "it"—it's doubtful that we'll validate ourselves, and it then becomes far too scary to disclose ourselves to other people. Even worse, we won't know *how* to show ourselves because we won't know who we are. Love and intimacy suffer in this alien climate of shame.

- Do you numb out to those feelings and aspects of yourself that have been belittled and rejected by others?
- Does it become too painful to let yourself experience your anger, sadness, spontaneity, or exuberance because you've been yelled at or humiliated for experiencing them?
- Do you shrink down to a more stunted self that you think will be acceptable?

Shame cuts like a knife to the soft core of your soul. You may experience it in these ways:

- Feeling small, weak, and insignificant.
- Having a gnawing sense of guilt.
- Feeling defective, defensive, unworthy, or worthless.
- Wanting to disappear in the face of real or imagined criticism.
- Feeling "less than" others, inferior, or inadequate.

The felt sense of shame is often a dreaded, sinking feeling in the pit of the stomach—a sense of feeling queasy or restless. As one man put it, "I'm terrified that someday I'll be seen as a fake. They'll see through me and realize that I'm not the cool, confident person I appear to be. They'll realize that when I say I'm doing fine, that I'm covering up how I really feel because I'm afraid I'll be rejected and condemned. I'm afraid of being judged for having flaws and weaknesses." As the saying goes, oftentimes when we insist we're "fine," FINE stands for freaked out, insecure, nervous, and empty!

A forty-four-year-old librarian put it this way: "I'm afraid that beneath my smile, people will see that I'm really insecure. Sometimes I feel like covering myself up and going to sleep. I just want to make everything go away." Hiding from potential humiliation kept her confined to her house on many nights. Her loneliness resulted from failing to risk showing herself. She stayed safe, but painfully secluded.

Shame Keeps You from Showing Up

At my high school reunion, I learned that an old friend didn't attend because he was embarrassed by his baldness. I felt sad that his discomfort about his appearance robbed us of an opportunity to reconnect. I was reminded how shame shatters our self-esteem and prevents us from bringing our true selves to each other. It keeps us from showing up.

Overcoming this sense of unworthiness begins with gentle honesty and warm acceptance about where you are right now. This means acknowledging that you feel shame while not allowing it to define who you are. You have shame from your social conditioning, but you are not shameful. This tenderhearted self-embracing is the starting point for healing your real or imagined flaws—and moving toward a deeper love that unfolds only in the gentle arms of authenticity.

EXERCISE:

Recall a recent incident where you experienced shame. It may be an embarrassing experience or a comment that made you feel small. Then list at least five qualities you like and value about yourself. You may choose from the following list:

I am:

honest · dependable · loving · compassionate · humorous · flexible · strong · a good provider · communicative · tender · intelligent · insightful · devoted · kind · a good mother/father · a good friend · a caring partner · loyal · creative · curious · humble · willing to learn and grow · willing to admit mistakes · a good person · generous · genuine · honorable

As you hold these positive traits in mind, go back over the embarrassing incident and see if you can turn it around. Can you put it in perspective, given your positive qualities? Can you view it in the context of affirming your gifts and talents? If others have shamed you, can you see it as a statement about them, instead of about you?

The fear of how others may view us is a core human fear—often-times so strong that it shapes our entire way of living. This is why surveys reveal that the number one human fear is the fear of public speaking, even surpassing the fear of dying! We're more afraid of dying of embarrassment than of dying of cancer!

Shame poisons your well-being by making you painfully self-conscious. Fearing an exposure to ridicule, you're unwilling to expose your vulnerability. Afraid of being disgraced or discarded, you don't take the risk of being real with people. Intimacy requires genuine-ness that shame demolishes.

Shame is a major drain on your joie de vivre—the spontaneous joy of being alive. Gripped by its darkness, you may feel that you have no place in the world—no right to take up space, no right to *be*. Shame, along with a fear of rejection and ridicule, may drive you to concoct a fabricated self designed to win acceptance. Sadly, this false self prevents you from showing your authentic heart and thereby keeps intimacy away.

Children need to be seen with adoring, smiling eyes. When they are frequently met with disapproval, they internalize shame, not love. They grow up feeling lacking, not lovable. The propagation of such belittlement produces a harvest of hopelessness. Over time, a tightly wound pain may implode on itself, producing a rage turned inward, which can trigger depression or teen suicide. Or rage may flare out-ward, leading to the school shootings or gang membership that is disturbingly common today. *Shame is the unrivaled incubator for the despair that leads to violence.*

When I was twenty-one I was driving with a friend and having a lively conversation. Suddenly, the car behind cut me off and I was forced to slam on the brakes. The driver then came running toward my car screaming obscenities. Being a peace-loving person, I told my friend to roll up his window and lock the door. "Oh, that's Phillip," he said, "I don't know what's gotten into him!" Phillip then proceeded to pound my car window so hard that I was certain he'd break either the window or his hand. Terrified, I was able to drive on the sidewalk to circumvent his car and drive away. I had no idea who Phillip was or why he was enraged.

Several weeks later, my friend saw Phillip at his junior college and spoke with him about the incident. Phillip said he was upset because he saw us laughing and he "knew" we were laughing at him. I realized how desperate and violent people can become when they imagine they're being slighted or insulted. This young man's self-worth was so low and his shame so deep that he was quick to imagine that people were making fun of him.

Shame Suppresses You

When we collectively realize how shame is responsible for not only immense personal misery but also colossal social ills, our new educational priority will be to nurture healthy, self-affirming, emotionally intelligent children who feel that they have a fertile future ahead of them. Achieving this goal requires creating structures that ensure that every child knows *and feels* that he or she is wanted, treasured, and protected. It also means teaching children to recognize and deal with their emotional pain rather than act it out by hurting others.

Ronald Brill, author of *Emotional Honesty & Self-Acceptance*, suggests, "Rather than focus on violence-proofing our schools, educators should use schools to violence-proof our children." It is only by learning to deal effectively with feelings that children will develop the healthy self-acceptance that creates a foundation for mature love and happy marriages.

Children are born with a miraculous capacity for joy, openness, and spontaneity. Life is vibrant with wonder and beauty. But as shame creeps into our lives, our joy and curiosity curdle into caution and mistrust. Our irrepressible spirit becomes dampened and dulled. Life is no longer joyful and juicy.

As we become adults, our shame-generated anger and frustration may be acted out in our marriages and with our children. Thus the cycle of shame-based violence propagates itself.

Fortunately, your capacity to love and affirm yourself is never destroyed, just impaired. The promise of facing shame is that you may overcome an obstinate barrier to showing your authentic heart—and fulfilling the promise of finding love in midlife.

Don't Betray Your Soul

Many of us can remember the excruciating embarrassment of being the last one chosen for the team, or being laughed at for giving a "silly" answer to a teacher's question. We pick up the clear message that love, respect, and acceptance depend upon our accomplishments, performance, and popularity. Falling short, we feel inferior because we don't compare favorably with those who are lavished with attention.

As a vulnerable child, you probably acted a role to fit in. If you grew up in a chaotic or unstable family, maybe you adopted the role of peacekeeper or appeaser. If you were neglected or if love was conditional, you might be eager to please to gain approval. If you were like most children, you learned to manage your anxiety about whether you were safe and lovable by sizing up your environment and performing according to expectations; you became an expert at impression management. Or, rather than submit, you may have assumed the role of a rebel. In either case, a reactive identity was created, not an authentic one.

Sadly, the more you're coaxed to stray from your real heart, the more you betray your own soul, and the more alienated you become from others and from life. Not feeling trusted, you learn not to trust others or to trust life. Rather than experience a natural developmental process that would usher you toward the trust and openness that support love, you become inwardly guarded and defensive. Your natural inner signals and instincts are lost in a quagmire of shame and fear. Your intuitions and insights yield to rigid roles and a desire for acceptance, even at high cost. All of this doesn't bode well for wise mate selection as an adult!

The loss of your authentic self has gloomy effects on your love life. The qualities in another person that attract you are subtly based on the wounds of childhood. You look to rescue or be rescued. You seek to lose yourself in merging rather than find yourself through genuine relating. The stage is then set to rage or withdraw when your wants are not gratified. There's no real self to come back to.

Because immature notions of love are interwoven with the wounds of childhood, it takes effort to develop a more mature view of love; it means transforming yourself. It means embarking on a path of growth where you heal old hurts, clarify your thinking, and crystallize your vision of where you want to go. You must distill out your self-worth from your achievements, status, and any abusive history that might have made you feel small and inadequate.

By understanding how the process of self-abandonment and disconnection began, you can better understand what may have propelled you into relationships. As you open the doors of perception, romantic illusions lose their hold and move you toward discovering your authentic heart.

The Fabricated Self

The frustrated longing to be loved prompts you to *manufacture* a self that will win approval and respect. Getting the message from parents and caregivers that your real self is not adequate to win love and inclusion, you fabricate a false self that will do the job.

The word "personality" comes from the Latin word *persona*, meaning mask, particularly one worn by an actor. We're often attracted to people who "have personality," but do we really know them?

The convention of showing a fabricated self is deeply ingrained in our society. I've occasionally browsed the personal ads and been bemused by suggestions to leave a voice mail greeting to lure a mate. I have come across advice to speak with a cheerful voice, or to share something exciting about your life, or to leave a voice mail greeting that's clever or funny. Rarely have I seen any mention of relaxing and showing your real self!

The split between our natural presence and our fabricated self with all of its narrow beliefs is generated by a society that uses shame to mold our way of being and behaving. As a result of this rift within our collective psyche, we've created a culture in which most of us don't know or trust ourselves or others. We numb ourselves to our alienated condition through the distractions and addictions of modern life, which fuel the market economy but foul the soul.

Being cut off from ourselves is at the core of today's crisis in marriage and family life and accounts for the larger social problems generated by isolation and frustration. Our self-disconnection also prompts the shallow views of love that are designed to rescue us from the loneliness and disconnection created by our shame. Losing ourselves creates anxiety as well. As Trappist monk Thomas Merton knew, "As long as you have to defend the imaginary self that you think is important, you lose your peace of heart."

The fear of criticism, humiliation, and isolation drives you to concoct an "acceptable" self. However, the experience of love and connection is only possible when you manifest your authentic self. You may have learned to trust your fabricated self because this false self has gained some modicum of "success" and approval—perhaps through the social rewards of status or wealth, or through a charismatic personality that can charm and disarm people. Herein lies your predicament: the more you invest in an artificial self, the more you abandon your genuine heart, which you must inhabit to experience mature love and intimacy. The more you're driven by shame, fear, and pain to polish and parade an acceptable self, the more you deny a heart that longs to be contacted and loved.

As your fabricated self operates on automatic pilot, you may experience a vague sense of loneliness and disconnection. But you may wonder why, since it appears to be functioning quite well. You might think, "I just got a promotion to senior vice president and my stocks are soaring, so how can I be unhappy?"

The construction of a counterfeit self constitutes your original self-betrayal. This disassociation from your authentic heart is the essence of what is called codependence, a condition in which you sacrifice your own feelings, beliefs, and needs in order to accommodate those of others. When you mistrust or neglect yourself, you don't know how you feel or what you want. Your very sense of self is built on reactions to others' needs and wants. Or it's built upon narrow identifications, such as your job title, sports car, or good-looking spouse.

When these adulterations of your authentic self aren't reversed, your prospects for love dim. Love requires connecting with a self that becomes ever more radiant as you embrace, affirm, and nurture yourself. Your authentic heart is expansive by nature; your fabricated self keeps you contracted and isolated.

Developing a fabricated self is synonymous with the religious concept of "original sin." The shame that prompts you to cover yourself in a garb laced with defenses and deceptions keeps you disconnected from yourself, others, and God (however you understand this). "Sin" is the original alienation from your authentic self, which passes from generation to generation. The way out is the way in. As Catholic priest Eugene Kennedy observes, "Salvation comes to those who are themselves."

Buddhism also recognizes the need to connect with your authentic heart. Bodhi-Dharma, the first patriarch of Zen, taught that "if you wish to seek the Buddha, you ought to see into your own Nature (hsing); for this Nature is the Buddha himself. If you have not seen into your own nature, what is the use of thinking of the Buddha?"

You can feel honestly loved only when you're committed to affirming and showing your true heart. Midlife relationships become lifeless if you live from a fabricated self crafted to gain respect and avoid the trauma of being rejected or denigrated.

The young attempt to wrest love through *fashioning* a self rather than *being* yourself is destined to disappoint you. Instead of valuing and showing the self you are, you become a contorted version of yourself. Trying to achieve "self-image actualization" rather than "self-actualization" diverts you from an authentic life and rich relationships. Although the world may sing your praises, you lose your soul.

Show Your True Heart

Mark, a forty-nine-year-old businessman, complained that women never warm up to him. Rather than look within, he sought solace in cynicism. He came to the conclusion that all women are self-centered and hypocritical and continued in a love/hate world of dating and dumping women.

During therapy, Mark began turning the mirror toward himself and gradually made some courageous discoveries about his *own* phoniness: "I'm always trying to influence people's perceptions of me. I try to be interesting. I try to manipulate people so they'll find me funny, capable, and caring. I follow a set of 'how-to-be's'—I'm the new liberated male. It's how I deceive people. I try to be more sophisticated than I really am so they'll find me desirable. But it never works."

Mark gradually realized that he needed to embrace himself with his strengths and weaknesses. Some people will be drawn to him; others won't be. He needed to accept rejection without concluding that he was flawed and hence fall into a pit of shame. Facing rejection is part of the risk of loving. His relationships became more enriched as he became more real. As he put it, "I need to keep asking, 'Who am I?' Then I need to find people who can accept me as I am. If they don't like me, what's important is that I still like myself! That's all that I have power over in a situation. I can't control others' perceptions of me!"

We may be slow to recognize that much of our lives has been

spent constructing a synthetic version of ourselves to please people. It's no wonder we become resentful and cynical! We resent being someone we're not—or someone we believe we have to be. Psychoanalyst Alice Miller addresses how self-inquiry is the first step in our journey toward authenticity:

> If a person is able . . . to experience that he was never "loved" as a child for what he was but for his achievements, success, and good qualities, and that he sacrificed his childhood for this "love," this will shake him very deeply but one day he will feel the desire to end this courtship. He will discover in himself a need to live according to his "true self" and no longer be forced to earn love, a love that at root, still leaves him empty-handed since it is given to the "false self," which he has begun to relinquish.

Many people spend their entire lives masquerading around a phony self. They rarely relax into their authentic heart, which has been encased with all kinds of desperate fears, judgments, and armor. They use willpower and intellect to determine what feelings are permissible and how to fashion acceptable responses to people.

At times, such adjustments are surely necessary, such as in a dysfunctional workplace. But if this is how we conduct our personal relationships, we lose ourselves. We betray ourselves by clinging to a self-identity forged during younger years when we so much needed acceptance.

You'll never know who your true friends are until you're true to yourself. If you win companionship because of an image you're projecting, you'll wonder whether your friends are attracted to you or to your image. As a result, love and connection will never deepen.

The word "intimacy" derives from the Latin *intimus*, meaning "innermost." By not showing your innermost nature, you'll never enjoy the deepening of intimacy that comes with a mature awareness and affirmation of who you really are. Satisfying, trusting relations remain a distant dream when you live with an abiding uncertainty about your worth and value.

This book is an invitation to be more kindhearted. But it's difficult to be honestly caring when harnessed by duty and obligation. The clamoring demands of your inner and outer critics create a pressure and burden that annihilates love ("If you love me, you'll sacrifice yourself and give me what I want"). Love flows most deeply and meaningfully in a climate of freedom. Love blossoms as your heart is so touched by another that you're genuinely moved to be there for him or her. Mature love cannot be forced; it cannot be compelled to fit some image of how love should look. For the authentic heart, love is a joy, not a chore. Love is limited when contaminated by concealed motives.

Most of us fear direct contact with others. We hide who we really are and what we really feel and want. Consequently, there's no authentic meeting of hearts, no contact that would nourish our soul. Alone and disconnected, we reach out in quiet desperation for some comfort, perhaps through sex, junk food, alcohol, or television. Or we try to control and dominate people to feel empowered.

The proverbial midlife crisis results only partly from getting older. More centrally, you're shaken by the realization that you're not being who you really are. You haven't found meaning in life; you haven't been living fully—and life might be growing short. This realization can dawn at any age, but it's more likely to strike as you grow weary of the old programming and beliefs that aren't delivering the goods, or when you face a crisis that challenges your innocence. An auspicious midlife passage means grieving the loss of your idealized, fabricated self—along with its medley of false hopes and questionable motives—and being reborn into the richness of your inviolate heart, discovering the exquisite beauty of your true nature.

Contact the Deeper Layers
of Your Authentic Heart

If your self-expression was repeatedly ridiculed or ignored in your youth, you probably learned to mistrust your genuine self. Revealing yourself became associated with hurt and rejection. It's scary to let people see your true self when you've been shamed and rejected for revealing your real feelings, wants, and viewpoints. Sadly, you may remain unacquainted with the depths of yourself because you've driven it into seclusion for so long. The passage into midlife love becomes fulfilling as you contact, show, and trust your authentic heart.

Most of us bounce between our shame-driven, fabricated self and our genuine self. We're aware of some of our feelings some of the time, but we never get to the bottom of what's really going on. We're aware of some slice of our experience but rarely embrace its totality.

For example, one of my clients would quickly show anger when she was actually feeling sad and afraid because her partner wasn't spending enough time with her: "Your work is more important than me!" Doris would shout at her partner, Dale. "I've had it with this relationship!" Dale would bark back sarcastically, "What does that mean exactly? You're just gonna walk out? That's a great solution!" Dale's hostility would trigger more rage from Doris. Hostility and accusations began feeding on each other, locking Doris and Dale in a battle of wills rather than a sharing of souls.

It may appear that Doris was being real by being honestly angry, but her resentment was a mere surface response—the first step toward uncovering more vulnerable feelings closer to her core, especially feelings of shame, hurt, and fear.

When they both realized that their verbal attacks were fueled by shame and a fear of losing love, their exchange became more mean-ingful, heartfelt, and productive. When Doris said, "I've had it with this relationship," Dale interpreted this as, "I'm not being a good partner (shame)" and "she might leave me if I don't shape up (fear)." Rather than notice more tender feelings, he immediately became defensive and attacked back. Similarly, when Dale reacted sarcasti-cally with, "What does that mean exactly? You're just gonna walk out?" Doris heard her own inner voice of shame ("I never say things right. I'm not important enough for people to hear me").

As Dale uncovered his deeper feelings, he could tell Doris, "It scares me when you say that you've had it with our relationship. I feel like an inadequate partner; I feel like a failure and I have guilt around that. I want to be a good partner for you. Tell me more about what you're feeling and wanting." This nondefensive response allowed Doris to feel safer and to share her more vulnerable feelings: "I miss you when I don't see you enough; I get lonely for you. I love you and enjoy our time together." Mature love grew as they discovered and shared ever deeper layers of their unfeigned hearts rather than spout-ing criticism and contempt.

The spoken word has potent effects. According to an old Sufi saying, a word spoken in haste can never be retrieved. When your fabricated self is busy protecting its image and safeguarding its security, you may say things that violate another's boundaries and not recognize how you've violated trust—until it's too late.

It is difficult to undo the damage of venomous words or hurtful actions. Sometimes marriage counseling can't save a relationship because the couple has sought help too late. By repeatedly slashing each other's sensibilities, they're unable to reverse the escalating tide of hurt, resentment, and mistrust.

Until the adolescent impulse to get your way yields to the mature ability to communicate from your honest depths, your relationships will languish. Not sharing issues and feelings at an earlier moment is like ignoring small cavities until the decay finally strikes a raw nerve. If you postpone looking at unpleasant truths, your partnership may need major root canal work, if it's salvageable at all.

Heed Instructive Guilt and Shame

Not all shame and guilt are injurious. In contrast to *destructive shame*, which is paralyzing, *instructive shame* is your wisdom trying to get your attention. It tells you when you've hurt someone or fallen short of your own values. By gently embracing appropriate guilt or shame, you can learn something about yourself. You can become a better person.

When I was in New York talking about my book *Love & Betrayal*, a man shouted sarcastically, "You've ruined my day! I now realize how I've betrayed many women and *you're* making me feel guilty about it!" Perhaps this man had so much shame that he had erected strong defenses against feeling any of it.

Mild shame or guilt is a vital part of forming a healthy, vibrant conscience, which can reliably guide your actions according to inner signals, not just noble ideas disconnected from your felt experience. When morality develops in close concert with your experience of life, it flowers into strength of character and integrity. It becomes a personal code of principles connected to your gut and heart. Being aware of instructive guilt is a corrective to our narcissistic culture of feel good-ism, where we pursue our own pleasure without awareness of how we're affecting others.

To paraphrase philosopher Martin Buber, guilt can be a call to be responsible instead of continuing to be irresponsible. We're not summoned to redo the past or wallow in shame about what we've done but rather to face whatever comes in the present with a keener sense of our true values.

"Mental morality" is skin-deep. It's ultimately unreliable because it's not grounded in your being, and you're prone to slip when you think no one's looking. "Felt morality" develops when you befriend your feelings and know yourself deeply. It reliably guides you through life's turbulent currents

Guilt Can Awaken Our Heart

The shame or guilt that naturally arises when you've hurt someone can arouse your intrinsic conscience. It can be an instructive signal that awakens your pure heart—a message to you to overcome narcissism and recognize how you're affecting people. Properly acknowledged, shame and guilt can open a doorway to understanding how you've hurt someone. If you never allow guilt or remorse to touch your heart, you will fail to develop empathy for people. As you become more entrenched behind your defenses, you're not much fun to be around!

Some people are so guilt ridden that they jettison any feeling that resembles shame. Lacking self-compassion and being afraid of being wrong, they have difficulty saying "I'm sorry" or "I was wrong" or "I blew it." Excessive shame keeps them in denial; no mistakes are allowable. Shame overload paralyzes your capacity for clear introspection. A "no flaws allowed" mind-set is the biggest block to noticing the effects of your actions and taking responsibility for them. No growth is possible without some small amount of shame.

The failure to acknowledge any regret or responsibility reflects fragility, not strength. It requires a denial of our human limitations. It represents the sin of hubris—exaggerated pride and confidence. As we become stronger and wiser during midlife, we can learn to be comfortable admitting, "I made a mistake and I apologize" without having it mean, "I am a mistake and I'm a bad person."

In a recent talk, John Bradshaw jokingly said he wanted to retitle his best-selling book *Healing the Shame That Binds You* to *Finding the Shame That Heals You*! If your body wasn't wired to experience shame, you wouldn't know when you'd gone beyond the bounds of human decency.

Something to watch out for: Some people newly affirming their self-worth misuse psychological jargon to dismiss every caring impulse as "caretaking" or "codependent" behavior. They justify a new kind of cruelty as a way to overcome their seeming powerlessness, such as after a breakup or during a child custody proceeding. Instructive guilt helps us find a way to balance self-empowerment with basic kindness.

4

Your Inner Critic: The Voice of Shame

The judge is the force in you that constantly evaluates and assesses your worth as a human being and thus limits your capacity to be fully alive in the present moment.

—Byron Brown

❦

"Y ou're foolish! You should know better! When are you gonna grow up!" When shaming words are served up over and over again, we get the impression that something is drastically wrong with our natural responses to life. These assaults breed a shame-driven "inner critic" that coerces us like a stern schoolmaster. We then no longer need others to control us; we do the job quite nicely ourselves.

This self-scrutinizing structure in the human psyche has been variously called the inner critic, inner judge, inner vulture, or super-ego. I prefer to call it the inner critic, but whatever it's called, this negative self-talk is the voice of shame.

If you notice the sensations associated with shame—perhaps a dull ache in your stomach, a tightness in your chest, or a heaviness throughout your body—you know that shame is operating. If you catch yourself talking in a contemptuous, critical manner to your-self, shame is nearby.

Denigrating self-talk often begins with phrases such as:

- Why can't you ever . . . (do anything right, get it right, suc-ceed, do the smart thing . . .)?
- You're always . . . (screwing up, a loser, saying the wrong thing, repeating bad habits, attracted to the wrong person . . .).
- You'll never . . . (win, amount to anything, accomplish any-thing, be happy . . .).
- You're so . . . (stupid, selfish, bad, vain, crazy . . .).
- When will you finally . . . (grow up, get it together, do it right, make enough money . . .)?
- If only you were . . . (better, smarter, more articulate, more competent . . .).

If you can identify such phrases in your head, you've taken the first step toward replacing them with kinder self-talk (more about this later).

The inner critic is the guardian of your constricted self. It is armored with a repertoire of self-talk that "rescues" you from your authentic self at every turn. For instance, at the first glimpse of a genuine feeling or need, you might control yourself with a phrase like, "Don't hurt people's feelings by telling them how you feel," or, "Stop being so selfish!"

It saddens me to see people berating themselves for normal human feelings. For example, those hurting from a failed relationship often say to themselves: "You should be over him by now," or, "How could you have been so dumb! You blew it again!"

Such declarations are intended to help, but criticizing yourself doesn't alleviate your pain. It perpetuates it. You won't learn from your experience when your inner critic is pounding on you. Growth takes place in an atmosphere of self-compassion and self-forgiveness.

Challenging your stern beliefs can be disorienting. By suspending self-critical thoughts, you may fear being engulfed by a sea of unfa-miliar feelings. And if you divulge these "strange" feelings to others, you may fear being ridiculed or being seen as repulsive or weak. Shar-ing your real fears, hurts, or concerns might unsettle people who've been trained to be repulsed by their own authentic self.

Another protective service offered by the inner critic is that it defuses potential criticism from others. If you are poised to berate yourself for an embarrassing comment or poor decision, then you preempt others from delivering the fatal blow; you beat them to the punch.

For example, when radio disc jockeys mispronounce a word, they often poke fun at themselves. Listening to my car radio one Labor Day, I heard a local disc jockey comment: "It's a beautiful day out there on this Memorial Day weekend . . . I mean *Labor Day* weekend. Where's my brain today!?" Perhaps like many people, he discovered the general rule that people criticize you less when you are quick to mock yourself.

A high price is paid for the self-scolding services rendered by your inner umpire, one who's forever evaluating whether you're safe or embarrassingly off-base. You're then beset with the chronic stress of not being yourself. Physically, you may get high blood pressure, rashes, or other diseases that have a body/mind link. Emotionally, you may become so self-preoccupied that you're unavailable to be empathic toward others and experience the delight of intimacy. Spiritually, you may abandon the place inside you where it's possible to experience deeper dimensions of love, joy, and union. Midlife is the time to get the inner critic off your back and relish the responsible freedom of being yourself.

Legacies of Your Inner Critic

Youthful love often fails because instead of being who you really are, you're playing out shame-driven roles that you *think* will bring happiness. Midlife development involves healing the residue of shame you carry and replacing its cognitive cohort, your scolding inner critic, with an inner voice that speaks to you gently.

Shame is a viral program that shuts down your heart. The emotion of shame and its mental comrade, your inner critic, team up to poison your spirit and keep your relationships shallow. When this dynamic duo operates, you live with the ongoing anxiety that you're worthless, unlovable, and inadequate.

You may be afraid of failing, which would "prove" that you really are inferior. You may be afraid of rejection, which would confirm that you really are unwanted. Less visibly, you may be afraid of succeeding, as success might make future failures more humiliating.

Shame and its associated fears operate like background noise: they're always present, but you may not notice how they're affecting you—how you're living with pervasive anxiety about your goodness and worth. The fear of being shamed or disrespected can make you shrink up inside. Dreading the prospect of getting hurt, you may protect yourself from being seen as you are. Living behind a defensive shell, you may guard your heart from real or potential blows of rejection or ridicule. You may become dispirited and inauthentic, not trusting that it's safe to come out of hiding and live and play from your authentic heart.

Fortunately, you're not condemned to be forever immobilized by shame and its vocal spokesperson, which is poised to count the ways you're just not good enough. Shame becomes more destructive when you're blind to its presence, or when you condemn yourself for having shame inside you, or when you allow that critical voice to live rent-free in your brain. Shame is more debilitating when you're ashamed of your shame, and when you don't catch and challenge the subtle and blatant ways your inner critic is jabbering at you.

Your shame repository may be so unwieldy that you split off your awareness from it. You may have felt so invaded and injured during childhood that you lost touch with your body. Byron Brown states it clearly in *Soul without Shame*: "The sense of invasion, rejection, or hurt caused by the parent's critical energy was often overwhelming to your sensitivity. So distancing from yourself (self-rejection) dulled your awareness of the attack to help you survive what was intolerable or unstoppable. In extreme cases of abuse or trauma, the only way to survive was to completely dissociate from reality in the moment." When you disconnect from yourself, all that may remain is a sense of feeling tired, hopeless, anxious, or angry.

An essential part of healing and recovery is reconnecting with your bodily experience of the sensations and feelings that reside in it (more about this later). But before you do this, it is helpful to identify the voice of the inner critic and all the subtle ways it strangles your authentic heart. Midlife is a time to recognize and heal the accumulated shame that holds you back from relationships of depth and delight.

Rather than allow shame to define you, realize that whatever shame you carry comes from society and your history, not your inherent nature. Understanding the subtleties of this process is often aided by hiring a therapist to help you with this kind of psychosurgery—separating yourself from the shaming, critical voices that create misery for you and those close to you.

Your inner critic may stifle honesty by serving up beliefs such as:

1. Nobody wants to know how you really feel.
2. If you show vulnerability, people will use it against you.
3. Nobody will understand you, so don't even try explaining yourself.
4. You're more likely to get what you want if you disguise your feelings, needs, and motives.
5. Why bother expressing yourself: who really cares?
6. You're such a poor communicator, so don't even try!

You can replace this critical self-talk with a nurturing inner voice:

1. Some people *are* interested in how I feel. Even more important, *I'm* interested in how I feel.
2. If I show vulnerability, it's an opportunity to feel closer and not carry everything inside.
3. People are more likely to understand me if I take a crack at communicating. Then I may find people who understand me, or I'll attempt to clarify further so they can understand me.
4. If I'm more direct, at least I'm giving people a chance to give me what I want. It takes less energy to be direct, even if it's a little scary.
5. People who care about me do want to hear my feelings and wants. I can take a risk to express myself. People may understand me better if I reveal more of myself.
6. I'm not a perfect communicator, but I can keep learning so I get better at it. It's okay to make mistakes; that's how I improve.

Remember that most people talk negatively to themselves and have difficulty talking to themselves in nurturing ways.

Shame doesn't heal by being ignored. If you live as if shame doesn't exist, it will drive you in destructive ways. It will become the power behind the puppet's strings and move you in ways to make you compensate for feeling inferior, perhaps by proving that you're better than others or being arrogant. Offensive and deceptive behaviors are often cover-ups for shame. You attempt to be big because you feel small. This overcompensation for feelings of inferiority alienates people, pushing love further away.

For Jason, a fifty-year-old executive, being respectable meant being the perfect gentleman: "My word is my bond" was his motto. One day, a crucial business meeting came up on the same night he had a movie date. He was caught in a double shame bind! If he didn't stay true to his word, he'd feel like a heel (shame). If he didn't attend the meeting, his business project might fail (shame).

At first, he tried to squirm out of his date with Wendy by suggesting that the movie reviews were bad and perhaps they should forget it. She reassured him that her friend loved the movie. "Well," he went on, "I've also been feeling under the weather lately and I don't want you to get sick." Again, he was being the noble gentleman—consistent with his self-image! But that didn't fly either because Wendy was willing to risk catching his cold. Feeling increasingly tense and frustrated by his inability to wiggle out of his commitment, he suddenly blurted out, "Look, I just need the night off, is that okay?"

This exchange left Wendy feeling stunned and confused. Something smelled fishy. Why was he so upset? Fortunately, they had enough commitment to talk. Jason finally acknowledged that a business meeting came up and he didn't want to disappoint her—or make her angry. Of course, she was much more hurt and angry by his tap dancing around the issue than if he had stated the truth without deception.

Jason gradually realized that Wendy wanted the truth, even if it was disappointing. This was better than the cutting comments that exploded from the pressure cooker of his shame! She felt more respected by getting the straight story from him rather than feeling the craziness of hearing one thing but sensing another.

To Be Human Is to Feel Shame Sometimes

Jason realized that unexpected things happen in life and that it's not shameful to change plans when necessary. He could maintain his integrity by speaking in a direct, kind way when he wants to change plans, and thereby loosen the rigid stance of his inner critic (always keep your word!), which was a setup for more shame and failure. He felt relieved to relinquish his self-image of being Mr. Reliable and replace it with the more realistic notion that he can only do his best, which doesn't mean being perfect. Communicating in a more authentic way enabled trust and closeness to grow.

Dispirited by shame, you may fear that you'll repel people if you show your real self. You may tell yourself, "This isn't the image that will win friends!" An inner struggle then brews between what's real inside you versus what you *think* you're supposed to show people to be acceptable. This agonizing struggle tends to alienate people because you're no longer really present. You're disassociated from your authentic heart. People often sense when you're being disingenuous, phony, or indirect, and that's what pushes them—and love—away.

Shame and fear begin to heal as you accept that these feelings are present and also recognize their destructive legacy. This means accepting that you're human, like everyone else, and that it's okay to have flaws and vulnerabilities. Midlife is a time to realize that you don't have to be a paragon of perfection to be loved.

Your heart becomes more accessible and your self-protectiveness melts as you warmly embrace yourself as you are—vulnerably showing your true feelings and wants. But first you must be honest with yourself. To be human is to feel shame, fear, and hurt sometimes, and this is okay, though it's not who you really are. Beneath your socially created shame lies your authentic heart waiting to be born—the larger you that longs to breathe freely, and to connect with people and life.

Brad learned to play it safe in life. During his student years, he rarely raised his hand in class, fearful of being wrong. As an adult, he inspected every word before speaking: "I'm always careful about what I say. I get self-conscious and come across as stiff and awkward. Inside, I'm afraid I'll say something dumb and be laughed at. So I say little."

Fearing ridicule, Brad would become quiet in his relationships. He gradually realized that people were shunning him not because there was anything inherently wrong with him but because holding back made him elusive—and even boring. As a result, he had no deep, trusting relationships as his fiftieth birthday was approaching.

While shame may lead one person to withdraw, it might lead another to become overly sociable. Paula, for example, talked a lot as a way to impress people while hiding her anxiety about not being good enough: "I talk when I get nervous. I become a chatterbox—especially when I like someone. I want to show how smart I am. I think they'll like me if I keep proving myself. When things get quiet, I get anxious. I'm afraid they'll find me boring."

Promoting the image of being interesting covered up a deeper insecurity: "I can't just relax and be myself. I think no one would love me for who I really am—with my strengths *and* weaknesses. But I push people away because I get so lost in talking that I don't listen. So I don't connect." Trust never grows when we're so busy constructing an acceptable self that a real connection never takes root.

Paula gradually gave herself permission to feel shy and nervous when meeting people. By taking one small step at a time, she found the strength to accept her real feelings. She allowed them to be part of who she is without shame or apology.

Your inner critic may block you from speaking authentically from your heart by saying:

1. You'd better keep your mouth shut so you don't embarrass yourself.
2. If you don't say anything, no one can attack you.
3. If you stay inside the house, you're safer. Why set yourself up for rejection or criticism?
4. If you keep talking, maybe you'll finally get heard. Also, you deserve the attention. You're very expressive, so use it to your advantage!
5. Be critical of others before they have a chance to be critical of you.

You can replace this critical self-talk with a nurturing inner voice:

1. It's okay to talk when I have something to say; it's okay to be silent if nothing occurs to me. I can participate by listening as much as by speaking, maybe even more so.
2. If someone denigrates me, that says something about them, not about me. I don't have to be perfect in how I express myself. It's okay to be shy. I can hold myself with respect, even if I fall.

3. The house is safer, but if I feel lonely, why not take a risk to go to a lecture, a concert, or an art show? What's there to lose? And how safe am I if I'm alone the rest of my life? If I reach out to someone and that person doesn't respond, at least I tried. There are other people out there whom I might click with better.
4. If I talk a lot, I don't give others a chance to respond. I may feel more connection if I learn to pace myself and listen to people.
5. Not everyone is critical. There's no need to be so defensive. Relax and give people a chance. If someone is critical, you can still affirm and love yourself.

Be Aware of the Ghost of Past Shame

Whatever shame you've stored from old relationships is readily reactivated in a new relationship. New shame acts as a fuel that ignites your volatile storehouse of shame, which can trigger reactions of rage, withdrawal, or hurt. You may also be restimulated by fairly innocuous circumstances that remind you of past ridicule. Light, playful teasing may remind you of the vicious teasing you received as a child. Or you may become furiously jealous when your partner looks at another man or woman, painfully reminding you of the affairs of a parent or former partner. When you distort the present by viewing people through eyes of the past, you may push love away.

To the extent that you grew up with criticism, ridicule, or neglect, you may feel unworthy and insecure. The repeated shame of having been denigrated or ignored creates an anxious anticipation of being humiliated again. If you endured physical or sexual abuse, you experienced further atrocities that create unspeakable wounds. Trusting isn't easy when it was broken so casually during vulnerable years.

We've all been exposed to shame in our society, whether in our homes, school, playground, or workplace. That's why respect and sensitivity are so important in relationships. They create the trust and safety we need to go deeper with each other.

We each have different emotional triggers that provoke the harsh voice of the inner critic. See if any of this self-talk sounds familiar:

- You're crushed because your fiancée calls off the marriage ("you're unlovable").

- You notice your hair turning gray ("you're unattractive").
- You hold a party, but few show up ("no one likes you").
- You no longer fit into your old clothes ("you're overweight and ugly").
- Your pulse quickens as you're attracted to a lovely man or woman, but you assume that he or she wouldn't be interested in you ("you're not desirable").
- The person you're dating says you're too old for him or her ("you're over the hill").
- Your partner leaves you for someone wealthier ("you're not as good as others; you're less than others").
- Your sexual partner tells you that you're not satisfying him or her ("you're not sexually adequate").
- You're offered a new job at a lower salary ("you're a failure in your career").
- Your partnership ends in divorce ("you always fail at relationships").
- Old age leaves you dependent upon others ("you're too old to be any good; you're just a burden").

In each instance, you may experience yourself as not adequate or lovable. But these "shame attacks" don't prove that you really *are* unworthy. They restimulate old fears and insecurities about yourself—the familiar story that you're just not good enough. They run counter to the socially conditioned image of how you *think* you should be (gorgeous, independent, superior, perfect). Seized by an attack of shame, you pull back from showing yourself to people. You lose touch with the simple goodness and beauty that's at the core of who you are. Midlife is a time to finally accept—and celebrate—yourself as you are.

Shame Prevents Depth

Shame creates a guardedness around your heart that cuts you off from your depths and from others' depths. How does shame keep you on the surface of life?

Shame distorts the experience of your deeper feelings. When

shame abounds, it acts like a glue that keeps *all* your feelings stuck. This is why shame has been called the "master emotion." John Bradshaw describes the contaminating effect of shame: "To be shamebound means that whenever you feel any feeling, any need or any drive, you immediately feel ashamed." The feelings and needs that have been blanketed by shame become associated with the belief that you're awful, stupid, or childish for having them.

One client described the noxious effects of shame as follows: "I breathe shame, it gets absorbed into my system, it feels like a poison inside me. I visualize shame as a dark cloud that prevents me from sensing my deeper feelings and needs."

Feelings are sometimes painful. But you're beset by a further agony when shame dominates. For example, you may feel tearful when ending a relationship. But if you feel ashamed to cry, you wage an emotional war within yourself. Your inner critic might chime in, "You've cried enough already! Don't make a fool of yourself!"

The shame of appearing weak or being disrespected may prevent you from surrendering to your wounded depths. By blocking your body's natural movement toward crying, you store your pain along with a multitude of accumulated sorrows. This unhealed pain keeps you stuck. Instead of opening up and trusting again, you hide behind defenses such as chronic resentment, blame, or withdrawal. *By avoiding necessary pain, you perpetuate unnecessary suffering.* By not trusting your authentic experience, you become distant from yourself. You hide your heart—even from yourself.

From Self-Criticism to Self-Acceptance

One man who was saddened by separation from his partner described his transition from shame to acceptance: "I used to say to myself, 'Rise up to your sadness and push through it! Be strong! Don't fall into that pit again!' But as I let myself feel my sorrow right now, it's so tender. It's like I've owned it now. I don't need to get away from it. I feel stronger now that I've gone into it."

What are called "feelings" are the sensations that arise from allowing yourself to be touched by life. The tragedy of being ashamed of *how* you are touched by life is that you erect a wall between yourself and your precious feelings—between yourself and life. When your inner critic cuts you off from the depth at which life speaks to you, you bypass vital information about how to live your life and how to love yourself and others more fully.

For instance, anger may be telling you to stand up for yourself and not tolerate abuse. Hurt may be a step toward healing your pain. Rejecting your shamed feelings cuts you off from those feelings and, more important, from life itself. You then reject the creative way that life is trying to move you. This contempt for life is spiritual suicide. Midlife is a time to replace self-criticism with a warm embrace of the full range of your feelings. *To love more fully, you must embrace life fully, including your life of feelings.*

When shame lurks in the background, you may be reluctant to make conscious contact with people. You may always close your eyes when making love. You may communicate indirectly, fearful of being further rejected. You may divert your glance when shaking hands with people—or gaze with stiffened, steely eyes. As one person put it, "I'm afraid to look directly at people. When I do look at them, my eyes are hard and cold. I don't let people *in* through my eyes. I keep them distant. I'm afraid that if I let them in, they might see me. I'm afraid of what they'll see."

Monica, a fifty-year-old nurse, came into a counseling session experiencing "a big sadness." She felt alone and unseen in her marriage. She had difficulty honoring the sadness as something valid. As she put it, "When I start to feel sad, I think there's something wrong with me. So I move away from it and blame *him* for our problems." Slowly, she was able to look beneath her shame and allow her sadness to be.

As sadness became unhinged from Monica's shame of feeling sad, something deeper emerged. "The sadness is saying, 'Listen to me, see me. I matter, I'm important.' There's a longing there for love. But it's scary to let people get close, to let them see how important they are to me." Tears now began to flow: "It hurts to see this. I'm afraid people will hurt me. I let people in *so* far, then I stop it. In the past, when I let people get close, it would hurt; I haven't recovered from that. I need to let go of that hurt so I can let in the good stuff. Otherwise, the good stuff just bounces off a piece of Plexiglas."

I asked her what would feel like a small step forward. After some moments staying with her feelings, she responded: "I need to let myself feel it. I need to be more honest with myself. I need to cry. Feeling wanted makes the feeling of *not* having been wanted more acute. The more I grieve what I didn't have, the more I can let in what I *do* have. I also need to let a few people know what's happening, instead of keeping all this to myself. I need to trust more."

As deeper tears released, another piece of the puzzle came together: "My husband can help me if I *let* him. It's hard to trust because I've been so hurt before. Letting him touch me and love me has been difficult because it brings up all the hurt of *not* having been loved in my life. I sometimes cry after making love because it's hard to believe I'm lovable. It's hard to trust that. But I haven't felt sexual for months, and now I realize it's because when I let him close, it brings up a sadness I've been ashamed of. I don't want to feel that. But I need to *feel* that if I want to let in love." Fortunately, she had a responsive partner. Trust and intimacy grew from this tender sharing of their hearts.

We damage trust when we blame our partner for something going on inside ourselves. As Monica realized, the partnership wasn't the problem. It was her shame that was paralyzing her from entering a deeper journey into her sorrow, which became a doorway to the love and caring that were available to her.

Your inner critic may stifle intimacy by insisting:

1. You don't deserve love.
2. If he/she sees who you really are or what you really think, feel, and want, he/she might get angry or leave you.
3. If you show insecurity, people will laugh at you or see you as weak.
4. Always show your best side and hide the shadow parts of yourself—the rough edges that are unsavory and unattractive.

You can replace this critical self-talk with a nurturing inner voice:

1. Everyone deserves love. I'm not better or worse than anyone else.
2. If he/she sees who I really am, I might feel more love and connection in my life.
3. If I show my insecurities, then I'm having the courage to show something that everyone feels at times. If people judge me, that's their problem!

4. Rough edges are part of what makes me human. People would feel intimidated if I seemed perfect. There's no shame in having foibles.

Shame Smothers Joy

Many people in midlife who seek therapy say, "I'm not unhappy, but I'm not happy, either. There's no joy in my life. I don't care much about anything. Life feels flat, and I have no idea why." Again, it's the abiding shadow of shame and the voice of the inner critic that are often responsible for vague discontent.

Shame not only buffers you from unpleasant feelings, it hampers your happiness. As a result, you inhibit your laughter and constrain your pleasure. A grimness and seriousness set in. Your aliveness and spontaneity become buried in an avalanche of shame.

As spontaneous feelings clash with how you think you should be, you may side with the protective voice of your inner critic. When your feelings are chronically experienced as a threat, your body armors against both positive *and* negative feelings alike. Struggling to become invulnerable to shame and other dreaded emotions, you stifle both your agony and your ecstasy. You become apathetic, numb, depressed. There's no way to develop relationships of depth and delight when you've lost enthusiasm for living.

In the touching movie *Shadowlands*, the main character, C. S. Lewis, said something profound as he grieved the death of his beloved wife: "The pain now is part of the happiness then. That's the deal." If you want to let in joy, love, and pleasure, you must be willing to experience their polar opposite: sadness, loss, and pain. You must embrace the full range of your feelings instead of judging some feelings as acceptable and others as unacceptable. You can't open to love unless you open to life.

Your inner critic may stifle happiness by saying:

1. You'll never be happy. If you get too happy something bad will happen. You don't deserve happiness.
2. You'll never amount to anything.
3. Don't get carried away with laughing or feeling good about yourself or your life.

4. Don't make a fool of yourself by singing in front of anyone or in the shower.
5. Don't expect too much from life.

You can replace this critical self-talk with a nurturing inner voice:

1. I have a right to happiness, just like everyone else. I'll deal with what the future brings when it comes. If I can't allow myself to feel joy, when will I ever be happy?
2. I can succeed if I work at it. In any case, my worth and value don't come from my accomplishments. They're based on who I am as a person.
3. I can laugh as much as I want and for as long as I want. There's plenty of times I feel pain and sorrow; when I feel pleasure, joy, or love, I want to relish it.
4. If I feel like singing, I'll sing. If others think I'm making a fool of myself, that's their opinion.
5. There's unlimited potential to find joy and fulfillment in life.

Shame Keeps You Self-Centered

Shame keeps you preoccupied with concerns about your performance and worth. "How did I come across? Did I make a fool of myself? Are other people getting ahead of me? How do I measure up?" These thoughts keep you in a small box of self-concern. You're always wondering how others are seeing and judging you. Life is all about you! Egotism is rooted in a pervasive shame that perpetuates self-absorption.

Healing shame means taking a leap beyond self-preoccupation. You become more genuinely concerned about others to the degree that you accept and love yourself. You see the world more clearly as you're less anxious about how others are seeing you.

Welcome to the Human Condition

The habitual ways we've been criticized and shamed by people—as well as the ways we criticize and shame others—are part of the human condition. We hurt people in similar ways that we've been hurt. Even in healthy relationships, we're bound to hurt those we love sometimes, even if our intentions are pure.

As we heal our shame, we become more authentic and less shaming and critical of others. We become emotionally available for the love and closeness we deserve. By refraining from shaming others, we create the safety necessary for love and intimacy to grow in midlife and beyond.

I hope that you'll hold yourself with caring and compassion as you identify how shame has held you back from blossoming into your full beauty and power. By uncovering and embracing the ways you've been hurt and closed down to love and life, you're on your way toward the deeper authenticity that's the foundation for mature love.

If you discover ways you've shamed and hurt people—and harmed your relationships—you may experience sorrow or remorse, but I hope you don't paralyze yourself with self-criticism. I can't emphasize enough that *there's a huge difference between self-blame and taking responsibility*. Wallowing in self-blame can be so debilitating that it prevents you from looking honestly at yourself and loving yourself.

A climate of self-compassion and self-forgiveness will help you take responsibility for how you may have contributed to difficult relationships. Rather than condemn yourself, you can create a climate that supports you and others in the effort to bring forth your true selves. You can develop the strength, wisdom, and compassion to live from your authentic heart while creating a safe climate for people to be authentic with you.

Identify and Heal Shame

1. Has shame affected your relationships? Do you hold back expressing yourself, fearful of being laughed at or rejected? Do you stay isolated or overly cautious to avoid getting hurt? Are you easily angered?

(Becoming aware of how you relate to people may help you get in touch with how shame holds you back and keeps you isolated or angry.)

2. Do you speak to others in the same manner you were spoken to as a child?

(It is a common tendency to transfer your guilt to others without realizing it. This protects you from working through your feelings. If you can recognize that there's self-contempt in you, then you can work with it internally instead of spreading it to others.)

3. Do you spend much time thinking about whether someone likes you or fantasizing about how to get that person's approval? Is it more important that someone you're dating likes you or that you like him or her?

(The lack of self-esteem created by shame may lead you to seek acceptance and approval because you have difficulty giving it to yourself. As you accept and love yourself more, you'll need that approval less from others, and you'll feel more comfortable and relaxed in your relationships.)

4. Does a shame-driven self-image make it difficult to laugh at yourself or have a sense of humor? Do you always take yourself very seriously? Do you allow yourself to take risks and have natural curiosity?

(When shame is operating, you become very serious. If you've been frequently belittled and laughed at, it may be hard to laugh and loosen up. You become hypervigilant, constantly evaluating whether a person is insulting you or liking you. What *you* think of *you* is what's most important.)

5. If you slur your words or say something that's incorrect, do you put yourself down before someone else gets the chance? If you forget someone's name, do you feel overwhelmingly embarrassed?

(This is a clue to noticing your inner critic. Talking to yourself in a critical way generates shame inside you.)

6. How do you talk to yourself when things don't work out? Is there a kind, reassuring voice that comforts you or a mean, harsh, critical voice that attacks and denigrates you? Are you aware of when these voices are active, either in the moment or sometime afterward?

(Noticing your self-critical voices is the key to transforming them into kinder self-talk. Being gentle with yourself is a key to opening your heart and creating relationships of depth.)

7. Is it difficult to identify and accept your flaws and limits? Is it difficult to accept others' flaws and limits? Do you notice any connection between these two?

(Being critical of yourself and critical of others goes hand in hand. Learning to be gentle with yourself is a key to being gentle with others. Working on being kinder to others may also help you be kinder to yourself.)

8. Are you comfortable apologizing when you're wrong or when you make a mistake? Do you overapologize? Do you feel uncomfortable with the notion that you fall short sometimes? How do you respond when you fail at something? Can you fail without allowing this failure to define who you are?

(The inner critic tries to protect you from being wrong or making mistakes. It "catastrophizes" failure and shortcomings. If you can give yourself slack to make mistakes and be imperfect, you can become more comfortable with yourself when you fall short.)

9. Is it hard to begin projects or pursue new directions because you fear failure? Does your inner critic have anything to do with your failure to complete projects or does it sabotage you in relationships?

(If you don't try too hard, then your inner critic can't fault you for failing. After all, you didn't really commit yourself to a relationship or project. If failure is seen as a natural and allowable part of life, then it's easier to take the risks necessary to succeed.)

ॐ

Summon the Courage to Affirm the Authentic You

When we come to the last moment
of this lifetime, and we look back across it,
the only thing that's going to matter is
"What was the quality of our love?"

—RICHARD BACH

5

Getting to Authenticity

The most frustrating aspect of the search for Intimate Love may be that we cannot pursue it as a direct goal; we reach it only as the by-product of our willingness to be open with each other.

—Jordan Paul

∽∾∾

The shaming inner voices born of social conditioning distort your authentic feelings and longings and throw you back to a false self that's incapable of loving and being loved. By recognizing how you become overpowered by the distorting voices within and outside yourself, you can begin to extract yourself from their toxic influence. The conditioned beliefs of your youth can then be supplanted by an empowering understanding that prepares your heart and mind for the authentic love of midlife.

It is only by discarding contrived models of yourself that you can begin to listen to the quiet messages of your soul that speak through the language called "feelings." Being in touch with what is truly alive and genuine inside you creates a climate that allows love and intimacy to thrive.

Midlife is a time to appreciate that authentic love flows from the inside out, not from the outside in. It doesn't grow when you're

trying to be somebody you're not—shaping yourself into some idealized way of being so that people will be impressed. Authenticity is
about being real, not looking good. You invite love toward you as you
bring awareness to how life is coursing through you from moment
to moment, coupled with the willingness to affirm and selectively
reveal the full range of who you really are—your sorrows and joys,
fears and fortitude, warts and wonderfulness.

Loving relationships require the courage to know—and reveal—
your innermost heart. However, you might be more gentle toward
yourself by recognizing that you needed the protection of a fabricated self during years when you felt unsafe and didn't have the
awareness and skills to be genuine. After all, in younger years you
hadn't yet developed the wisdom to realize that something was rad-
ically wrong. As one fifty-nine-year-old put it, "I never would have
survived if I didn't build a wall to protect myself. It would have been
too painful to face rejection and ridicule if I stopped being the 'perfect wife' and showed my true fears, hurts, and needs. But hiding
isn't serving me anymore. I've been lonely in my relationships. I'm
ready to be myself and see who likes me as I am."

Realizing that you had little choice but to hide your inner light
amid a less than perfect family and society can free you from self-
blame; it can instill compassion in your struggle to reclaim what the
Chinese philosopher Mencius calls your "original heart"—a simple
openness and presence to life. As you heal and grow, you live with a
more open heart, allowing yourself to be more receptive and transparent. As you age with vulnerable openness, your heart becomes
more pliable and touchable. A climate for love is created.

Shed the Fabricated Self

By midlife it's likely that your fabricated self—and all of its spurious
calculations—has drawn you into one or more partnerships, thereby
ensuring their destruction. As one relationship after another crashed
and burned, your reflective intelligence may have started to wonder,
"Am I missing something here? Am I just choosing the wrong people
or is something deeper going on?"

A crucial breakthrough is to realize that the false self's idealizations of love will never lead to satisfying love. Nor will an atmosphere

conducive to intimacy be fostered by trying to fit yourself into some idealized image of how you should be, or by trying to control the impression you make on others. Midlife dignity means valuing your true feelings while relinquishing the self that was constructed to secure love. As you distinguish your honest self from its stand-in twin, you increasingly welcome who you really are and bravely allow love to be guided by your innate wisdom.

Relinquishing the fabricated self begins through a process of *shedding*. Rather than adding something to your old self—making it shiny and new—you're invited to surrender and let go of your usual control. Rather than trying harder to construct a more sophisticated version of your false self, you're invited to notice what already exists— or what lies just beneath the surface, longing to be born. You're asked to engage in a process of *emptying* so that your fullness and beauty, your tenderness and power, your passion and peace may come to full fruition.

What do you empty yourself of? Genuine love emerges as you replace juvenile notions with more reality-based views. For example, during your youth, you may have seen love as a rescue fantasy, not realizing that love's growth rests on developing inner qualities such as self-awareness, wisdom, and compassion.

Your authentic self continues to unfold as you relinquish disempowering beliefs absorbed from parents and society or self-sabotaging beliefs based on disappointments with early love:

- "You'll never have a good relationship."
- "You're a failure and don't deserve love."
- "Everyone is screwed up!"

Shaming and blaming yourself and others only serves to prop up your well-defended, phony self. Instead of succumbing to these voices, try affirming "I no longer need these beliefs to numb myself to pain and the fear of failure. I'm moving on now." Assign your inner critic a new role: "Tell me when I'm getting off track, but be my caring consultant, not my overbearing boss." As you notice and disclaim what's old and outdated, you're preparing yourself to honor the deeper feelings and aspirations of your authentic heart.

You need faith in yourself and in life to open up to new possibilities. You need to affirm that no matter how much hurt you've endured, you're willing to keep your heart and mind open to love again. You may also need to affirm that you—like all human beings—deserve love. As authors Judith Sherven and James Sniechowski put it, "No one can give you what you are convinced you cannot have."

By understanding what it means to accept yourself as you are—your light and dark side, your triumphs and failures, your joys and heartaches—you no longer fight and resist being who you are. You move toward greater peace, joy, and freedom. As you open to dormant aspects of your authentic self, you heal and awaken. As you embrace who you really are, you have more of your whole self to bring to your relationships. The foundation for midlife love is then set—one forged between hearts that are more open and less defended.

What Does Being Yourself Really Mean?

The commitment to being yourself raises the question, "Which self am I being—my fabricated self or my authentic self?" People misuse the expression "I'm being myself" to justify the abusive ways they treat others ("I can't help it, I'm just being myself!") or as an excuse for their rigidity ("I'll never change, that's just the way I am!"). Others are afraid of being truthful, fearful that if the defensive walls came tumbling down and their true nature was revealed, they'd unleash a demented beast who'd be out of control.

The comforting truth is that the core of your being is kind and loving, not destructive. During moments when you're most connected to life and self—perhaps while viewing a sunset, engaging in prayer or meditation, or making love—your thoughts and impulses are filled with benevolence and good will. The spontaneous, self-sacrificing behavior of rescue teams after major disasters, such as the earthquake in Turkey, or of the good Samaritan who helps a neighbor in need reveals the goodness in us.

The impulse to hurt others reflects a disconnection from your core self. The plague of domestic violence is a dramatic example of the refusal to acknowledge vulnerability. Physical and emotional abuse are brewed in the bitter cauldron of shame, fear, and hurt. Controlling others is a manifestation of an inability to acknowledge and make peace with these feelings. For example, when you're criticized, you may become enraged to protect yourself from feeling shame and hurt. Or you may attack with words or fists when you're fearful that your partner may abandon you. As you develop the capacity for self-soothing—calming yourself by embracing what you're most deeply feeling—you soften inside (more on this in the chapter on self-soothing).

The Process of Unlayering

The rage inherent in verbal or physical abuse, as well as in other kinds of manipulation, is not an expression of authenticity. Rage and hostility are often secondary emotions (except when in response to abuse or injustice). They are covers for underlying hurt, fear, or shame—impotent attempts to control a situation or person. It takes courageous awareness to embrace your primary feelings, understand their source, and share them openly.

Connecting with deeper feelings beneath your anger is good for your health! Physician Dean Ornish has cited studies revealing that frequent anger is a risk factor for heart disease. Couples in long-term marriages who constantly argued had weakened immune systems. Newlyweds who expressed hostility toward their spouses showed negative immunological changes. Uncovering and expressing your feelings not only deepens intimacy and lessens conflict, it may help you stay healthy and live longer!

Like most people, you probably see yourself as a genuine person. But it's too simplistic to think that you're a person who's either real or not real. You're a process, not a fixed thing—a verb, not a noun. While your shame-frozen, fabricated self-image is static, your authentic self is fluid and changing. Sometimes you know how you're feeling, perhaps hurt or afraid, but most often your feelings are vague and fuzzy. Sometimes you know what you want, perhaps a hug or reassurance, but oftentimes you're not sure.

You may think you know what you feel and want, but this awareness is often the tip of the iceberg. You may think you're being real by declaring your anger about a messy house, but is that your truest longing? If the house were suddenly immaculate, would you be happy? Or is your anger shielding you from something deeper, such as:

1. Feeling hurt or shamed by a partner's comment.
2. A lack of affection and connection.
3. A fear of being left or abandoned.
4. Feeling unworthy of love and closeness.
5. Feeling insecure or anxious about the relationship or something in your life.

The ability to contact your more vulnerable feelings and wants reflects a self-awareness and wisdom that grow as you mature. The courage to disclose your true self is a potent way to nurture love at any age.

In truth, your authentic self is not really a solid self. It's more accurate to use the term "authenticity" than "authentic self." Otherwise, you might try to perfect some image of an authentic person, making it into a rigid construct of how you should think, feel, or behave. Trying to polish yourself into a shining image of who you think you should be is a manifestation of a contrived self. When I use the term authentic or real self, my intention is to point you in the right direction—toward the process of becoming awake to who you really are, to the different shades of your rainbow of consciousness that happen to be present in a given moment.

The Process of Awakening

Authenticity is about inviting ever deeper layers to unveil themselves in their own fluid way. Uncovering these layered depths allows you to relate more intimately, first with yourself and then with others. What's called "personal growth" results from awakening to—and embracing—the constantly changing feelings and meanings that arise within the recesses of your being rather than trying to control them through fixed ideas of how you *should* be. The word "awakening" conveys the active process of growth. Such awakening cannot be rushed. It's a gift of time and courageous awareness, which is why midlife is a fertile coming of age.

Whatever you may experience is real for you. Even if it's only the tip of the iceberg, that's an important start; it's the beginning of a journey into your authentic heart. But there's usually something more, something deeper, if you only take the time to be still and listen to its quiet voice.

Even feelings you may find distasteful, such as rage, lust, and greed, are natural human experiences, although you have a choice about whether to act on them. Condemning yourself for shadowy feelings makes them more problematic. Pushing them into a dark corner of your psyche permits these untamed emotions to fester unconsciously—eventually closing your heart to life and love.

The Simplicity of Your Authentic Heart

Being authentic is quite simple. You may make it difficult because you're afraid of painful consequences: being rejected, ridiculed, or abandoned. If you permit yourself to be a hostage to your fear of being unworthy, hurt, or alone, you betray your integrity. You ignore or minimize your legitimate feelings, needs, and viewpoints to perpetuate a pseudoconnection with others, which you suppose is better than no connection at all! But deep down you're unhappy because you know you're not being real. The fear of being abandoned leads to the anxiety and depression of abandoning your true self. It takes inner strength to face the consequences of affirming what's real for you.

When you feel insecure or afraid, you may cover up such natural feelings. Like a pompous politician, you insist that you're right, which compensates for the shame of being wrong or the fear of being judged as weak or incompetent. As one man put it, "I always had to be right because I couldn't stand the thought of being wrong—or *appearing* to be wrong or uncertain. Letting my guard down made me too vulnerable, so I always had to look confident, even though I had no idea what was really going on. I was good at *pretending* to know, even when I was totally lost." Desiring to be right, this man would ride roughshod over his partner's feelings and opinions, which led to a separation.

This presumption of knowledge is a telltale sign that your defensive self is up to its old tricks, providing the illusion of conviction, control, and security. This illusion protects you from the embarrassment of uncertainty, even though there's nothing shameful about being uncertain. You must find the strength to embrace the insecurity of not knowing before you can really know what's stirring in your depths. As philosopher André Gide warned, "Believe those who are seeking the truth; doubt those who find it."

This isn't to suggest that you should be constantly absorbed in some tiresome task of searching for your deepest feelings and truth, but that you make an effort to regularly attend to your inner world so that you don't stray too far from yourself. Experiment with finding a balance between looking within, being spontaneous, and practicing new behaviors that feel more genuine, even if they are scary or awkward at first. Being real becomes increasingly spontaneous and gratifying as you learn to trust your experience of your genuine feelings.

It isn't easy to extricate yourself from old programming and a continuous media barrage that coaxes you to venerate a false, socially acceptable self-image. You may not even be aware of your self-deception. Like Mephistopheles tempting Faust to make a pact with the devil in exchange for everlasting power, you are constantly indoctrinated into trusting your false self. You're persuaded to bow before the Madison Avenue edict, "You are the image!" If you buy into the media-driven belief that your value and worth are tied to your image, you are lost. The very realization of how you're not being genuine is the beginning of authenticity.

Beware of Spiritual Seductions

Even those who appreciate that their basic nature is one of goodness and beauty may take winding detours in the process of finding their true selves. For example, a spiritual or New Age perspective can degenerate into the belief that if you're not continually happy, something's wrong. So you pressure yourself to put on a happy face, thinking that is your real self.

Not long ago I attended a conference with a spiritual theme. A friend introduced me to a vibrant woman who asked, "How are you?" Just getting over a cold and feeling tired, I took a risk by honestly replying, "Not so good today." Apparently displeased with my answer, she quickly responded, "What do you mean, not so good? What's that about? It's a beautiful day today." I felt that my authentic self wasn't welcomed here. Later, I discovered that she was one of the workshop leaders.

If you have spiritual inclinations, you may feel embarrassed that you're not living up to your spiritual potential if you feel sad, angry, or fearful about something. You may wonder, "Will they think I'm not spiritually evolved?" If a relationship ends, you may cover up sorrow with the self-berating inquiry, "How did I create that?"

Some spiritual systems of belief reflect an adolescent spirituality that comes with a subtext of rules and prohibitions about how you should and shouldn't be. As a result, you run the risk of creating a self-image of being happy and peaceful that may be just as fake as all the other images you have worked so hard to free yourself from.

A forty-eight-year-old computer programmer put it this way, "Meditation helps me feel safe, but I use it to keep distant from my feelings and from people. I go into my own private world so I don't get hurt in relationships. But it's not working because I'm lonely inside and really need to connect with people. I'm starved of love in my life." No longer using meditation as a defense, he continued valuing its benefits while also reaching out for the connections he wanted.

When true love exists in a relationship, you can truly be yourself. You can feel safe being just as you are, knowing you'll be accepted, not judged. How freeing it is to envision a partnership in which you don't have to create a false version of yourself to feel accepted—where you can get up in the morning, go through your day, and go to bed at night being exactly who you are.

6

Celebrate Your Authentic Self

A great deal of energy in close relationships is wasted due to one or more persons trying to keep feelings hidden. Our feelings are central to life—they are made of the raw energy that drives and motivates our existence—and to be cut off from them is to suffer a slow, silent erosion of the spirit.
—Gay Hendricks and Kathlyn Hendricks

∽∾∾

Loving connections with others are possible to the degree that you connect with yourself. What does connecting with yourself mean? It means experiencing life through your own eyes. It means trusting your senses and intuitions rather than letting others' opinions or beliefs displace your own. It means affirming your own experience of people and life and being willing to declare that the emperor has no clothes if that's what *your* eyes see. It means trusting yourself to deal with the feelings that life brings up in you, even if they are difficult ones. It also means tapping deeper aspects of your soul—discovering qualities such as compassion, strength, tenderness, joy, openness, and love.

How wonderful it is to give birth to who you really are. One woman in her fifties described her search this way: "I always thought

I was real, but after more soul-searching, I realized, 'Well, maybe not.' I went through old photos searching for a picture of when I thought I was authentic. I looked at the face, the smile, and the pose in order to see when the break with my real self began. I finally found the picture. I was six months old! The face is absolutely honest—no forced smile, no phoniness. There was no separation from my real self. I put that photo on my dashboard to remind me that it's okay to be myself."

Being authentic requires enough self-worth to acknowledge blind spots and blemishes. As a person in process, you'll never quite arrive. There will always be limits to your achievements, looks, knowledge, understanding, and ability to love. However, as you allow yourself to experience what's really there, you nurture qualities that enable you to feel fulfilled, complete, and whole. You come to rest in the depths of your authentic heart.

It Takes Courage

Authenticity requires courage because you're exposing yourself to criticism and ridicule. You're not going along with the program of adjusting yourself to win approval. By differentiating yourself from others, you risk rejection and isolation. But this developmental task of becoming an awake, strong self allows a depth of intimacy that the immature lover can only dream about.

What's genuine is a function of personal experience. The task of midlife growth is to summon the courage to see what's true and real for *you*. However, I've observed commonalities among people in midlife who are growing more comfortable living from their authentic heart:

- Embrace your feelings.
- Embrace your needs, wants, and longings.
- Embrace shame and underlying sorrow.
- Embrace yourself as you are.
- Embrace shyness.
- Embrace risk.
- Embrace solitude.
- Embrace death and loss.

Embrace Your Feelings

In order to be yourself in midlife, you must learn, as Socrates and others have taught, to know yourself. This involves a commitment to be honest with yourself about how you really feel, what moves you, and how you want to live. It also means bringing awareness to the darker folds of your heart that your fabricated self finds threatening to its agenda of self-protection and control.

The love that grows through authenticity is rooted in self-knowing. You contact your true self to the degree that you bring awareness to the changing flow of inner experience—your dynamic inner process. This process includes your naturally arising needs and longings, sensations and feelings, and insights and intuitions—and what holds meaning and purpose in your life, perhaps raising a family, caring for the environment, and making a contribution to the world. Your inner process also contains qualities of your deeper essence—your beauty, your strength, your warmth, your wisdom, your love, your value, and your humility. Midlife is a time to nurture these gifts of your human endowment.

Embrace Your Needs, Wants, and Longings

Your inner self has needs and longings. An important facet of being yourself is to embrace these longings rather than be ashamed of them. You become troubled, and then trouble others, when your deepest needs and longings go unheeded. Abraham Maslow, after twenty years of personality study, concluded that psychological ill-health is a *deficiency* disease: "It is born out of being deprived of certain satisfactions which I called needs in the same ways that water and amino acids and calcium are needs, namely that their absence produces illness." Well-being and happiness rest upon meeting basic needs, which include:

- Safety
- Touch
- Acceptance
- Respect
- Affection
- Intimacy
- Love

Such needs are the longings of your heart. What is called "mental illness" or "psychopathology" isn't a disease in the usual sense—it's a sickness of your soul. You suffer when your longing for loving, intimate relationships is repeatedly frustrated. Gradually, you lose touch with the yearning itself, becoming depressed, hardened, or tired as you enter the second half of life. You become a "rugged individual" who doesn't depend on anyone—the Marlboro Man or Woman who's always cool and aloof—refusing to acknowledge that you're a creature with needs and wants.

Affirm Your Basic Human Longings

Midlife is a time to finally declare, "Yes, I have needs and longings. There's nothing shameful about that. It's okay to let people see that I'm vulnerable. I'm a sensitive human being with a tender heart that's easily hurt—just like everyone else, whether they acknowledge it or not."

You cannot exert some athletic willpower to squash your needs for acceptance, recognition, and love. Of course, you might *try* to violate the basic human blueprint in an attempt to deny your longing for connection. However, your frustrated yearnings will eventually surface in one way or another, whether it be through angry outbursts, depression, physical symptoms, or addictions that numb the pain of unmet needs.

Ignoring your basic needs keeps you preoccupied with meeting them. Your well-being is then clouded by vague anxiety and desperate searches down blind alleys, such as seeking power and control. As you begin to satisfy legitimate needs, something inside you relaxes. You're then freed to grow toward what Maslow calls "higher needs." These are the deeper longings of your heart.

Most people are content to develop to a certain point and never to venture beyond. They pay their bills, endure their jobs, and manage their relationships. Success is measured by social status or by having a warm body lying next to them at night. But if they never ask, "Is that all there is?" they'll never discover the deeper promise of midlife: more rewarding relationships, creative pursuits, and spiritual fulfillment.

Needs and longings connect you to people and life. By denying them, you squash a sacred life force. When the protective voice of your inner critic condemns these powerful promptings from within, you create a split in your soul. If you push them away, you'll never awaken to a deeply embodied spirituality rooted in your interconnectedness with life. Instead of maturing into a self that's both strong and vulnerable, you'll isolate yourself while clinging to rigid ideas of who you should be.

People feel less threatened by you when they know that *you know* you're human, too. They feel valued knowing they can contribute to your life. As a channel opens between two authentic hearts, there's a giving and receiving of love that is nurturing.

One forty-six-year-old man, Ralph, who prided himself on his intelligence and wit, realized how he'd fallen into a trap: "It's so liberating to just *be* myself instead of putting on my lookin' good self. It brings me and my partner closer knowing I can let down my guard and just hang out and be real. As I've gotten into my forties, I care less about what people think of me. I'm realizing that I'm okay as I am, and that many people like me that way. If they don't, I'm more comfortable saying, 'It's not my problem.'" Instead of performing for others, Ralph found the satisfaction of living for himself.

Midlife maturity means affirming yourself, while being flexible and receptive. If you don't value yourself, you're at risk of collapsing into a shapeless puddle of mud when life doesn't go your way (therapists call this "fragmentation" or "dissociation"). However, if you remain rigidly independent and untouchable, you'll never be intimate with anyone.

EXERCISE:

Can you acknowledge and express your needs and wants openly or do you hide them? Which feelings and wants are okay to express and which ones do you tend to hide?

(You may hide certain feelings or needs because they embarrass you. As you accept yourself and overcome your shame, you may express them more openly. This frees you to be yourself more and more.)

Uncover Your Authentic Experience

Partnerships blossom as you find the everyday courage to discern and express what's happening inside you. For example, my client

Sam would yell at his wife, Amy, whenever she lost her car keys: "Someday you'll get more organized!" She'd then retort sarcastically: "Yeah, I'll get compulsive like you." This bickering created a cycle of mistrust and distancing. As they uncovered their deeper experience, they stopped lobbing hand grenades over the wall of their defenses. As Sam discovered, "I showed anger when I was really feeling frustration. Beneath that, I felt guilty that I wasn't able to help her—as if that was my job! Wow, where did that come from? I was trained to be a rescuer; I was taking too much responsibility for her."

As Amy looked deeper, she realized how she was colluding in their lack of intimacy. Instead of *reacting* by attacking, she began *responding* by disclosing her authentic feelings and needs. In a heartfelt way, she looked at Sam and said, "I feel hurt when you criticize me for losing my keys. I'd like you to back off and let me look for them."

Through the simple magic of contacting and showing each other what they truly felt, they took a step toward each other's world. Sam and Amy grew closer as they developed the awareness and courage to reveal deeper layers of their authentic selves.

As I'll describe later, identifying and embracing what's really happening inside you creates a basis for effective boundary setting and communication—further essential ingredients of midlife love. By contacting and disclosing your inner experience, you assume a new level of responsibility for nurturing closeness.

As you unveil your hidden world of feelings, needs, and motivations, something can shift *within* you—and then *between* you and your lover. By knowing yourself more deeply and sharing what's really happening, you allow your partner to see your true self. As you become more real and transparent, it's easier for a person to see into your heart and connect with you. If you're received in a sensitive, nonjudgmental way, intimacy deepens. As the fear of being real gives way to the satisfaction of being understood, you may be blessed with the gift of a deepening love, trust, and intimacy.

Embrace Shame and Underlying Sorrow

As I've explained, shame distorts the experience of your authentic self. However, the shame that is directly embraced loses its power to freeze your feelings and stifle your zest for life and love. As the fog of shame begins to lift, you discover the feelings it has obscured, including your sorrow and pain. By touching your sorrow with love, you hollow out a tender place in your heart, thereby enlarging your capacity to love and be loved.

Life affords you ever-increasing opportunities to face sorrow and loss: the death of a parent or friend, sudden illness, seeing your children leave home, or losing your job. How you deal with loss and change makes the difference between whether you connect more deeply with yourself or become resigned to bitterness or depression.

Research has established a link between loss and a host of physical and psychological ills. As you learn to welcome sorrow rather than steel yourself against loss in order to "stay strong," you open to life on life's terms. By courageously acknowledging your grief, you stay resilient.

Have you ever skidded out of control on an icy road? If you jam on the brake and turn away from the skid, you'll flip over. But if you turn your wheel in the direction of the skid, you stay safe. Frantically resisting what you cannot control only spins you further out of control. If you turn your attention toward your feelings and flow with changes on the icy roads of life, you will be more available to enjoy the love and delight that's also part of life.

The Value of Pain

Are you hurting? Are you in pain? Modern science has the answer: better living through chemistry. Pop an aspirin for fast relief!

No, I'm not proposing that you empty your medicine cabinet; thank God for medical science! The point is that physical and emotional pain are seen as an enemy by our society—something to conquer, not value. We get the message: "Don't even consider that your pain may have something to do with what's happening in your life! Just get rid of it!" But what price does our soul pay by ignoring a vital message that our body is trying to give us in the best way it knows how? By sedating the messenger, we may never get the message.

Rather than deaden your pain, is there something you can learn from it? Rather than depend on prescription drugs to deal with a dysfunctional lifestyle, perhaps you need to change your lifestyle.

Instead of relying on medication to fit into a sick society, why not build a consensus to change society?

Most people now in midlife formed their self-image during a time when showing pain meant being a crybaby. Men especially were trained to believe that acknowledging pain isn't okay. Be a tough hero like John Wayne, who gets shot in the shoulder and says calmly: "It's only a flesh wound." Or laugh it off like President Reagan, who after being shot quipped, "I should have ducked."

Showing pain is shameful and unwelcome in our society, as Senator Edmund Muskie discovered when he lost the presidential nomination because he was seen crying. Authentic expressions of sorrow are not the ticket to public office. Most voters want officials who have their "act" together, who have a self-assured manner and overconfident answers to knotty questions. But then we're disappointed when our elected leaders aren't real. We can't have it both ways.

If we want honest politicians, we need to make it permissible for them to show us their genuine selves, not their act. We should commend them when they say, "I don't have an answer for that," or, "I'll need to think it over and get back to you." We need to applaud them when they honestly change their minds rather than cling to an artificial consistency. After all, we get the politicians we deserve.

Hiding pain reflects ignorance, not strength and maturity. It bespeaks antiquated values that need to be updated.

When I played baseball in Little League I was a good pitcher. My career peaked at twelve, then went downhill fast! I struck out many batters with my curveball. Occasionally, the ball forgot to curve and would hit the batter. It hurts to be hit by a hard ball! But even at the young age of eleven and twelve, many kids would trot off to first base, quietly bearing their bruise. They'd already gotten the message that being men meant being tough and not revealing "weakness." The fabricated self was already well in place.

If we belittle men for crying or being afraid, we can't later expect them to express tender feelings and share emotional intimacy with a future companion. The human personality isn't that malleable; patterns get set. If we want to prepare men for peaceful, loving relationships (the ultimate family value), we need to teach boys that expressing hurt, fear, and pain is just as virile as being a warrior—if not more so. We need to create a society where people feel safe to be genuine and open.

The Taoist text *Tao Te Ching* speaks clearly to the paradox of strength:

Nothing in the world
is as soft and yielding as water.
Yet for dissolving the hard and inflexible,
nothing can surpass it.

The soft overcomes the hard;
The gentle overcomes the rigid.
Everyone knows this is true,
But few can put it into practice.
Therefore the Master remains
serene in the midst of sorrow.

Women, of course, also need to express authentic feelings, perhaps especially anger and outrage. Yet many women have been taught that being a lady means not being angry. They're trained to be "sugar and spice and everything nice." So legitimate anger goes underground. It may then leak out destructively, shocking their loved ones when pent-up emotions finally explode or seep through the casing of their courteous self.

The Shame of Pain

Unfortunately, being strong is often defined as:

- Not acknowledging hurt or sadness.
- Not admitting fear.
- "Sucking up" or stuffing your feelings.
- Not being needy or not having needs.
- Not displaying vulnerability.
- Performing and achieving even when you're hurt or sick.

By pushing away unpleasant feelings, you award them power over you. Although you might think you're controlling your pain, it's controlling you. You might think you're done with it, but it's not done with you! Like a hurting child, it wants attention. Painful feelings won't leave you alone until you gently turn toward them and embrace them warmly.

In order to suppress pain, you armor yourself. You unconsciously tighten your muscles and constrict your breathing, which is both a reaction to stress and a cause of further stress. Your body may rebel through back pain, high blood pressure, depression, anxiety, or baffling ailments. These symptoms are messages that your body is trying to give you. As you enter midlife, these physical communications can become more problematic—until you face your feelings directly and listen to what they're telling you about your life.

If you can accept that you have hurt, shame, and fear in you but recognize that this doesn't mean that you're awful or ugly, then you no longer need to protect yourself by proving your worth or criticizing others. You have access to a quiet strength that no one can shatter as you befriend these feelings—over and over again.

Befriend Grief to Grow Stronger

However hurt you are, you may strengthen yourself by finding meaning in the tragedy. As the philosopher Nietzsche said, "What doesn't kill me makes me stronger." Therapist Daphne Rose Kingma also offers an optimistic outcome: "While these tragedies do certainly leave their marks, they often make our hearts stronger: stronger in openness, stronger to be aware of what love truly is, stronger to let love in—but only if we've resolved them." As physicians know, a broken bone often becomes stronger once it heals.

Rather than bracing yourself against hurt, you need to embrace your hurt. Until you develop a healing way to deal with the loss of love, you'll block yourself from fully opening to its delightful depths. Rather than trying to banish the pain of loss, you need to develop a *relationship* with loss. Losing is part of loving. You can't dance in the light unless you embrace the darkness.

When you feel it's safe to allow yourself to have feelings you've battled for so long, you will develop more compassion toward yourself and others. As you accept and embrace the full range of feelings that comprise your vulnerability, you become "invulnerable" in a curious way. You're no longer subject to the ravages of your disclaimed emotions. That's the good news of midlife maturation.

Knowing you can ride the rapids of difficult feelings and not drown, you will develop real strength, which prepares you to love and be loved as never before. You nurture a true, quiet power. This is what St. Paul meant when he said: "When I am weak, then I am strong." Author Thomas Moore reflects the same notion: "It is not rare for genuine personal strength to be clothed in gentility and quiet."

Experience Feelings to Strengthen Your Immune System

Allowing yourself to have strong feelings can be good for your health! A study conducted at UCLA by Margaret Kemeny, a psychoimmunologist, found that strong feeling states such as happiness or sadness produced an increase in "killer cells" that fight disease. Contacting feelings can strengthen your immune system, whereas the absence of emotions suppresses it.

Research has also established a link between loss and a variety of physical and psychological ills. Gail Sheehy, author of the best-selling book *Passages*, offers a strong argument for people in midlife to deal with loss in a healthy way: "Exit events that begin to pile up in the second half of life: loss of social status, the departure of grown children, sudden deaths of friends—these and other occurrences are now considered portents of physical problems. The literature remarks on how an individual under high stress—especially men—is unaware of its existence and its impact on his life."

By replacing juvenile images of strength—biting your tongue and toughing it out—with a mature embracing of grief, you'll not only feel better, you may also protect yourself from heart disease, depression, and other ailments.

In addition to the health benefits of *contacting* your feelings, evidence suggests that *disclosing* your feelings by talking about losses and traumas enhances immune functioning and may prolong life. Researcher Dr. James Pennebaker and his colleagues have suggested that social support helps keep you healthy if you're willing to be communicative. According to Dr. Pennebaker, "Social support only protects your health if you use it wisely. That is, if you have suffered a major upheaval in your life, talk to your friends about it. Merely having friends is not enough."

Most people believe that showing pain, hurt, or fear will repulse their friends. But part of a truly caring, intimate relationship is to talk about the pain that inevitably arises from being in a relationship and being alive. Jordan Paul says it well: "Openly sharing our painful feelings and receiving the warmth and acceptance of another is profoundly intimate. When our pain opens our partner to his or her own pain, we both connect to the common fears and hurts that affect us all."

EXERCISE:

> Think of a recent event or interaction that brought up feelings for you, whether joy or sorrow. Can you allow yourself to embrace those feelings in a caring, gentle way? Do you tend to judge some feelings or longings as unacceptable and try to push them away? Can you bring more warmth and acceptance to yourself?

Embrace Yourself as You Are

One of life's most profound discoveries is so simple that it's easily overlooked: your innermost self is a lovable self. By embracing who you really are, you cultivate a growing kindness toward yourself that manifests itself as increased attentiveness and gentleness toward others. Being more present, you're more approachable. Being and showing your authentic heart invites people toward you.

Princess Diana was an example of a vulnerable and accessible person. By revealing to the world her eating disorder (bulimia) and her struggles with life and love, she endeared herself to millions.

If you show the world only a fabricated self, then that's all people will see. Being a false self is safer; if people reject you, then you won't hurt as much because you haven't exposed your true vulnerable identity. Of course, if your superficial self is accepted and loved, then that doesn't do you much good because you're not being loved for who you really are. You're then burdened with the task of maintaining your image to ensure continued approval. And deep down, you're haunted by the knowledge that you're being phony, and by the gnawing fear that you're really unlovable.

Being loved for your image doesn't supply the nurturing you need. It's like watering the leaves of a plant while the roots wither. For love to soak into the inner place that needs to be touched and nourished, you must first relinquish the protection of your facade so that your more vulnerable and lovable self can thrive. This doesn't mean that you should open yourself indiscriminately. You must be discerning about whom, when, and how much to trust. Such wisdom grows through experience.

Here's an example of the power of authenticity and the high price of not showing your genuine heart. As I'm getting to know a woman, I may begin to like her. But I'm shy to tell her. So I hide my feelings and continue to play games. I call infrequently and stay cool and detached when we're together. Not surprisingly, she concludes that I'm not very interested and pursues other men. She's confused by the split she senses in me—an incongruity between what I'm putting out and how I really feel. She sees me as cold and closed, when I'm actually quite fond of her. By the time I express my honest feelings, it's too late. She's moved on.

The opposite scenario is that I may pursue her aggressively. Under the spell of young love, I may call her every day. I tell her I'm crazy about her and that I love her. Of course, I don't really *know* her after just a few weeks. She's likely to interpret my eagerness as romantic infatuation. She's seen this before with men who come on strong then fade quickly.

A third scenario is that I find the middle ground between frosty withdrawal and hot obsession. As I muster the courage to "make a fool" of myself and express my authentic heart, I may say something like, "I feel shy to tell you this, but I really like you. I'd enjoy seeing you more often." If she's a mature woman, she's likely to appreciate such an honest disclosure, even if she feels uncomfortable or shy. If she has hardened herself against the softer feelings within herself, she might think I'm a wimp and judge me as weak. She may not appreciate that my genuineness takes strength.

If she receives my feelings graciously, a deeper closeness may develop. If I'm met with rejection, I may feel hurt for a short time, but I know where I stand. I'd rather know this now than pursue someone who's not available for me. Then I'm free to move forward rather than obsess over someone who's not interested. And I can appreciate myself for having had the courage to be vulnerable.

By midlife, I've had enough experience to know that people have differing preferences for a partnership. Rejection doesn't mean there's something wrong with me, although I'm open to looking at how I might be pushing people away.

Trust Your True Self

Of course, before divulging deeper feelings I would want to build some trust by revealing myself in small ways and seeing if I'm accepted. However, trust and connection can only deepen if we take some risks to be open. If I want others to be forthright, I need to do the same. Courageously revealing your authentic self to trusted people—and being gently attentive when others disclose them-selves—is a prescription for deepening love and intimacy.

It takes steady trust in yourself and in the unfolding process of life to be real with people and to trust that your authentic self is an endearing self. Life often invites you to live on faith alone, trusting that being yourself will provide the best opportunity for connecting with people and that by continually reaching out from who you really are, some courageous and sensitive souls will appreciate you as you are.

EXERCISE:

Think of three times you took a risk to be your real self with someone and let the chips fall where they may.

1. What happened?
2. Was it a positive or negative experience?
3. What did you learn?
4. If your experience was negative, is there anything you can do differently next time that might make it more positive?

(If you've had a bad experience being genuine, it may be dif-ficult to value honesty. Although some people don't appreciate honesty, most do, as long as you communicate with respect and sensitivity. Once you've had some positive, gratifying experience of being genuine, you will find it increasingly easy, and even some-times exhilarating, to act from your true inner being.)

Embrace Shyness

As you release the pretensions and idealizations of the fabricated self, you might notice a curious feeling—"shyness." It might manifest itself as butterflies in your stomach, or as an uncomfortable "icky" feeling when you are complimented or hugged. You might find yourself averting your eyes from people or feeling hesitant to approach someone you like.

If you experience shyness, consider it a blessing. Shyness is an entrance into a tender fold within your authentic heart.

When children feel shy, they are experiencing a delicate opening to an unknown situation. As their caution recedes, they will smile openly, delighting those around them. This natural openness, innocence, and receptivity is something we love about children; it's very endearing. How destructive it is when obtuse adults squash these precious qualities.

Feeling uncomfortable with their own inner child, many adults never avail themselves of the deeper contact that's possible with children. Instead of sharing a pure moment of openheartedness, they distance themselves by becoming observers and commentators. Entrenched behind their own defensive walls, they make comments like, "Look how shy you are," or, "Don't be so bashful." Such statements are subtly demeaning; they prod children to become self-conscious. Told that there's something wrong with being vulnerable, children become afraid, recoiling from those who've failed to reflect back their sensitivity and openness. Sadly, they learn that being shy is something bad.

Avoiding shyness may prevent you from connecting with people. Susan, a fifty-two-year-old manager, put it this way: "One of my defenses was being overly confident. It was a false confidence that I mistook for strength. It was really a cover for not letting myself slow down and feel connected with people. It was an exuberance and perkiness, which was a cover-up for a shyness that I didn't know I had. Exuberance was a way to show people I was witty and interesting. But it prevented me from feeling what it was like to connect with them. When I took time to notice the other person, I felt shy for the first time. I thought, 'Oh, this is interesting. I'm here with this person and we're connecting and I don't know what will happen next. It could be good or could be bad.' I felt vulnerable. There we were as two real human beings. There was an intimacy there that was a little scary, but very enlivening."

Shyness may appear to be a frailty, but it's a powerful solvent for cynicism and rigidity. The moment you embrace it, you're no longer hardened; you've reawakened to your tender yearning for closeness. As the armor around your heart melts, you're more emotionally available.

Shyness may begin as a sense of embarrassment when uneasy emotions arise—when tears well up during a movie, or when a friend is affectionate, or when you're not sure someone will like you. You feel shy to be glimpsed in your vulnerability. Your exposure raises fears about whether you'll be valued. If you can summon courage to embrace shyness, it can yield to sweet, loving contact. Midlife is a time to balance wisdom with self-assured innocence, which keeps your heart exquisitely alive.

Shyness as a Friend

If you can allow yourself to experience shyness when it arises—if you can gently turn your attention toward the place in your body that feels this shyness—then it becomes a friend, not a threat. Embraced shyness transforms into tenderness and sweetness. At first, you might notice yourself breathing more tensely or tightening your stomach or chest to get rid of it. If you can open to your bodily sensation of shyness without being judgmental, you might find yourself softening. Shyness may then transmute into a harmonious sensation of joy throughout your body. As your tolerance for shyness grows, there are greater possibilities for breakthroughs into the exhilarating pleasure of connecting.

Anthony, a fifty-two-year-old programmer, expressed it as follows: "I used to see shyness as weakness. When I was younger, it almost paralyzed me. I'd be terrified to ask a girl out on a date. But now that I've come to accept myself more, I use it as a strength. When I go *with* it—instead of fighting it—I can be shy *and* reach out. It makes some people uncomfortable, but others find me more approachable. Those are the people I want to know."

If you never allow yourself to experience shyness, you're likely to develop a rigid character structure rather than a liquidity of being that enables you to connect with your own core and that of others. Embracing shyness in midlife is a courageous step toward relationships of mutual vulnerability and respect—and the deepest intimacy.

EXERCISE:

The next time you reveal something you feel vulnerable about with a friend or partner, notice if you feel any shyness. If so, what does it feel like in your body? Is your belly tightening and your breath constricting? If you experience an electric openness of being that accompanies shyness, you're on the verge of deeper contact.

1. Do you notice yourself wanting to retreat because you fear this close encounter?
2. Are you afraid of sensations and feelings that arise within you from the contact between you?
3. Do you divert your eyes, walk away, or talk rapidly to override genuine relating?

If you accept your shyness, you may begin to enjoy sustained connection with a partner or friend. This requires that you both develop a tolerance for deeper contact, if not a positive taste for it. As you allow yourself to sense whatever feelings arise within you as you relate—whether anxiety, excitement, or relief—you may gradually rest in the nurturing closeness for which you've longed.

Befriending shyness enables you to find peace within the very midst of your fear of making contact. As you integrate maturity with childlike openness, you come to luxuriate in wise innocence—one of the further fruits of midlife growth.

The Benefits of Befriending Shyness:

1. Experience your tenderness.
2. Open yourself to contact.
3. Soften into your authentic heart.
4. Embrace yourself as you are.

Embrace Risk

Relationships grow when you take intelligent risks to extend yourself to others. Without continuing self-awareness, authenticity, and kind communication, a relationship is likely to wither, just as your body deteriorates if you don't nourish it with healthy food and exercise.

A forty-eight-year-old scientist, who was happily involved in a one-year partnership, attributed his new success to a commitment to total honesty: "I used to think, 'What will *sound* good?' I didn't have any idea what would *feel* good to say. It feels good to have the integrity to tell the truth."

But once his new relationship was going well, he began reverting back to his self-protective habit of withholding his real feelings and needs. The relationship began slipping into a familiar pattern of distance and discontent. "I was becoming complacent. I stopped being open and honest because I was afraid it might jeopardize the relationship. I didn't want to lose another partner. But honesty is what brought us closer! By being overprotective, I was causing the relationship to slip away."

When he deviated from the path of being authentic, he sensed a distance creeping into the partnership. Fortunately, this awareness helped him get back on track: "Now I realize that being open and honest isn't something you do once or twice—and then expect to live happily ever after. I see what people mean when they say relationships take work! But the rewards are tremendous."

Mature love grows as you risk being yourself *again and again.* As you develop a history of facing the abyss and making a soft landing into the arms of a warm and understanding person, the tender strands of trust and affection strengthen. As love grows, you feel less scared to be yourself. Being genuine becomes a natural, comfortable way of being with someone you're growing to trust and love.

Embrace Solitude

Being authentic raises the possibility of being rejected when you're most vulnerable. The resulting fear of being alone and isolated is a core human fear. You need to face this fear courageously so you don't manipulate to get love, collapse into defeat if you're rejected, or languish in an abusive relationship. When being alone becomes an acceptable option to you, you're freer to risk being yourself and loving openly.

You can't force anyone to love or want you. Part of your strength comes from knowing you can be alone if necessary. The more you can embrace solitude, the more you can warmly extend yourself to people. The more you have yourself and a life apart from the relationship, the less desperately you need a particular person. *There's less to lose when you have yourself.* You're more willing to risk rejection when you can stay creatively engaged with life if the relationship ends. You can grieve your hurting heart without losing heart. You can relish time alone to reclaim the connection with yourself.

Juvenile love often involves an unhealthy merging and a loss of self; mature love requires some space between you. Unable to find solace in solitude, you become desperate for connection. The poet Rilke describes this loss of self: "Young people err so often and so grievously in this: that they . . . fling themselves at each other, when love takes possession of them, scatter themselves just as they are, in all their untidiness, disorder, confusion. . . . Thus each loses himself for the sake of the other."

As you take steps to develop a meaningful life, you can make space for a relationship to enter that life. The more you "get a mid-life," the more you become a *host* to a potential partner, not a *hostage.* You become, in the words of Rilke, "two solitudes [who] protect and border and salute each other."

Fear of Aloneness and Unhealthy Dependency

Is your fear of abandonment so overwhelming that you surrender your real feelings, longings, and dignity to please others? Fearful of being alone, do you retreat from being honest with yourself and others? If so, love and intimacy are likely to atrophy in this alien climate of inauthenticity.

Your relationships may take on a sticky, clinging quality, which can suffocate them. One couple who jointly ran a business described their personal time together as being stuck in oatmeal: "We don't feel satisfied spending so much time together. But we don't know what to do with ourselves when we're *not* together."

The spark of love matures into a steady flame as you give it air to breathe. Time apart makes time together more lush and meaningful. In order to reduce dependencies that lead to stagnation, you must courageously face your aloneness and learn to find refuge in solitude. Abraham Maslow, a founder of both Humanistic and Transpersonal Psychology, reminds us that "In the later stages of growth the person is essentially alone and can rely only upon himself." Midlife is a time to balance the richness of solitude with the fulfillment of connection.

Some therapists believe that a major purpose of a partnership is to heal hurts that originated in childhood. If you are part of a committed couple, you may help each other heal by providing some of what was missing in childhood. But no one else can *fully* restore you to wholeness. A lover can be responsive to your needs and wants, but he or she is not responsible for your life.

Love matures as you:

1. Spare your partner responsibility for your childhood wounds.
2. Appreciate your partner for whatever nurturing he or she provides.
3. Heal and support yourself apart from the relationship.

Rather than be too dependent on your companion, it's often helpful to seek out a trusted therapist or counselor to further you in resolving old wounds that block current relationships. Such an investment in yourself can advance your prospects for attracting and nurturing love during middle age and beyond.

Anna, a forty-five-year-old massage therapist, was often irritable with her husband, Brent, who was left feeling that he was never good enough for her. Anna often badgered him to dress differently, talk more, and make more money. As Anna uncovered her deeper feelings, she realized how her fears were operating in the marriage. She was attempting to shape Brent according to her romantic wish for a husband who'd satisfy every desire. But instead of bringing him toward her, she was pushing him away.

As Anna wrestled with her complicity in the problem, she realized that she was seeing Brent as the source of her happiness: "I thought if I could get everything to look right, I'd be happy. I tried to make him give me everything I wanted; I didn't trust that I'd get what I need by just loving him. I now know I have to find my own inner strength. When I give him space, he comes toward me." As

Anna discovered, a deeper love can develop as you focus more on connecting with yourself than on shaping your partner.

Something to watch out for: It would be a mistake to equate maturity with lack of conflict. Some couples need to argue and hash things out as part of their process, especially if one of them keeps dragging his or her feet. Each couple must decide how much conflict they're willing to accommodate and deal with differences in ways that are productive.

Although life can be richer with a loving partnership, it's liberating to realize that you can create a satisfying life without a mate. When being single is an acceptable option, you can enter relationships from a position of strength and choice, not fear or obligation.

The increasing capacity to embrace aloneness in midlife doesn't mean that interpersonal needs vanish. But instead of narrowing your options by pursuing "The Relationship," you may increase them by developing a network of meaningful connections:

- Look for occasions where you can meet potential friends.
- Join a church, synagogue, or meditation group.
- Exercise in a gym or yoga class—with other people.
- Participate in a twelve-step program.
- Volunteer for a cause you are interested in.
- Take up a hobby you can do with other people: dancing, bike riding, etc.

The American obsession with being happily married overlooks the rich connections possible with people in your community. As you feel more connected in your life—even if not with a sexual partner—you can become more comfortable being single.

As you courageously confront the demon of aloneness, it can become a comforting ally, not a dreaded enemy. As you become more adept at embracing the various layers of your authentic self there is less to fear. One client who was skeptical about the possibilities of positive solitude discovered its value in midlife: "I no longer feel the loneliness of being *by* myself, I feel the richness of being *with* myself. When my partner isn't around, I don't feel so antsy anymore. I used to make fun of her when she wanted time alone. Now I trust there's a rhythm of being alone and coming together."

The French philosopher André Gide commented that many people suffer from "the fear of finding oneself alone, and so they don't find themselves at all." As you learn to enjoy your time alone, you're freer to risk being yourself. If you're unwilling to stand alone, you may seek companionship that offers no real intimacy. You might hold on to a relationship that's toxic to your well-being. Fearful of losing something that you never really had, you may go through the motions of having a relationship, when no real "relating" is happening. Staying together "till death do us part" is scant accomplishment if you're perpetually miserable.

The realization that solitude not only enriches you but also enriches your relationships often doesn't dawn until midlife. The problem many couples face is finding time alone—and time together—as life gets busier. It takes a certain vigilance to ensure that time spent for "being" isn't subsumed by time spent for "doing."

Embrace Death and Loss

Perhaps the ultimate sense of aloneness strikes as you face the loss of loved ones and, eventually, your own death. As you enter the second half of life, the realization of your mortality hits home in a new way.

You can live more authentically as you peer at death soberly. When your relationship with death and loss is one of denial, your relationship with life is one of avoidance. Although the thought of dying may frighten you, there is no more potent reminder of what's important in life.

Since death represents the ultimate loss of control, those who've had difficulty relinquishing the control of their fabricated self are especially prone to fear death. They haven't had much practice being real and facing life honestly. Such people may glibly minimize their feelings: "Hey, we're all gonna die someday, so why think about it? I'm not afraid of dying!"

Death is especially distasteful for people who haven't lived fully; it's a tragic end to an unlived life. Dying at any age is premature for people who haven't surrendered to life. The part of them that knows that their deeper potential hasn't been realized fears letting go. Surrendering to death means forever surrendering the possibility of living an authentic, fulfilling life. Not having been born fully, they fear the death of their unrealized potential.

Maintaining a gentle awareness of your inevitable death is a potent reminder to live *now*.

- Do you express appreciation to people you love?
- Do you relish the freedom to be yourself, especially with those you trust?
- Can you do something more creative than watching television tonight?
- Do you make eye contact with the clerk behind the cash register and share your warmth with people you encounter during the day?
- Do you notice the beauty of the cloud formations as you walk to the market, or the wildflowers along the road?

Remember What's Important

When your relationship with loss is distorted, so is your relationship with life and love. In *Journey to Ixtlan*, Yaqui Indian Don Juan reminds Carlos Castaneda to keep the spirit of death over his left shoulder as a way to remember what's meaningful in life.

You'll deal with death the same way you've dealt with life. If you haven't permitted yourself to experience strong feelings in life, then you'll sidestep difficult ones that accompany illness and death. The lifelong avoidance of your feelings makes the experience of dying more tormenting—both for yourself and for family members witnessing your anguish.

As a popular Zen Buddhist saying puts it, "Those who die before they die do not die when they die." By facing the little losses in life, you're better prepared for the final letting go. As you live more honestly, you die more peacefully.

There's little urgency to grow when you don't give death its due. In India, where bodies are cremated in public view, there's the reminder that death will greet us all. Midlife is a time when people you know die with increasing frequency. As you learn to face loss and embrace sorrow, you come to live with greater poignancy and presence.

EXERCISE:

> Think of three things you'd like people to remember about you after you die. They may be things you've accomplished or, more important, qualities that you'd like to be appreciated for. Being aware of them will remind you to cherish and cultivate these qualities while you're alive.

Loving Life

When a loved one dies and the taste of loss lingers in your soul, you may appreciate life in a new way. You may be freshly inspired to "seize the day" and live with more passion and purpose. The awareness of the finitude of life can remind you to

- Treasure your loved ones.
- Cherish moments of contact and caring.
- Be kinder to people and other living things—while there's time.

I've been fortunate to know people who've found genuine peace at the end of their lives. Dying is easier to embrace when it becomes the next step in living.

Living with an authentic heart provides the best practice for dealing with death. One woman I was privileged to know had a large capacity to accept what life brings. She was well practiced in the art of embracing her feelings. As she opened to the fears accompanying dying, these fears would pass, as feelings usually do when embraced just as they are. Even though her physical pain was sometimes insufferable, it would diminish as she gently allowed it to be instead of fighting against it. Two days before her death I asked if there was anything she wanted me to tell people. Smiling radiantly, she replied, "Tell them that dying isn't so bad."

When death draws near, what's important in life suddenly becomes clearer. In my work with the terminally ill, I've never heard anyone regret not working late hours at the office or vacuuming their house more often. Instead, people ask:

- Did I follow my path in life?
- Did I take enough risks?

- Did I hurt anyone badly?
- Did I love well?

As St. John of the Cross reminds us, "In the evening of life you'll be judged by love alone." By finding the courage and wisdom to love more fully during midlife, you can live with more meaning and die with greater dignity and serenity.

Expand Your Capacity for Authenticity

1. Are you willing to risk the rejection that may come from being who you really are, or have you become adept at impression management? Is it more important to be yourself or to please people?

(We are conditioned to please people in order to be accepted. Being authentic means being more committed to honesty than to fitting in.)

2. Do you have difficulty letting go of control? Do you fill in "awkward" lulls in conversation, or can you enjoy periods of silence to reconnect with yourself or enjoy a quiet connection with other people? Can you rest in your heart and relax in your breath?

(Moments of being genuine may be ones in which you don't know what to say. However, as you become more comfortable with pregnant silence, your presence and participation come through. Experiment with allowing for silence and noticing the connection that becomes possible.)

3. Are you quick to offer solutions, or is it enough to offer kindness and caring? Can you allow for feelings of shyness and awkwardness?

(Men are especially trained to offer solutions to problems. But this may leave the other person feeling even more isolated. If someone seeks a solution, you may offer one, but people usually need empathy and understanding first. This creates the connection they need most when they're hurting.)

4. Do you avoid feelings by using drugs or alcohol, overworking, smoking, eating, gambling, shopping, having compulsive sex, and so on?

(Various addictions numb feelings and are ways to avoid embracing your authentic self. If the addiction is strong, you probably need to end it before you can work on embracing your true feelings. You may need help for this, because it's very difficult to do alone.)

5. Have you found a balance between solitude and time with people? Can you grant your partner time alone or do you feel threatened by that?

(It's easy to expect your partner to meet all of your needs. But this will put pressure on the relationship. You need to find other ways to meet your needs, including creative times alone.)

6. Can you allow for feelings of loss and sorrow, as well as joy and pleasure? Can you let go into crying and laughter?

(Many people try to seek pleasure and avoid pain. This is natural. But trying to avoid unpleasant experiences usually perpetuates them. Facing whatever life brings you is a wiser way to develop equanimity. If you do not hold on to pleasure or pain, you may discover that they come and go in their own rhythm.)

7. Do you view your feelings as a friend or as an adversary that can destroy you?

(A big leap in personal growth is to view your feelings as a friend, not an enemy to be avoided. Trusting your feelings means making peace with yourself. You can't be comfortable with yourself and develop true self-confidence until you befriend the full range of your human feelings.)

8. Do you believe that your core self is a lovable, beautiful self, or do you believe that you're basically defective, flawed, and unworthy?

(Recognizing your basic goodness and beauty is a step toward loving yourself and bringing love toward you.)

❦

Respect Yourself through Boundaries

A key to my boundaries is knowing my inner life. My inner life includes my beliefs, thoughts, feelings, decisions, choices and experiences. It also includes my wants, needs, sensations within my body, my intuitions, and even unconscious factors in my life. If I'm unaware or out of touch with my inner life, I can't know all of my boundaries and limits.

—CHARLES WHITFIELD

7

Boundaries as a Foundation for Intimacy

A boundary is based on a process of checking in with ourselves from moment to moment about how much and what kind of contact we want. A wall, on the other hand, is rigidly in place and is rarely responsive to our inner or outer environment.

—Chris Evans

◦∽◦

Most people think it's not doable. Having a partnership *and* having yourself seems like mission impossible. Relationships are about compromise and sacrifice, aren't they? They're about losing yourself to love!

After nearly twenty-five years of practicing psychotherapy, in addition to living my own life, I've seen that relationships flounder when we're not being true to ourselves. We can actualize the tender promise of love to the degree that we know ourselves and "have" ourselves. Midlife is a time to deepen love and intimacy not by giving ourselves away but by being ourselves ever more fully.

Partnerships struggle when we lack awareness of ourselves—our real feelings, thoughts, wants, values, and longings—and also lack the skills to communicate our experience clearly, respectfully, and nondefensively. We don't need to work harder to fix ourselves or to fit into our partner's world. We need to find, respect, and reveal ourselves.

One of life's curious paradoxes is that you can't have intimacy without boundaries that define and protect your autonomy. You can't relish the joy of union until you're comfortable being alone. You can't "have" another person until you differentiate yourself *from* that person—and thereby "have" yourself. You can't expect another to hold you tenderly unless you learn to hold yourself with kindness and caring. Without being rooted in yourself, what is called "union" degenerates into sloppy enmeshment; what is called marriage is a loss of self, not a discovery and expansion of your inner beauty and selfhood.

The joy of sharing your authentic heart can't safely occur until first and foremost your heart belongs to yourself—and to the larger life of which you're part. When two become one, beware! It's hard to move around in your life if you're too attached. Relationships thrive when two whole people are becoming ever more whole. Love doesn't mean losing your heart to another person. It means finding it as a loving resonance awakens your heart.

One thirty-nine-year-old woman expressed a common dilemma: "I got lost in *his* world. I was so eager to please that I gave myself away. I thought if I kept loving him, he'd love me back. I tried so hard that I neglected my own interests, friends, and career. I became the self-scarifying martyr—pushing my own needs aside—until I couldn't stand it anymore! Then I'd blast him with blame and anger, which pushed him further away." These destructive cycles tore this couple apart.

As she learned what it meant to validate, instead of vacate, herself—respecting her feelings and wants—she could express herself before a toxic buildup occurred. Her calm assertiveness began to draw healthier men as there was no longer a threat of her previous abrasiveness, which had been born of self-denial and the mistaken belief that she had to suppress herself to have a man.

Partnerships are the source of our highest highs and lowest lows. Oftentimes, we've felt so lost and overwhelmed that we're thoroughly confused about what it takes to move toward lasting love. How can we have a relationship in which we actually relate person to person—without losing ourselves?

The way forward lies in your ability to surrender to love and intimacy while having the backup ability to maintain a certain kind of boundary that keeps you connected to yourself. Understanding how to create flexible personal boundaries—differentiating your world from another's world—creates a healthy foundation for midlife love.

The Antidote to Enmeshed Relationships

The delights of intimate relating will evade you until you can respond to the following questions:

- What do you want in this relationship apart from real or imagined pressure to supply what your partner wants?
- What are your needs apart from your partner's?
- Can you remain respectful of your partner's needs while honoring your own?
- Are you willing to deal with the consequences of not giving your partner what he or she wants?

Until you learn to distinguish your own reality from that of others, you'll remain painfully enmeshed in your relationships, perhaps without being aware that you've let yourself fade into oblivion. Only by having clear boundaries can you, in the words of Kahlil Gibran, give your hearts, "but not into each other's keeping. . . . And stand together, yet not too near together." Boundaries keep you disentangled in a way that supports the healthy growth of love and intimacy.

To assess your own boundaries, consider these questions:

- While listening to people, do you compulsively nod your head in apparent agreement when you actually disagree or don't understand what they mean?
- Do you laugh at jokes you don't find funny?
- Do you try to get people to like you without considering whether you like them?

- When people accidentally bump into you, or when your carts bump in the market, do you apologize, immediately assuming that *you're* at fault?
- Do you avoid conflict because you want approval and acceptance?
- Do you seek conflict, not respecting others' boundaries?
- Have you been physically or verbally abused and assumed that *you* were doing something wrong?

If you've answered yes to some of these questions, relax. You're in good company. To be human is to want acceptance and love, so it isn't easy to live within the boundaries of your own skin. It's a lifelong project.

Boundaries Support Intimacy

Haphazard boundaries keep you confused and overwhelmed in relationships. If you are unable to sort out your own feelings and needs, your reality will become enmeshed with your partner's reality. For example, one client who wanted more lovemaking with his wife accused her of being "closed down" and "selfish." But was she obligated to provide sex if her wants and rhythms were different from his? Or did she have a right to experience different needs?

Another client wanted to visit her friends one night a week. She'd ignored them when in a previous partnership and realized how important friends are. Her partner was annoyed that she wanted a life apart from his and insisted that she stay home. His refusal to let go of control and to respect her boundaries eventually led to separation.

Without sturdy boundaries, you're easily dominated and controlled—if not abused—by others. Your reality is subsumed by their world. If you are unclear or timid about your own wants and needs, you become easy prey for those who confidently express their wants. Your sense of self will become overshadowed by the way others treat or view you.

For example, Patrick criticized his partner Nancy for spending money: "You're incredibly extravagant and materialistic!" But did these accusations automatically mean that she was guilty as charged? Or did they say more about Patrick's values and preferences? Was

Nancy required to comply with his request? Or did his criticism mask his own blind spots, his own stuff? Maybe he is too conservative and self-denying! Better yet, why judge either of them for how they are? Helping each of them affirm their authentic needs while respecting the other's preferences is more beneficial than a futile argument about who's right.

During one of this couple's sessions, Patrick asked Nancy with disgust, "Do you really need more clothes? Don't you have enough? You love to spend money, don't you?" These accusations often led her to give in. She then resented herself for submitting and losing her voice. At other times, she'd overreact by buying more clothes to prove that no one could control her! Either way, they both lost. A growing resentment and power struggle kept them distant.

Set Boundaries from Your Heart

How could Nancy set boundaries with Patrick's critical comments without shutting down their communication? How could she affirm her right to buy what she wants without overreacting? And how could Patrick express what's happening in his world when she spends their money? Can they both express their needs with an open heart?

The shift came when Nancy learned to set limits about what she could and couldn't hear from Patrick and when Patrick learned to communicate his *feelings* about Nancy's behavior, not his *judgments*. Nancy's intention wasn't to stonewall communication; she wanted to hear Patrick's feelings. She loved him and wanted to know how she affected him. But she didn't want to receive blame and accusations, which reminded her of her disrespectful father and the pain of not being trusted to make her own decisions.

During one session, Nancy told Patrick, "I feel angry and hurt when you're critical and tell me what to do. I want to feel free to make my own choices. I was never allowed to do that growing up. I want to hear your feelings, but not your judgments." Nancy felt more empowered by setting a clear boundary with Patrick regarding what was unacceptable. Expressing herself with quiet strength, she made it clear that she didn't want to be shamed and criticized. She discovered greater dignity knowing that her choices weren't limited to complying or rebelling. She could communicate her boundaries.

Patrick recognized that trying to change her backfired because Nancy felt controlled and demeaned by his sarcasm and hostility. As I helped him look deeper, he realized that underlying his manipulative comments lay fear around money. He was anxious about losing his job in an industry prey to downsizing and mergers. Also, in his family, money was tight with no frills allowed. His ethic was one of saving.

Patrick received more empathy as he communicated from his heart without putting her down: "When you buy clothes, I feel anxious. I'm worried that if I lose my job we'll have no savings. And I feel inadequate because I'm not earning enough. It's hard to tell you my fears and limits; I'm afraid you'll think I'm a wimp, and that I won't make you happy and you'll leave."

Hearing him express his insecurities in an open, vulnerable way, she was touched. She became willing to reduce expenses in order to have a less worried husband. Feeling heard, Patrick found it easier to understand her need to make choices, and he became more flexible and supportive. This heartfelt sharing led to a trust and closeness that had eluded them.

The Power of Internal Boundaries

As your self-worth becomes less influenced by others, you're less susceptible to being injured by others' judgments, sarcasm, or opinions. By knowing and affirming yourself, you're not predisposed to giving people the power to judge you. You can evaluate others' opinions and either accept or reject them based upon your self-evaluation.

Criticism may still sting, but your hurt will be less enduring if *you give your assessment of yourself more credibility than others' opinions of you.* Nancy described this important internal boundary as follows: "As I get stronger, his negative judgments don't matter so much. What's important is what *I* think!" As your identity derives from a source within yourself (the affirmation of your authentic self), you have more of the inner stability necessary to love.

Still, it may serve you to hear people's feedback, even if clothed in a distasteful garb. By being deaf to all but the kindest communications, you might dwell in a comfortable but self-deluded bubble. By finding the strength to hear a hurtful comment or criticism and then separate the wheat from the chaff, you might learn something about yourself. It takes a great deal of self-affirmation to listen to people without giving them carte blanche to attack and define you.

The ability to know and affirm your authentic self protects you from prematurely opening your heart to someone who might hurt you. If you neglect monitoring your boundaries, you may allow yourself to merge with an alluring man or woman before knowing him or her. You may become emotionally attached before you have ascertained whether your tender heart will be held kindly in this relationship.

For example, if you tend to have sex too early, you may not want to jump into bed until love is present. You may want children, but does he or she? If you're considering living together, wait until you trust that this person respects your feelings, values, and viewpoints—and that you can communicate well. By moving adroitly, like a fox on ice, you're less likely to fall through the cracks.

Through clear boundaries, you become more resilient in your relationships. You're free to:

- Move toward people or move away from them.
- Let people "in" when that feels right; set firm limits when so inclined.
- Monitor your degree of openness so that you permit yourself to be drawn closer as you feel accepted and understood.

Therapists Merle Fossum and Marilyn Mason use a zipper analogy to describe boundaries. If you have poor boundaries, you have your zipper on the outside, which gives everyone the power to unzip you—and violate your dignity—at any time. But if you have clear boundaries, you have your zipper on the inside. You can then decide on your own barriers to entry, allowing people close when that feels consistent with your wants and integrity.

Trust Your Backup System

As you grow confident that you can calibrate your boundaries as needed, you're freer to surrender to the spontaneous joy of loving. Trusting your ability to set firm limits as a "backup system," you can extend yourself to others in a warm, easygoing way. Then, if you're hit with a sneak attack, you can "fight back," so to speak, by firmly stating that you don't want to be judged or criticized, or by expressing your hurt or anger.

You're also free to end the relationship. This ultimate boundary may be set during the early stage of dating if you feel mistreated or if it's clear that things just don't feel right. If you're more involved, you're free to separate when your repeated best efforts fail to dislodge a major impasse. Trusting your capacity to take care of yourself provides a foundation for growing closer without losing yourself.

As you feel self-assured about your ability to maintain your sense of self, you can trust yourself to become more relaxed and spontaneous. Deeper levels of intimacy unfold when the border between two people softens. It's important to have control over these borders— control over when to let the drawbridge down and allow someone access to your authentic heart.

Live with Dignity

"Boundaries" is simply another word for knowing yourself and taking care of yourself. It means discovering and affirming your limits—knowing what you can and can't accept in a relationship. It means finding a refuge within yourself—treasuring the deepest chamber within your heart that no one can defile. It means realizing you're a separate person—a human being who deserves dignity and respect, like every member of the human family. While all this may be obvious, it isn't easy to maintain self-supporting boundaries, especially when your self-development was disrupted through abuse or neglect, which weakened your will and self-worth.

Through boundaries, you give yourself the space you need to identify your feelings, discover your needs, and assert yourself freely. Without boundaries, you may become overpowered by the press of others' feelings and demands. You then have no means to counteract others' criticism, hostility, or abuse. As a result, you become ineffective in your life and get swallowed whole in your relationships.

"I used to let my partner walk all over me," lamented one woman in midlife. "I thought if I tried harder, he'd treat me better. It never happened. I didn't stand up for myself; being *me* felt like I was being *mean.* I could never do anything right in his eyes. I feel freer knowing I don't have to accept that." By newly affirming her world of feelings and wants, she no longer fell apart when his opinions or demands blew her way.

When your boundaries are healthy, you listen to people and weigh their words against your own experience. You're free to agree or disagree with others' beliefs. You may reveal that you disagree or simply know it in your own mind.

When people express their feelings, these are *their* feelings. If they are angry or critical, you may listen without assuming that you've done anything wrong. If others are hurting, you offer compassion, but without trying to rescue them. If you're feeling overwhelmed and don't want to listen anymore, you can say so. In short, by keeping closely connected to your true heart, you don't lose yourself.

Inner Experience

As you increasingly come to know yourself in midlife, you can set boundaries that match your deepest and clearest sense of self. Freeing yourself from shame, you can trust your inner signals as a reliable guide to living. If someone wants something from you—time, attention, affection, a favor—you can check whether or not you want to give it. You can ask yourself, "Do I feel comfortable with that?" If yes, you can comply. If not, it isn't mandatory to feel guilty about saying no. Or you can say no even if you feel some guilt. People will ultimately trust you more when they sense that you're a person who knows your "yes" and your "no." By hearing your "no," they can trust that when you say "yes" you really mean it—you're not just being polite. Trust grows in this climate of freedom to be yourself.

Boundaries ensure privacy, which is different from keeping a destructive secret, such as hiding an affair. Knowing your boundaries means you can choose to share or not share something about yourself. You're not obliged to tell people everything. You may even want to conceal some tender areas from your closest friends. If you feel pressured to reveal too much too soon, you can simply respond, "I don't feel comfortable talking about that right now."

The point is that you have a choice. You have control over how much and how quickly you want to reveal yourself to a person.

With some people, you may want to play with your edge of discomfort, taking a risk to go over the line a little to see if you're met with a warm response. With others, you may rightly be cautious because your experience has taught you that this person doesn't handle your heart with care. Trust your intuition by listening closely to your guiding heart.

Psychotherapy, meditation, or any approach that helps you clarify and embrace your actual experience is invaluable in your effort to set boundaries. Until you know your truest feelings and wants—what upsets you, what nurtures you, what scares you, and what fulfills you—your boundaries will not be clearly aligned with your inner experience.

EXERCISE:

The next time you want to end a telephone conversation, notice how you feel about saying so. Do you feel guilty? Are you stern and abrupt about it? See if you can find a way to end the conversation while also keeping your heart open to the other person. For example, you might tell the other person you enjoyed your conversation (if this is true) or let him or her know that you need to move on to some other activity.

Boundaries Support Yourself and Others

By honoring your boundaries, I express respect and caring. If I love you, I don't want to hurt you by violating your boundaries. I don't want you to abandon yourself to please me. If you're clear about your limits, then I'll do my best to operate within those bounds if I want a trusting relationship of equals. Of course, this can get tricky if honoring your boundaries means that my vital needs won't be met. This is when communication becomes essential.

You may not always know when you've violated someone's boundary. Part of getting to know a person is getting feedback that you've overstepped your welcome. Boundary violations can happen in otherwise good relationships because you simply don't know the other person well enough. However, if you continue to transgress the same boundary, then you display disrespect.

Boundaries Protect Relationships

I serve you *and myself* by respecting your boundaries. I don't want to provoke you to distance yourself or hurt me in return. This would further erode the intimacy we both want. For example, if you agree to see a movie that you'd rather not see, you may have a miserable evening—and then be no fun at all! Or you may resent me later. Then you'll face a conflict that could have been averted through clear boundary setting. I'd prefer that you take care of yourself by declining my invitation rather than holding it against me later. By taking care of yourself, you're also taking care of *me*, and you're wisely taking care of *us*.

Rigid versus Flexible Boundaries

There may be times when you need to be vehement in order to protect yourself. For example, Fred, a forty-four-year-old client who was experiencing the hurt of separation, decided to eliminate contact with his former partner for at least a year and then see whether he wanted to be friends: "I need a lot of space from her right now. She just sent me an e-mail with her picture attached. Then she called to say 'hello.' It stirs up too much stuff to hear from her. It reminds me of how much I still miss her and want to be with her. I need to cut off *all* contact for a while so I can let her go—and open myself to someone new. Later, I'll see if it feels okay to be friends."

Sally, a forty-two-year-old secretary, needed to separate from her partner without discussion. Whenever she'd broach the topic of breaking up, she'd be persuaded to change her mind through his clever arguments and empty reassurances: "He says things will be different this time. He gets that apologetic little boy look on his face. So I start thinking there's hope—maybe this time he means it. But then he reverts back to the same old ways of being critical—and steamrolling over my feelings. He refuses to acknowledge that *we* have a problem and to see a couples therapist." Rather than get hooked back into an unworkable relationship, she was finally determined to end it, which was the beginning of reclaiming her life.

Newcomers to the art of creating boundaries may do so in a blunt, hurtful manner. This is one of the unfortunate excesses that can occur when someone discovers the word "codependence." Realizing they have eagerly tried to please, while abandoning themselves, they may now displease in a struggle to affirm themselves. Driven by shame to acquiesce to others, they may now be driven by a different kind of shame—the shame of *not* being the assertive person that codependence groups encourage.

Setting boundaries isn't about being reactive; nor is it just another name for cruelty or narcissism. Others will respect your boundaries more readily when they're expressed with kindness. As you grow stronger, you can express your boundaries without numbing your heart.

As you become more confident in setting limits, your boundaries can progress from being rigid to being flexible—from being fierce to being fair. You can exercise your right to care for yourself while maintaining an awareness of your impact upon others. Rather than dismiss caring as mere "codependence," you can balance commitment to yourself with consideration for others' well-being. Balancing self-assertion with openheartedness is a further step in midlife growth.

To Be Touched or Not to Be Touched

Nowhere are boundaries more pertinent than in monitoring your desire for physical contact. Many people have been physically or sexually abused as children. When the most basic human boundary has been casually violated, touch becomes associated with trauma and a desecration of one's dignity. It takes much healing and awareness to reappropriate the right to be touched or not touched.

The need for human touch has been well documented. Hundreds of studies have shown that infant development is crippled without sufficient touch. A study of HIV-positive men revealed that massage for one month significantly increased immune response. Those suffering from irregular heartbeats in a coronary care unit had a significant reduction in irregularity when the nurse or doctor touched the patients when taking their pulse. Dr. Dean Ornish concludes, "The simple act of touching someone is a powerful way to begin healing loneliness and isolation."

Sadly, we're a touch-deprived society. Americans are reluctant to touch one another compared to other cultures. A study by Sidney

Jourard observed how many times couples casually touch each other in cafés. In Paris, known as a romantic city, couples touched each other 110 times per hour. In Puerto Rico it was 180 times. But in the touch-phobic United States, couples touched twice per hour! At least we're ahead of London, where couples never touched.

Boundaries are essential to feel safe and comfortable. But how safe are you if your reticence blocks you from getting the physical contact you need to be emotionally and physically healthy?

EXERCISE:

The next time someone wants to touch you, notice how you feel about that. Do you feel comfortable with this or not? Can you say no to sex and touching? Can you say yes to sex and touching?

(It's vital that you let people touch you only when you feel comfortable with it.)

Be Yourself While Respecting Your Partner

After packing her bags and leaving an angry note, Pam came to my office for a session. "I always give in," she told me with a new resolve. "I've finally had it!"

When you're first learning to set boundaries, you might be paralyzed by inaction due to overconsideration of the effects your limit-setting might have upon others. You might hear the unruly voice of critical self-talk jabbering at you, perhaps declaring that you're being too selfish by asserting your rights and wants. So act you must, even if a bit insensitively. Sadly, however, some people take it too far; they act impulsively without thinking through the consequences. Short-term satisfaction often leads to long-term suffering.

Years later when she returned to my office, Pam recounted a common story. "After I moved out, people told me to fight for everything I could get: 'Why shouldn't you screw him? What did he ever do for you?' Now I regret listening to them because the fighting hurt our kids—and created bitterness between us. It wasn't a good way to deal with my anger, hurt, and fear."

The misguided attempt to fight for herself by hiring an aggressive attorney rather than negotiating what was fair was emotionally and financially traumatic for Pam's family. Rather than achieve a satisfying completion with her partner, the resulting hurt and resentment elongated the healing process and created despondency in the children as they had to watch their parents caught in an adolescent power struggle.

Flexible boundaries enable you to share power *with* people rather than wield power *over* them. You then have autonomy while maintaining intimacy. This delicate dance involves the art of fine-tuning your boundaries so that you may *honor your own needs while being sensitive to your impact upon others.* As you become stronger, you can express yourself in a way that affirms your truth but allows others to express their truth. You then find the middle path between suffocating dependency and lonely independence: the give and take of interdependence.

As you affirm your rights while respecting the rights of others, you can set boundaries in a manner that combines strength with gentleness, assertiveness with sensitivity, and firmness with flexibility. You become ready for lasting, midlife love as you balance loving yourself with respecting others' rights and sensibilities. By knowing and safeguarding your authentic heart, you connect with others in a deeper, more loving way.

Know Your Boundaries

1. Is it okay to disagree with someone's thoughts and opinions, or do you give the impression that you agree even when you don't?

(It's often easier to go along with people than "rock the boat." But if you do this frequently, you may feel disempowered in your life.)

2. Did people touch you inappropriately as a child? Do you let people touch you now even when you're uncomfortable with it? Can you ask for what you want and say what you don't want?

(It's important to know your physical boundaries. You can allow yourself to be touched when that feels comfortable and say no when you want to.)

3. Do you find yourself getting into triangles? Do you feel a need to take sides when others are disagreeing or in conflict?

(This involvement may mean that you have a difficult time standing on your own. You may be overly protective of people.)

4. Do you find yourself rescuing people who are in pain? Can you allow them to have their pain and simply be with them in a caring way?

(Through healthy boundaries, you allow others to experience their feelings without rescuing them. You offer compassion more than solutions. Being present and caring goes a long way toward helping people feel better.)

5. Can you keep people's private sharings private? Can people trust you with their confidences?

(Trust is fragile and easily broken if you reveal sensitive things that people tell you. Confidentiality is a cornerstone of psychotherapy because if people don't feel safe, they won't open up. The same principle applies to close relationships.)

6. If you raise a touchy issue with a person, do you first check if he or she is comfortable talking about it?

(Rather than violate people's boundaries, try to respect whether a person is willing to hear a complaint or issue you have. If a person is caught off guard, or if this isn't a good time to talk, the conversation may go poorly. If this person is never willing to talk, then it's probably his or her resistance to hearing your feelings, and you may need to be more vehement about your need to talk.)

7. Did you have a hard time saying no when you were growing up? Or was your "no" respected? How comfortable are you saying no to people now?

(Boundaries mean having a healthy sense of control over when to let people close and when to keep them distant. Unless you know how to say no, you can't really say yes.)

∽◌∾

Practice Self-Soothing and Self-Connection

The person who inwardly feels worthless is the one who must build himself up by selfish aggrandizement, and the person who has a sound experience of his own worth, that is, who loves himself, has the basis for acting generously toward his neighbor.

—ROLLO MAY

8

The Softening Ingredient

Liberation isn't about breaking out of anything; it's a gentle melting into who we really are.

— Marianne Williamson

∽o∾

Living from your heart means living less defensively. It means shedding the facades and pretensions designed to protect you from the world. Instead of retreating from life—playing it safe to avoid shame or ridicule—you emerge from hiding and let yourself be seen in your essential humanness. This more genuine life means being exposed to life's thorns and thistles. You could be judged or ridiculed. You could be rejected. You could get hurt.

What You Have Control Over

Personal boundaries help protect your tender heart. However, while boundaries offer essential protection, they can make you stiff or self-righteous without a softening ingredient that's essential for midlife loving: the capacity for self-soothing.

What comes your way from *outside* yourself is unpredictable. But you can influence what happens *within* yourself. You have choice over how you relate to events—not total control, but enough choice to make a difference. As Jean-Paul Sartre put it, "Freedom is what you do with what's been done to you."

You're free to respond to circumstances with greater serenity. You can go inside yourself when you're upset or frustrated and talk kindly to yourself. You can fold your arms around your hurting heart rather than harden and contract against your pain and thereby increase your suffering. The capacity for self-soothing safeguards you from collapsing into depression or blindly reacting with rage and blame when things don't go your way. As you develop a comfortable container for a full range of experience, your capacity to love expands—and your boundary setting comes from a more responsive, less reactive place.

There's an old story from Hinduism and Buddhism about how to protect ourselves from the harsh roads of life. One option is to cover the earth with leather to make our path smooth. But this would take some doing! The other option is to find a good pair of walking shoes. Self-soothing provides the protective shoes we need to walk the rough patches ahead of us.

Self-soothing is a term coined by Self Psychology, founded by Heinz Kohut. It describes your capacity to calm and comfort yourself, which is one vital aspect of a well-integrated self. Another school of thought known as Object Relations Therapy offers a similar concept called "containment."

Rather than abandon yourself when facing something difficult, you need to maintain the basic integrity of your being. Without this skill of holding yourself lovingly, you'll remain a victim of how others treat you. You'll be apprehensive about life and feel fragmented when problems arise. If you lack a coherent self to deal with challenges, you'll be unable to love wholeheartedly.

Children learn self-soothing as a gradual developmental process. As their feelings and needs are heard by responsive, accepting parents, children gradually feel safe to discover and express themselves. They can explore their world assured that a trusted parent is available when they need comforting. Trust grows as they experience the devoted presence of at least one caregiver who is *adequately* consistent and nurturing.

"Good-Enough Parenting"

Of course, no parent can be constantly attentive. The passed baton of developmental wounds from generation to generation, in addition to life's ongoing demands, makes it a formidable task to attend to a child's needs. When we have so many needs of our own, it's quite a feat to be there for others' needs. If we made a poor mate choice when we were young, it may further confound our child's longing for stability and safety.

Over time, when there has been what is called good-enough parenting, children internalize the steady, reliable presence of their caregiver(s). Thus begins a remarkable process of becoming an autonomous person—a miraculous journey of awakening an inner source of strength, confidence, and serenity.

Sadly, these inner resources don't develop ideally in most children, to say the least. Childhood trauma or abuse prevents the positive attachment necessary for healthy development. Repeated ridicule, criticism, or neglect disrupts the bond of trust with self and others. This leads to a life with a strong imprint of anxiety, isolation, and/or depression.

Becoming an adult under these conditions, you may not do well with adversity or change. The risk taking necessary to succeed in life and love becomes infused with the fear of failure and rejection—or the fear of success. There may be alarm at the prospect of real intimacy if connection and fulfillment have not been a familiar component of your childhood diet.

The developmental gap created by "not good enough parenting" leads to a frantic search for someone—oftentimes anyone—to make life safer and less empty. In your quiet desperation for love, you may:

- Bond too hastily with a person, clinging to what you like and ignoring the rest.
- Remain in a destructive relationship, fearful of losing whatever comfort you're getting.
- Alienate people with your excessive expectations and demands, assigning them the job of making you feel comfortable.
- Carry a low-level resentment or rage that pushes people away, and that leaks out whenever you're disappointed or unhappy.

The developmental gaps born of disruptions of trust hinder your adult relationships. Unfounded suspicions, jealousy, and concerns about whether you're loved may reflect difficulty in trusting. Fearful of losing love, you become emotionally destabilized, reacting with rage, criticism, or withdrawal whenever real or imagined threats arise. Without the ability to soothe yourself, you will have a low frustration tolerance—and a high propensity to act out your pain destructively.

Mature relationships require the capacity to connect with yourself, especially when things don't go well. You need a way to rest in the refuge of your own heart. You need to replenish yourself apart from a relationship. You need to bring just enough acceptance and compassion to your inner experience so that you can comfort yourself instead of cajoling or controlling others so they'll comfort you.

You need to manage your own emotional life, not manipulate others. Although you'll continue to have interpersonal needs to give and receive love, life goes better as you develop resources within yourself to deal with frustrations and disappointments.

Self-soothing is a process of lifelong learning. You can keep improving at this art of self-care, just as learning to love is a lifelong process of growth.

Self-Soothing through Relationships

Relationships are a powerful vehicle for healing childhood wounds and learning to soothe yourself. But it all depends on how you hold and view a particular relationship. If you believe the other person is obligated to make you happy, then you'll lose your balance in unrealistic expectations. If you keep rehashing the same old story that no one's there for you, then you'll push love away, even when it's tapping at your door. You'll keep finding evidence that reinforces your belief that people aren't safe.

The hope of healing through relationships is to find a natural rhythm between outgoing and "ingoing." The key is to *let in* whatever connection, caring, and love are present and allow these blessings to heal your heart and warm your soul. If you're unable to receive deeply, you may want to explore the blocks or fears that keep you painfully locked inside your head and tightly armored within your body instead of resting receptively in your heart.

As you learn to let in that you're valued and cared about, you relax internally. You feel your worth and goodness. A maturing inner strength and serenity develops, which forms the basis for self-soothing. Some of what was missing in childhood is then remedied through your adult relationships.

Self-Soothing through Therapy

Psychotherapy may provide a more reliable way to develop self-soothing. Briefly stated, through regular contact with a caring, insightful therapist, you create the stable connection you may not have enjoyed as a child. This is why psychotherapy is sometimes called "reparenting." Through an ongoing therapeutic relationship with someone who's a good match for you, you begin to internalize qualities that enable you to feel a more calm, comfortable connection with yourself.

Psychotherapy isn't just about solving problems—finding quick fixes for heartbreaking conflicts, anxiety, or depression. More fundamentally, therapy is about awakening the inner resources you need to respond to life's challenges and to give and receive love more fully, thereby creating fulfilling relationships and family life. "Psychotherapy" derives from root words meaning "attending to the soul."

Wrestling with complex enigmas isn't readily embraced in a culture of instant gratification. The managed care solution of severely time-limited therapy is seen by many therapists as a cruel joke—a betrayal of a person's real needs. Unlike the skills necessary to program a computer or fix a flat tire, healing a human psyche takes plentiful patience and perseverance. It takes time and commitment for clients to build enough trust and connection with a therapist to really "open up"—to reveal their authentic heart to both themselves and the therapist, which leads to learning how to trust and soothe themselves.

Even if you had good-enough parenting, a supportive relationship with a skilled therapist can boost your ability to know and affirm yourself more deeply. Some therapists also teach self-soothing skills as part of their approach. Long-term therapy can foster your ability to connect with a person who really gets to know you, thereby deepening your ability to connect with yourself and the people in your life.

Aspects of Self-Soothing

As a relatively new concept, self-soothing needs further development so that the arcane language of psychology can be digestible for people without graduate degrees in that discipline. My own understanding of self-soothing leads to an expanded exploration of its physical, cognitive, emotional, and spiritual aspects.

Physical Self-Soothing

Learning ways to physically care for yourself creates an environment of support for your life and relationships. Proper diet and exercise are essential for physical health and vibrancy. Midlife is a good time to affirm a commitment to yourself by eliminating destructive health habits, such as excessive drinking, poor dietary choices (without being fanatical), smoking, and getting too much sun.

Although the physical beauty of youth fades, you can do much to care for what you have. By initiating an aerobics program, exercising at the gym, or taking hearty hikes, you can look and feel your best.

I've know many good-looking people whose relationships are always a mess. How you feel *inside* is the main impetus for attracting and having healthy relationships. You become eminently appealing when there's love in your heart, generosity in your soul, and a sparkle in your eye. As you move into your forties, fifties, and beyond, the physical attraction of youth can gradually metamorphose into the soulful attraction of a radiant, self-aware, wise person. As a Chinese fortune cookie says, "There is no cosmetic for beauty like happiness."

Sadly, many people stop caring for themselves after being disappointed in love. Self-neglect and self-contempt cast a spell of depression and pessimism. Such people may engage in self-destructive habits like drinking or overeating and then wonder why few people are attracted to them.

Physical self-soothing reflects an attitude of positive self-care that keeps you connected to yourself. Your body is resilient. Even after years of neglect it responds positively to efforts to care for it, within the limits imposed by your genetic makeup. The key is to cherish and nurture what you have rather than wish you were someone else. Loving yourself as you are right now eases your way forward.

The Aesthetic Connection

Physical self-soothing can be facilitated by attending to the aesthetics of your environment. Having beautiful objects, artwork, or plants in your home may lift your spirit, as long as you don't get seduced into a compulsive buying syndrome as a fleeting form of self-soothing. Japanese tea gardens, for example, help people enjoy the serenity of nature.

Doing simple things for yourself may also create an environment for self-soothing:

- Buy flowers.
- Get a massage.
- Take a hot bath or sauna.
- Enjoy the beauty of nature.

By caring for yourself in creative ways, you can more easily gain access to other ways of self-soothing.

Pets are a great comfort to many people. Some studies suggest that pet owners are healthier than people who don't have pets. Stroking your cat or dog appears to be soothing in a way that improves immune functioning.

NATURE WALK EXERCISE:

Allow yourself a few hours for a leisurely stroll in a quiet, natural setting: a park, the ocean, a lake, or perhaps around your neighborhood. Put aside thoughts and worries as best you can. Bring awareness to the simple experience of your breath. Now experience what it's like to put one step in front of the other, noticing the sense of movement. Be aware of the feeling of lifting your foot, moving your leg, and placing your foot on the ground. As you walk, notice what's around you—feel the air on your face, notice the sights that draw your attention, and hear the sounds of birds or other creatures. Be present for the beauty all around you and notice how you feel when you let it in.

Cognitive Self-Soothing:
What You Think, You Become

"Get over it! You're a mess! You'll never measure up!" According to cognitive psychology, your thoughts help create your reality. If you continue talking negatively to yourself, you perpetuate painful experiences. For instance, if you're hurting because a partnership failed, you might conclude that *you* are a failure. Or your inner critic may berate you mercilessly: "You should be over him by now," or, "How could you have been so dumb to have gotten involved with her!" These declarations pile additional suffering atop whatever pain you're already experiencing.

Buddhism also teaches that "We are what we think, having become what we thought." If we keep perpetuating thoughts about how awful or abusive someone is, we breed hatred and ill-will.

The cognitive approaches of Aaron Beck and others would have you identify and challenge these unrealistic, dysfunctional beliefs. Talking to yourself in a kinder, self-soothing way, you might say, "Wait a minute. Why am *I* a failure just because the relationship failed? I'm a valuable, worthwhile person who did my best. And why should I be over it by now? This was a serious relationship; it's natural, normal, and understandable that I'm still feeling sad about it."

If a relationship fails, you may reassure yourself with these self-affirming thoughts:

- I made the best choice I knew how to make at the time.
- It was courageous to take a risk to love.
- I learned a lot that I can use in my next partnership.

These comforting thoughts are more compassionate and realistic ways to view yourself and the situation; they help you heal.

Inner Calm: A Step toward Responsibility

Self-soothing can help you take responsibility for your part in a past or current relationship breakdown. By tightening up in a spasm of self-criticism, your attention isn't available to ask yourself, "Is there some way I co-create relationship problems?" Perhaps you have a habit of becoming defensive or critical, which pushes people away. Self-soothing creates a safe climate to look calmly and clearly at your role, and it moves you toward self-forgiveness.

Self-soothing prevents an emotional avalanche that can destroy relationships. For example, the prospect of visiting your in-laws may make you feel explosive inside, bouncing between your wish to please your partner and your desire to avoid a bad scene. Rather than feel trapped, you can take your inner child by the hand and be reassuring: "Your wife will appreciate this. You can limit your time with her family if it feels uncomfortable. You can bring a book, and if things get really bad, you can excuse yourself and take a walk or call a friend." Rather than "catastrophizing"—scaring yourself with disastrous thoughts—you can calm yourself with sober reassurances.

Replacing irrational, catastrophic beliefs with more sensible, self-comforting ones is an important step in your movement from self-scolding to self-soothing. You're then no longer hostage to the critical voices within you.

Cultivating Nurturing Thoughts

Cognitive self-soothing creates an inner climate that allows your authentic experience to emerge. When the mental chatter born of fear and shame subsides, you can see what's really going on inside you.

For example, after a separation, you may sink into apathy generated by your inner critic: "I'm incapable of loving," or, "I'll never find another person to love." You may see yourself as a powerless victim. In a peculiar way, you may become comfortably laced in the familiar garb of your depression or cynicism. If these reactions begin to define you, you'll never get over the simple sorrow of your loss.

Having been deprived of role models and guidance in embracing your feelings, you may revert to dysfunctional strategies for coping with loss and grief. Succumbing to your inner Big Brother, you might control yourself through frightful admonitions such as:

1. If you let yourself cry, you'll go crazy.
2. You'll repulse your friends.
3. Crying means admitting defeat and failure.
4. Admitting to hurt means you'll let him get to you, or you'll let her win.

You can replace these false, destructive beliefs with soothing, gentle reminders:

1. It's okay to feel hurt. I'm more likely to go crazy if I don't allow my feelings! I'll let myself cry for as long as I need to.
2. I don't need friends who won't accept my feelings.
3. Painful things can happen to good people through no one's fault. It takes strength to embrace sorrow.
4. It's not about winning but about being true to myself.

When shaming, fearful voices don't allow you to embrace your natural grief, sorrow, or even joy, you don't heal or grow. You hold on to what's old rather than make way for the new.

Develop a Calm, Clear Awareness

Suffering can be greatly exacerbated by critical thoughts, but usually your thoughts are not totally responsible for creating your pain. Experiencing hurt and pain is simply part of being human. Heartache and trauma can't be totally healed by reconfiguring your beliefs. You also have to make room for your feelings.

Soothing yourself with kinder self-talk is often the first step toward emotional self-soothing. It's hard to know how you're really feeling when you're berating yourself; whatever you feel is then magnified greatly by your critical beliefs.

Fortunately, you're not condemned to be forever ruled by your shaming inner critic. Gradually, you can shed the shell of your fabricated self and emerge as the beautiful being you are. But first you must recognize the subtle voices and confining beliefs that keep you suppressed. You're then well on your way to uncovering deeper levels of yourself. Bringing a calm, clear awareness to your inner experience delivers you to a sanctum where emotional self-soothing can take place.

Emotional Self-Soothing

The emotional aspect of self-soothing means bringing gentleness and caring toward your authentic experience. Discovering what's authentic within yourself begins by cultivating a sense of presence, and directing it toward your varied experiences. Being present means being open and available—being here in the moment, without getting lost in thoughts about the past, fantasies about the future, or other distracting mental chatter. You experience what's before you, free of analysis, judgments, and self-criticism. Like caressing a cat or feeling tender toward a crying child, you're fully present with what's here.

The Power of Presence

Poets are skilled at conveying a poignant sense of presence through an artful blend of words and images. Many of us love poetry because it invites us into a tender presence with life. Consider this poem by Liu Yu Hsi from eighth-century China:

> I have always been sorry
> Our words were so trivial
> And never matched the depths
> Of our thoughts. This morning
> Our eyes met,
> And a hundred emotions
> Rushed through our veins.

In that moment of meeting each other, there is depth and richness; there's a visceral process beyond words and thoughts.

Nature also invites you to be present both to yourself and to the life outside yourself. An awe-inspiring sunset or falling star may move you to suspend mental preoccupations, at least for a few pregnant moments as you experience the compelling beauty and power of life. The Hale-Bopp comet of 1997 inspired millions with wonder and delight.

Children abide in this moment-to-moment presence, but it becomes obscured as they're pressured to create a false self. If you're interested in expanding your capacity for love, you must recover this presence to yourself, to others, and to life.

Society offers countless distractions from being present to your authentic self:

- Drugs and alcohol distort your experience.
- Television and other entertainment may distract you from your core aliveness.

- Repetitive, noncreative work may dull your awareness.
- People who misuse their power may dishearten your spirit.

These and other forces make it difficult to live in your sensitive heart, until you change some of the things you have control over.

Open Up to Direct Experience

Connecting with your authentic heart means connecting with your direct *experience* of yourself, other people, and life. This experience includes the feelings and sensations that arise within you as you interact with the world.

We often mistake our felt experience of life with thoughts about life. Thoughts are reflections on our experience, which all too often distort reality. We replace our felt experience with beliefs, assumptions, and projections, which may or may not be true. Jacquelyn Small, a prominent leader of workshops on addictions, explains how these attachments keep us blind: "One of the hardest addictions to release (or die to) is our addiction to dogma, judgments, and opinions . . . this loss is the beginning of our awakening into Truth."

Your assumptions may put distance between you and other people. For example, if you're hurt or angry because your partner is late, you may fume with judgments that he's self-centered or inconsiderate. You may bitterly conclude that he doesn't value your time. You may assume that he doesn't care about you and decide to write him off.

In reality, your partner may have been stuck in traffic or caught in a meeting. Unable to soothe yourself when life throws a curveball, you may rage, blame, or withdraw—and give yourself high blood pressure.

Of course, if there's a pattern of being late, there may be something deeper going on. But even then, you're better off talking about your feelings and exploring together from a calmer place what his lateness may mean.

If you are submerged in a swamp of groundless opinions and conclusions, there's little chance for a shift in how you're experiencing a situation. There's little opportunity to preserve trust and connection. In contrast, by holding your fear, hurt, or anger within your warm embrace, there's more possibility of resolving your feelings rather than acting them out. By being with yourself in a gentle way, you'll be more connected to what's really going on inside you. Sharing whatever hurt, fear, or anger remains may then be done with more respect and kindness, and less blame.

Stay Inside Your Skin

Why do you automatically slink away from your direct experience? You jump outside your skin because it's uncomfortable to stay inside yourself when humiliation or insecurity arises. Judging and attacking protect you from unpleasant feelings, such as the fear of abandonment, the shame of being slighted, or the possibility that you're wrong.

In the short run, it's satisfying to blame and vent. You attempt to preserve your dignity by stripping others of theirs. You protect yourself from the unpleasant experience of shame or anxiety by unloading these feelings onto others. As Gershen Kaufman explains it, "Such strategies of transfer aim at making someone else feel shame in order to reduce our own shame."

Staying aware of what's happening within yourself means tolerating the ambiguity of a situation. This requires more inner resources than does pinning a negative label on people. It takes staying inside yourself and tolerating—if not welcoming—whatever inner experience arises. Soothing yourself when your partner is late would mean considering the possibility that there's a good reason for his or her tardiness and then embracing whatever disappointment or other feelings remain.

Attune to Your Body

Whereas opinions and judgments are artifacts of your analytical mind, feelings live in your body. Although you may recognize the value of "getting in touch with your feelings," you may have difficulty doing so until you learn what it means to be in touch with your body. Psychologist Rollo May states it clearly: "To be tuned to the responses throughout one's body, as well as to be tuned to one's feelings in emotional relations with the world and people around him, is to be on the way to a health which will not break down periodically."

By becoming present to the mystery and miracle of your body, you reclaim sensibilities that may have been numbed during painful relationships. As you reawaken to all that your body contains—the stored pain and the potential pleasure, the old shame and the wish for acceptance, the secret fears and the longing for love—you become exquisitely present to your direct, moment-to-moment experience of life.

This is not to suggest that you jettison your mind. A clear, creative mind is essential for cognitive self-soothing and other essential tasks. But as with many people, your mind may have become so controlling and disconnected that you need to resurrect the lost wisdom of your body in order to integrate body and mind into a unified whole. As poet Robert Browning put it, "Where my heart lies, let my brain lie also."

Jim Dreaver, author of *The Way of Harmony*, a lovely book on finding balance, makes a helpful distinction between clear thinking and heady analysis:

> People who are too analytical get stuck in their heads. They are usually very tight in their bodies, stiff in their movements, controlled in their behavior and actions. Such people are often referred to as being "anal." You might even say anal-ytical! They can get so bound up in words and concepts that they become mentally constipated. . . . The trick is to not waste energy in unnecessary thinking. Be aware, be open, be present. Learn to use thought when needed. It is a marvelous, creative tool. But don't miss life, the fullness of the moment, by always being in your head.

Think in the Marrow Bone

The need to reconnect with your body explains why the term "body-mind" has become so popular. As the fields of medicine and psychology mature, there is a more integrated understanding of how body, mind, emotions, and spirit work together. Disconnecting from any aspect of your humanness creates dis-ease and disconnection in your relationships.

Charles Whitfield, a leading writer on codependence and recovery, reminds us that "recovery cannot proceed successfully only in your head. It must also be experienced in your heart, guts and bones—in the deepest fiber of your being." The poet W. B. Yeats expresses a similar sentiment in "A Prayer for Old Age": "God guard me from the thoughts men think in the mind alone; he that sings a lasting song thinks in the marrow bone."

Through awareness of your body, you can recover your lost self—the core of your being that reflects the beauty of who you most deeply are. The age-old word "soul" has gained new popularity through many best-selling books, which reflects a collective longing to reconnect with your lost self. Whatever word you choose to refer to your core essence, you can never define it precisely. For it is fluid, subtle, and nonconceptual—a whisper lost amid the blaring voices around you and within you.

Embrace Sensory Experience

You're untrustworthy to the degree that you're disconnected from yourself or to the degree that you're so identified with fragments of yourself that you ignore the totality of who you are. For example, when secret fears or hurts lurk within you, they may leap out unexpectedly and unpredictably, harming those you love. If your partner is even slightly inattentive, your rage may be ignited. This rage may be covering up a deeper shame of being unimportant. Or, feeling sadly misunderstood, you may harbor a secret resentment that manifests itself by your connecting with your favorite sitcom rather than with your partner. Unless you identify and embrace your underlying feelings and longings, they'll become silent players in the drama of trust-shattered relationships.

People who are anxious or unhappy often tell me, "I'm not sure what my feelings are! How do I get in touch with them?" Even those who pride themselves on knowing their feelings may be aware of only *certain* ones—for instance, anger or sadness. But the feelings they most need to unearth go unattended, leaving them with the seemingly unrelated question, "Why don't my partnerships ever work out?" Looking outward, they conclude, "I just haven't found the right partner," or they may denigrate the opposite sex. In reality, they are keeping people distant by failing to contact and convey a fuller, truer sense of their feeling life.

Your body holds the key to reconnecting you with the sensory aspect of feelings and emotions. Learning to experience your vaguely felt bodily sensations is the shrouded pathway to your depths. Part of maturing into midlife love is to become more comfortable with the feelings and sensations that arise from your interactions with the world.

The Language of the Body

It is interesting that our language contains expressions that convey the bodily felt component of experience. We get "choked with emotion," we "burn with anger," and we are "heavy with grief." We get "butterflies in our stomach" and suffer a "broken heart." We carry the world on our shoulders. Some people are a pain in the neck—or other places.

Some expressions offer tangibly felt images: We get "bent out of shape" when people mistreat us. We feel "up against the wall" when there's a deadline. We're "walking on air" when we're elated. We also get wound up, wired, and uptight. Although we often ignore this bodily component of experience, our body nevertheless is exquisitely responsive to its environment—whether it is caring or hostile, accepting or rejecting, or reflecting the warmth or coldness we receive from others.

If you patiently noticed your everyday reactions to people and events, you'd observe that each experience has a physically felt component. These responses are usually quiet and subtle—and quickly dismissed, if noticed at all. But they contain messages that offer vital clues for our lives.

EXERCISE: Allow yourself five minutes for this exercise.

> Visualize a person who is critical of you or who has been critical in the past. Notice the sensations in your body and where they are. How do you feel in your abdomen area, chest, face, and other areas of your body? Are you holding your stomach or tightening your neck? Are you noticing any constriction in your breathing or elsewhere in your body? Are you aware of any emotions as you notice your bodily sensations?
>
> When you feel complete with this, take a minute to be aware of your breathing as a transition to the second part of this exercise. Now visualize a person who accepts and loves you—or who has accepted you as you are. Notice your bodily response. How do you feel in your abdomen area, chest, face, and other areas of your body? Or simply notice and allow whatever other feelings

might be present. Do you notice any easing in your stomach or chest? If you experience a warm flow of energy around your heart, this might be called love, closeness, or caring. Don't worry if this exercise was difficult. It takes practice to become aware of the felt dimension of experience.

Your Body Is Your Prism to the World

The more you're connected to your body in an open way, the more clearly and directly you experience your world, including its magnificence and its madness.

People react differently to similar events. The important thing is to notice and accept whatever *you* are experiencing. The stage is then set to be with your felt experience and perhaps understand it more deeply. Opening to the full panoply of your experience leads to equanimity because it brings you into harmony with yourself rather than keeping you in conflict with yourself. Self-soothing is a natural by-product of embracing your inner world.

Your bodily response to events may speak so faintly that it's easily overridden by familiar, defensive habits. For example, the slightest hint of criticism may prompt a barely noticeable tightening to defend against uncomfortable feelings of hurt or fear. During such a moment of pulling away from yourself, people may sense you pulling away from them! Or you might quickly lash out before getting your arms around how you really feel inside. This habit is especially common with people who are abusive. Impulsive lashing out with fists or words means you're far away from the self-soothing that comes from being gently present with yourself.

Unable to soothe yourself in healthy ways, you may resort to self-destructive crutches, such as smoking, drinking a few beers, and bingeing on a quart of ice cream—while watching television. Shopping sprees are also a short-lived attempt to soothe yourself. Addictive behavior derives from an inability to tolerate and soothe uncomfortable feelings. Defense mechanisms are those habits that protect you from the discomfort of opening to your authentic feelings.

The ability to self-soothe:

- Relaxes and nourishes your body, mind, and soul.
- Makes you more emotionally accessible and available.

- Helps you become less defensive.
- Allows your heart to be present to people and life, thereby increasing your capacity to love.
- Helps you to be happy.

Notice Instead of React

Calmly attending to your bodily felt world gives you some space between events in your life and your immediate reactions to them. Why is this important? You then have an opportunity to see what's really happening inside you rather than acting out familiar patterns that keep wounding yourself and others. Instead of being a slave to your surface reactions to others, you can find some distance. You can gently notice and welcome what you're feeling deep down. This embracing of your authentic experience is at the heart of self-soothing, and is an essential foundation for loving.

Jean and Sam were locked in a cycle that's common. Jean wanted more contact; Sam wanted space. The more she pursued him, the more he distanced himself. The more he distanced himself, the more forcefully she demanded contact. The more he said no, the more irate she became, which pushed him further away.

Jean justified her pursuit of Sam: "I deserve love. He's my husband and I have a right to spend time with him." Slowly, Jean realized that this sense of entitlement wasn't working and that she needed a new approach. Sure, she deserved love (don't we all!), but that wasn't the issue.

The authentic heart can't produce love on demand; it can only love in freedom. Jean's challenge was to approach Sam in a way that was more likely to *invite* love and closeness. She needed to create a self-soothing climate—out of which trust and love could flourish.

With my help, Jean directed her attention inside herself. As she began embracing her bodily felt experience, she noticed a tightness in her chest that was related to her anger. Allowing herself to experience it, she became aware of an ache in her stomach.

As she stayed with that ache, it led to a feeling of sadness and loneliness. She then took time to embrace these feelings in a gentle, caring way—that is, with an attitude of warmth and kindness toward herself. She took some slow, deep breaths and felt the sensations related to her sadness and loneliness. At times, she tenderly placed

her hand on her stomach, where she described sensations of "tightness" and "jumpiness."

Jean felt more connected to herself as she accepted and welcomed the fear, hurt, and loneliness that she'd been afraid to feel. As she recognized these deeper emotions, she began developing a relationship with them—and consequently a deeper relationship with herself. This provided an inner resource that allowed a more intimate, harmonious relationship with her husband.

Jean's movement to a more mature love blossomed as she began supplying for herself what she was expecting her husband to furnish. When she approached him with her deeper, more tender feelings, she enjoyed the warmer response she'd been wanting. As she described it: "If I do some inner work to get clearer about how I really feel and what I really want *before* I go to him, then there's a better chance I'll get what I want. When I recognize that I'm actually lonely or sad—then I can take some time to be with those feelings and then talk to him in a vulnerable way, rather than an attacking way. I can say with a softer voice, 'I feel lonely for you. We haven't been connecting lately and I'd like to connect.' I used to complain, 'You're not spending time with me! When are you going to be a responsible husband?' He responds better when I don't lay those trips on him."

By opening to her bodily feelings, Jean found a pathway that connected her more deeply with herself. This shift came as she began to create a warm container for these feelings, instead of making *her husband* the container for *her* feelings. This new level of personal responsibility—not stuffing her emotions down or demanding that he respond to them but developing a caring presence toward them—enabled her to express feelings and wants in a respectful, heartfelt way—and be willing to take "no" for an answer. "Of course, he doesn't always accommodate me. But now I trust that if I give him more slack and accept a 'no,' he's more inclined to say 'yes' later. Knowing I can come back to myself and soothe myself makes a huge difference."

Just as a child can't communicate what's really going on during a temper tantrum, Jean couldn't express what she was really feeling and wanting while fear, shame, and hurt were silently screaming inside of her. But as she began to gently hold these feelings, the tumultuous undercurrents of emotions subsided. She could then notice the quieter pulse of her authentic heart—the tender feeling and longings stirring within her.

This deeper sharing touched a resonant chord inside Sam. A climate of trust and closeness was being created, perhaps for the first time.

I'm always awed to witness how intimacy deepens through heartfelt sharing born of self-embracing. As Jean took the courageous step of being present with her real feelings—soothing herself by saying "hello" to them and communicating them with a warm, nonblaming tone of voice—Sam was able to relax and trust more. This helped him connect more vividly with his own yearning for contact. Sam's own self-soothing also enabled him to:

- Hear her feelings and requests without bracing for the worst.
- Become less defensive and reactive.
- Respond from a deeper, calmer place within himself, which increased intimacy.

Self-soothing is simple, but not easy. But then again, life isn't easy; building loving relationships isn't easy at any age.

You need to rest more deeply inside yourself to undercut destructive patterns that rob you of the unspeakable richness that's possible in relationships. You need to look within yourself in a sensitive way rather than take solace in blame or bitterness. Your midlife challenge is to find a path to your creative depths.

The intention to affirm, understand, and soothe yourself provides the foundation for this path. As one woman discovered shortly after separating: "It's more satisfying to blame *him:* 'I was betrayed!' But there's lots of sadness beneath that. As long as I hold on to blaming him, there's a tightness in my body. When I let myself feel that sadness and remember to be gentle with myself, then I can let go. That's the way to rebuild my self-esteem and find peace."

9

Focusing: A Path to Befriending Yourself

No matter how tangled or simple your life may become, your body will always know where your best routes to happiness and well-being lie.

—Eugene Gendlin

❦

There are many useful approaches to embracing your bodily felt experience and soothing yourself. The one I've found most helpful over the past twenty years is called "Focusing." It's based on Eugene Gendlin's research at the University of Chicago into key factors that make psychotherapy effective. This research earned him the Distinguished Psychologist of the Year Award issued by the Clinical Division of the American Psychological Association in 1968.

Gendlin and his colleagues studied hundreds of tapes of therapy sessions with therapists who had different approaches. They also administered psychological tests to see if there were positive changes in clients. After detailed examination of the tapes, the researchers could determine after the first or second session whether therapy would be successful.

The Wisdom of Being Inarticulate

To the surprise of Gendlin, the key to successful therapy wasn't what the therapist was doing. It was what the clients were doing within themselves! Focusing teacher Ann Weiser Cornell describes what the researchers found.

> What they heard was this: at some point in the session, the successful clients would *slow down* their talk, become *less articulate*, and begin to *grope for words* to describe something that they were feeling at the moment. If you listened to the tapes, you would hear something like this: Hmmm. How would I describe this? It's right *here*. It's . . . uh . . . it's . . . it's not exactly anger . . . hmmm." Often the clients would mention that they experienced this feeling in their bodies, saying things like, "It's right here in my chest" or "I have this funny feeling in my stomach."

Clients who made progress had the capacity to hang out with vague, blurry, fuzzy feelings and allowed their feelings to unfold in their own time and way. They attended to their inwardly felt world in contrast to "being in their heads"—talking about events and ideas. They were *present to their experience* rather than standing outside of themselves and talking *about* themselves in a detached way.

These naturally gifted clients had the ability to sense inwardly and contact the ever-changing flow of their moment-to-moment experience without being overwhelmed by their feelings. They were also able to gather subtle meanings and insights arising from their unclear feelings. They slowed down and took time to sense their feelings, and they listened to whatever message these feelings were trying to convey. This process enabled them to take the next steps forward in their lives.

Gendlin called this natural process "Focusing," and he developed teachable steps so that others could learn how to attend to their inner process. Colleagues of Gendlin, especially Peter Campbell and Edwin McMahon, have encouraged an attitude of "caring, feeling presence" toward one's inner world. This attitude highlights the self-soothing aspect of Focusing.

Although its origins lie in a psychotherapeutic setting, Focusing has been developed as an educational tool. It is being used in spiritual development, relationships, healing, parenting, creative writing, dance, and stress-reduction. When used for personal growth, Focusing can be practiced alone or, often more productively, with a guide or "Focusing Companion" who can listen openly and caringly. The Guide to Resources in the back of the book offers places to learn Focusing.

Tap the Wisdom of Your Body

The human tendency, especially for men, is to rely on reason and rationality, like Mr. Spock in *Star Trek*. This approach works well in science and engineering, but not when applied to relationships.

A common strategy for handling relationship problems is to insist that *our* solution is right and that our partner should have the decency to go along with our viewpoint. But genuine resolutions require creative input from a wellspring of wisdom largely ignored by our goal-oriented society. By trying to *be right* rather than finding the *right manner of approach*, our partnerships get mired down in:

- Self-righteousness ("I'm right and you're wrong").
- Demands ("Do it my way now!").
- Sarcasm ("When are you gonna grow up?").
- Blame ("It's all your fault!").

Attempts to coerce your partner are resisted because he or she feels insulted and pressured, not respected and included.

The key to Focusing is allowing yourself to be inwardly drawn toward your "bodily felt sense" of personal concerns. By resting attention within your body (where feelings and intuitions live), you lessen your tendency to analyze and control. You encourage a more creative part of yourself to reveal what *it* knows about the varied circumstances of your life. Gendlin refers to this process as "trusting the wisdom of the body," which unfolds as you welcome the bodily dimension of your experience.

Discover Your Body-Brain

Some people have referred to this place of deeper wisdom as your "body-brain." By directing gentle awareness to your heart, stomach, or entire body, you can calm your mind's anxious tendency to force a solution. By directing attention inward, your true heart has an opportunity to be heard, seen, and felt, whether through words, sensations, images, or memories.

Focusing involves an openness to the present moment—a felt inquiry into what is happening in the core of your being, beneath your mind's tendency to freeze the flow of experience into lifeless thoughts and analysis. Creative change, growth, and freedom emerge as you live in harmony with the ever-changing flow of your inner-most experience. As you give up trying to change and cajole your-self in the usual way (through your inner critic), you awaken to the greater richness of who you really are.

FOCUSING EXERCISE:

1. *Preparation:* Take a few slow, deep breaths. Allow your attention to settle into your body, especially noticing how you're feeling in your chest and abdomen area (this is where we tend to feel things the most). Allow some problem or difficulty to come to mind. (For the purpose of this exercise, don't choose a prob-lem that is too large or for which you might need professional help. Feel free to stop at any point if anything feels too uncom-fortable.)

2. *Get a Felt Sense:* Ask yourself if it's okay to be with this issue. If it feels too big or overwhelming, choose another issue. If it's okay, notice how this whole thing feels inside your body right now.

- Where do you feel it in your body (abdomen, chest, neck, face, all over)?

- What does it feel like (tight, jumpy, cold, queasy, hard)?

Take some time to sense it apart from your thoughts about it.

3. *Allow It to Express Itself:* As you take time to embrace how your body is experiencing this whole issue, allow a word, phrase, or image to come to mind that resonates with how you feel inside. Or perhaps a memory or a sense of what this is about will arise. Just let yourself be with that whole sense of (whatever word, phrase, image, etc. came up). If anything more wants to come, then stay with that.

Continue in this way, staying with each new thing that arises. Don't force anything. If nothing comes, that's fine. If something particularly painful arises, see if you can be with it in a gentle, caring way. Gentleness and self-acceptance are the key.

When you feel that something has shifted, or have a sense of completion, or feel that you just want to stop, then you can end the exercise.

4. *Appreciation:* Allow yourself to be with how you feel inside now. Appreciate whatever steps you may have taken.

Replace Control with Trust

Focusing involves letting go of your tendency to control life and allowing experience to unfold from within. Such experience ensues; it cannot be pursued. You calmly direct attention inside yourself, then be receptive. Trust that whatever feelings, perceptions, or understandings need to emerge will gradually unfold. Place your trust in a larger process that can't be coerced.

Peter Campbell and Edwin McMahon express the gentle attitude that is the essence of Focusing:

> Can I find some way to be a little more friendly with my feelings that are so hard to deal with? . . . This is a special way of being more gentle, more open, less argumentative, and kinder toward a hurting place in ourselves. . . . Most of us only feel our uncomfortableness with a problem or our need to control it. Rarely, however, do we experience what it is like deliberately and consciously to be *in* the body's sense of negative issues without immediately being pressured either to control or eliminate whatever hurting, scary, or other feelings are there. This openness to bodily knowing within the Focusing process sets the stage for real and sometimes dramatic change as hurting places are allowed to unfold.

During a Focusing session, a creative image came to Charles, an overwhelmed accountant: "I feel like I'm holding an aquarium that isn't glued on any of its sides. If I don't keep it all together, it'll fall apart." The more he struggled to keep everything intact, the more anxiety he felt.

As Charles began relinquishing his effort to control things, new perspectives emerged. Initially, he felt afraid of failing in his relationship and job. He grew up with strong pressure to succeed in every venture, which led to a perfectionism that was strangling him. Seeing more clearly how harshly he was treating himself, he noticed some tears. "It's hard for me to let myself cry—or let myself feel anything. I keep tight control over my feelings. I tell myself, 'Get a grip! Don't feel sorry for yourself. Just keep pushing ahead!' I'm afraid I'll fall apart if I let down my guard. I'm actually falling apart by *not* easing up on myself!"

Give Yourself a Spacious Pasture

Charles felt relief as he embraced the fear of failing in a caring, gentle way; he felt less overwhelmed by treating himself more kindly. He learned to take time for himself and live a more balanced life.

Eugene Gendlin expresses the value of "going with" troubling emotions: "Every bad feeling is potential energy toward a more right way of being if you give it space to move toward its rightness." By accepting the full range of your experience, you're in control of your life in a wider sense—not by avoiding unpleasant feelings or being resigned to them but by allowing them to be. As the Zen Master Shunryu Suzuki put it, "To give your sheep or cow a large, spacious meadow is the way to control him."

By being kind and gentle toward your feelings rather than self-critical, you reconnect with the integrity of your organism. You find some inner peace, even in the midst of a difficult situation. You may experience further relief and peace as you understand the meaning of your feelings. Like the Greek messenger God, Hermes, feelings may be trying to deliver a message to you:

- Anger may be a message to stand up for yourself. Or you might realize it's a defense against feeling pain and helplessness.
- Fear may be a message that you're approaching an uncomfortable but important truth about yourself. Or it may be a danger signal to keep away from a person or situation.
- A heavy feeling in your heart may be a sadness that's asking you to be gentle with yourself and to trust that it's okay to let go.

Reside Closer to Your Core

Focusing is especially helpful when you feel emotionally over-whelmed during a conflict. Rather than attack your partner or with-draw, you can go inside yourself and notice your breath and the sensations in your body. As you gain calm and perspective, you can express what you're feeling or needing with more clarity and less emotional charge.

Buddhism encourages a similar attitude of embracing your moment-to-moment experience of life: Zen master Shunryu Suzuki asks: "When you are sitting in the middle of your own problem, which is more real to you: your problem or you yourself? The aware-ness that you are here, right now, is the ultimate fact."

By helping you resolve inner and outer conflicts, Focusing can bring you closer to the core of your being, and to the core of Being itself.

The Tortoise and the Hare

The self-soothing attitude of Focusing encourages you to face fears and hurts at your own pace rather than push yourself, which usually backfires. Fears and resistance are respected, not blasted through. As you bring warm, nonjudgmental attention to them, they gradu-ally melt and you move forward.

At each juncture of the process, ask yourself, "Is it okay to be with this?" If it's not okay, perhaps because you're too frightened, feel free to stop for now and explore more later. If you've been Focusing alone, you may seek the support of a guide or therapist. The gift of another person's caring presence may help you be more gentle with yourself and explore issues more productively.

Our habitual tendency of mind is to solve difficulties through the quick fix of:

- Finding answers (spinning your wheels and getting nowhere).
- Getting others to change (sparking resentment).
- Pushing yourself harder to "get results" (generating shame and undermining self-worth).

Your efforts to gain control are sometimes necessary, as in the workplace. But in your personal life, the struggle to stay in control may spiral you out of control. Campbell and McMahon state it clearly: "God help you if you have no control over your life, but God help you even more if *all* you have is control."

More than just another technique, Focusing involves a natural way of living. You have probably "focused" at one time or another:

- While holding a sorrow gently in your heart, you had a new realization about a relationship difficulty.
- You felt better by finding a word that expressed your true feelings.
- Once you gave up trying to solve a problem, your next step forward suddenly revealed itself.
- During a walk in nature, you felt a deeper sense of being present and alive.

The gentle and accepting attitude of Focusing can quietly permeate your life, fostering an attitude of love, caring, and compassion for yourself and others.

Practice Self-Soothing to Enhance Creativity

Life becomes less of a battleground as you surrender the struggle to design a particular outcome. For example, as I'm writing this book, I sometimes feel frustrated when words don't flow freely. Nevertheless, I may stay glued to my desk, thinking, "I should be working on the book!" Oftentimes, when I look back on that day's writing, the creative quality of my work is dissatisfying, and I rewrite entire sections.

On other days—when I'm less controlling and more aware of my struggle—I'll take a break when I feel stuck. I'll just sit with my inner tension and frustration in a self-soothing way. Or I'll take a walk, work in the garden, pet my cat, meditate, or exercise. As I feel more connected to myself, I return to my desk later in the day. Simpler ways to express complex themes then emerge with a clarity and ease that surprises me. By noticing and relinquishing the tendency to push myself, I work smarter, not harder.

Spiritual Self-Soothing

In practicing meditation we're not trying to live up to
some ideal—quite the opposite. We're just being with
our experience, whatever it is. . . . We can be with what's
happening and not dissociate. Awakeness is found in our
pleasure and our pain, our confusion and our wisdom.
                                        —Pema Chodron

❦

Spiritual self-soothing is the result of connecting with your
essence—relishing the richness of dwelling in the core of who
you are. You have probably experienced quiet moments of being
present with life, when your mind became calm, worries faded, and
you enjoyed a sense of wholeness. Perhaps while walking along the
beach, making love, or reading a passage from a book, the cobwebs
in your mind suddenly cleared, and you delighted in a precious connection to the mystery and miracle called Life, Soul, or God.

Many people find peace and spaciousness through simple activities, such as knitting, gardening, journal writing, or browsing in a
bookstore. Others delight in listening to music, playing a musical
instrument, or sketching or painting. Still others participate in sports
or pursue dancing or rock climbing. Anything that focuses and
quiets your mind—or connects you with something larger than your
normal sense of self—can be a form of meditation.

I never saw my father more peaceful than when he was fishing on a boat in the bay. That was his way of meditating.

Tapping into a deeper, calmer part of ourselves is rare, and all too fleeting. The practice of sitting meditation can be a helpful way to reinforce the connection with ourselves.

Traditional religion and psychology have often overlooked the deeper possibilities of personal development. Many religions have adopted the Greek premise that body and mind live in opposition. Flesh and the spirit are seen as antagonistic, not complementary. St. Francis referred to our body as "brother ass." Being spiritual has often meant using mind and will to dominate the wild, "evil" impulses of the body. However, you can find lasting peace only when you're living in harmony with yourself, not fighting or condemning yourself.

Both the psychological and religious mainstream have failed to recognize the need to integrate body, mind, emotions, and spirit into a unified whole. This integration allows richer contact with yourself, which opens the door to trusting relations with others. The field of Transpersonal Psychology is bringing greater recognition of the spiritual side of being human.

Meditation and Self-Soothing

Meditation has gained recognition through abundant research documenting its health benefits. Many physicians now recommend meditation for patients recovering from illnesses, as well as for people interested in preventive maintenance.

Physiologically, meditation reduces stress, lowers blood pressure, and decreases heart rate, thereby facilitating physical self-soothing and reducing susceptibility to a heart attack. Psychologically, meditation has been found to reduce fears, phobias, and anxiety, thus demonstrating an emotional self-soothing aspect. By enabling the body and emotions to relax, you're freed to experience the present moment in all its splendor.

Research suggests that meditation allows perceptual abilities to become fresher, which implies an ability to perceive inner experience more clearly. As psychiatrist Roger Walsh observes, "More experienced meditators note that what tends to emerge . . . is an underlying calm and non-reactive equanimity so that a greater range of experiences can be observed and allowed without disturbance, defensiveness or interference." By discouraging intrusive thoughts and encouraging inner calm, meditation helps you connect with your authentic experience.

There are many methods of meditation. Tai Chi, aikido, or martial arts are active forms. Quieter methods focus on one object, such as repeating a prayer or mantra, focusing on a scripture verse, or attending to your breath. Whenever your mind wanders, which it's sure to do, you gently return attention to this primary focus.

"Insight" or "Mindfulness" meditation also has a primary focus, such as the breath. However, if your attention wanders to other experiences, such as feelings, bodily sensations, or sounds, you gently bring awareness to them. The following discussion involves these "Insight" methods, which dovetail well with Western psychology.

Within the tranquil environment of attending to your breath, deeper parts of yourself have an opportunity to emerge. Finding some distance from your usual thoughts and preoccupations, you may connect with ignored aspects of your authentic self. As you notice such feelings or experiences, you give them space; you allow them to be, without pushing them away or overdramatizing them. As they pass, you return to your breath.

A certain kind of relaxed, yet alert watchfulness is needed to attend to yourself in this moment-to-moment manner. It's not a passive activity, as may appear from the outside. That's why it's called meditation "practice." There's much happening beneath one's seemingly impassive face.

At times during meditation you may experience:

- A delightful sense of presence.
- A clear, calm sense of being alive.
- A compelling glimpse into your deeper nature.
- A larger, more expansive sense of yourself and life.
- An increased sense of love and compassion as you develop a connection with your authentic self, which connects you to humanity and life.
- Uncomfortable or difficult feelings that you've been pushing away but that are calling for your attention.

Meditation is more helpful as you become familiar with your feelings. Meditation then enhances the ability to experience deeper dimensions of your interior life.

Meditation can be misused, just as anything that is normally helpful can be abused, such as exercise or religion. Some people use meditation to avoid or suppress feelings that yearn for attention. Instead of being present to their inner world, they succumb to the allure of altered states of consciousness or cultivate a passivity that reinforces depression and isolation.

Ryan, a forty-year-old physical therapist who had spent years in an Asian monastery, came to realize that for him, "Meditation was a false refuge. I didn't want to face my anxiety, so I meditated to alleviate it. Every time I started to feel uncomfortable about something, I escaped into meditation. I still want to meditate because it reduces anxiety, but then I want to explore my discomfort when it comes up in meditation. I want to accept my feelings and learn what they're trying to tell me."

Whenever Ryan experienced anger, sadness, or other feelings he tried to "let go" of these emotions rather than accept them as an aspect of his world. Then, when he entered a relationship with a woman, he didn't know how to deal with his emotions. After developing the habit of pushing feelings away, he found they'd eventually announce themselves through rage or withdrawal.

Ryan realized that his emotions were more powerful than his will to transcend them. Gradually, he made room for feelings in his meditation and his life, which led to improved relationships as he entered his late forties.

MEDITATION EXERCISE: Allow 10 minutes.

Take a few moments to let your attention settle into your body. Become aware of your breath. Notice how your abdomen rises as you inhale and falls as you exhale. Bring your awareness to these sensations of "rising" and "falling." Don't try to change your breath. This isn't a breathing exercise; it's an awareness exercise. Simply be present with your breath as it is, without trying to change it. No matter how many times thoughts may arise, just notice them, and return to your breath as they pass. If body sensations, sounds, or feelings arise, simply allow them to be.

Experience them just as they are, and as they pass, return your awareness to the breath.

As always, if you begin to feel too uncomfortable during this exercise, you may stop at any time. If you want further guidance, refer to the Guide to Resources in the back of the book.

Quiet Your Monkey Mind

No doubt, your mind drifted uncontrollably during this meditation. Some worries may have surfaced, or you may have been distracted by thoughts about work or someone you're dating or would like to date. Don't be discouraged. This is part of the human condition.

Our mental "in basket" receives so many impressions each day that we have little time to process them all. So they float into awareness during meditation or dream states. Even if you seem totally distracted, something positive is happening as you bring awareness to your inner world.

According to Buddhist psychology, the mind is like a drunk monkey. You can't stop your compulsive chatter through an act of will. But you can create an inner climate where it slows itself down. As your mind dominates you less, you can live more in present time. You can more comfortably connect with the various aspects of your genuine self. Slowing down and being present also set the stage for connecting with others.

By attending to the subtleties of your inner world, you walk a path toward yourself. You become less agitated, less critical of yourself and others, and more unified with your essence.

Meeting yourself makes it easier to meet others. If you don't know how you feel, what you want, and who you are, how can you expect others to understand you? An intimate link with yourself is the foundation for being intimate with others. The more you inhabit your core, the more you invite others into a rich world of midlife loving.

The art of meditation is sometimes misunderstood as indoctrination into a set of beliefs to which people must blindly adhere. I have found Insight Meditation (sometimes called Vipassana Meditation) to be particularly helpful for Western people who want to learn a nonsectarian approach. Various forms of Insight Meditation (and some forms of Zen meditation) have taken root without the religious trappings of gurus, rituals, or other cultist accoutrements.

Insight Meditation originated in the Buddhist tradition, which has remained resilient by adapting itself to whatever culture it enters. Many scholars believe that Buddhism is more of a psychology than a philosophy or religion.

Similar to Focusing and other experiential approaches, Insight Meditation has as its key tenet to trust oneself and honor one's own experience rather than conform to another's version of truth. One is invited to check things out for oneself rather than blindly adhering to beliefs that sound reasonable to the intellect but don't necessarily resonate with the heart.

This nonauthoritarian, psychologically healthy attitude is finding fertile ground among people searching for respectful, nondogmatic ways of tapping their depths. There are even many Christians and those of other faiths, including priests and nuns I've known, who've found a deeper connection with their Judeo/Christian roots by nurturing inner silence in this way. The stillness that comes through meditation can deepen your connection with self, others, and the larger mystery of which you're part.

Meditation Helps You to Love

Insight Meditation refers to your ability to "see things clearly" or "see things as they are." Unclouded perception is the antidote to viewing things as you'd like them to be—according to your biases and preconceptions, which is a hallmark of young love.

Rather than seeing people as they are, you may size them up according to how they might gratify your own desires. Instead of seeing how you might serve *their* needs and *their* growth (mature love), you focus exclusively on serving yourself.

Meditation cultivates a spacious acceptance toward whatever arises inside you. This awareness can then extend to accepting people as they are, which demonstrates your love. A sixty-five-year-old man learned through meditation: "I've become more comfortable being uncomfortable. I don't have to know everything. I have more tolerance for disappointment or hurt when things don't go my way. I can accept my partner as she is. There's a deeper trust between us now—

and more connection. When people ask why I meditate, I say, 'It helps me love better.'"

Within the context of self-connecting meditation, you're more aware of what's occurring within the boundaries of your own skin. You attend to the subtle feelings, sensations, and perceptions that otherwise go unnoticed. With your body still and your mind steady, your awareness can penetrate beneath surface thoughts and emotions to what's really happening inside you, including feelings you normally bypass, such as fear, shame, and hurt. Bringing these to awareness provides an opportunity to resolve them, thus moving you toward a new world of loving from your authentic heart.

This deeper work of self-connection and self-soothing creates a greenhouse for love to grow. The more you can embrace your pain, the more you can be there for others' pain. The more you can accept yourself and embrace whatever comes your way, the more you can accept differences in relationships. Conflicts are less threatening as you gently embrace whatever feelings they bring up for you.

Recognizing a link between body, mind, and spirit, Stephen and Ondrea Levine observe in *Embracing the Beloved* that "armoring of the heart is recognizable as a hardness in the belly. When there is holding, self-protection, fear, distrust, the belly armors. This hardness reminds us to soften, to let go into healing. Soft belly is open belly, is direct access to the heart. . . . We begin to feel the whole body opening to receive sensation, to let life in at last."

SOFT BELLY EXERCISE: Allow ten minutes (I've borrowed from the Levines).

> Sitting comfortably, bring awareness to your body. Notice the sensations in your abdomen. Feel the belly fill as you inhale and empty as you exhale. Let your belly soften as you receive the sensation of breath. Allow the hardness and holding in the belly that resist the breath, that resist life to melt, to soften. If you notice hardness, fear, pain, or distrust being held in the belly, just let them be. Meet them with gentleness and love; let them release as you exhale. With each inhalation, breathe in kindness, compassion, love.
>
> As your belly softens, notice if room opens up in your heart.

When you're ready, open your eyes. Be gentle with yourself when constriction and tightness return; practice softening your belly during your day.

The Comfort of Your Inner Refuge

Through the equanimity created by the proper practice of meditation, hazy parts of yourself are more readily seen and touched. By directly opening to your actual experience, you discover the richness of what's authentic within you. As you embrace this truth—that is, as you allow yourself to *have* your untarnished experience—you become stronger; new resources ripen within you. Through gentle acceptance of what is, you're actually loving yourself in a soulful and intimate way. Gradually, you learn to rest in a still, tranquil pool deep within your being. Inner qualities of peace, joy, and freedom are more vividly felt as you mature in this practice of befriending yourself.

By embracing a full range of inner experience, you become more comfortable with who you are—and more confident that you can deal with whatever life delivers. As you find a safer refuge within, there's less to fear, less to be ashamed of. You experience your worth and value more tangibly, which provides a foundation for gentle empowerment in your life and relationships.

Meditation and related practices help you connect more securely with your very essence. Without this ability, your mood becomes tied to the ups and downs of your external life: you're doing well when your partnership is doing well or when your stocks are going up. As you allow yourself to be nourished by this deeper stream, relationships become an enrichment to your life, not an elixir that fills a vacuum.

The more practiced you are at soothing and renewing yourself, the less you fear criticism, rejection, or loss. Identifying less with your image and more with your essence, you don't take things so personally. You can hear people without getting defensive. You can set limits, tolerate differences, and be more patient with people's shortcomings. You can deal with conflict without losing yourself. The waves of life may wash over you, but they don't drown you. By closing your eyes, taking a few slow, deep breaths, softening your belly and connecting with the life that's always pulsing within, you return to your inner sanctuary.

As you gain access to your quiet depths, you touch a place within yourself that opens a rich realm of interpersonal connection. A delightful dimension of love and intimacy emerges as your mind and heart are rested and renewed through meditation. Through your quiet presence, calm gaze, and tender touch, you can participate in another's depths while remaining grounded within your own being. As shame and fear diminish, you may enjoy moments when the usual boundaries between yourself and others dissolve. You tap into a wider ground of being of which you're both a part, which is simultaneously soothing and enlivening. Standing before each other, it's as if you're saying, "I am here, are you here too? I'm grateful for this lovely connection."

There is boundless potential for deeper relationships among people who meditate or pursue a spiritual practice. The Vietnamese meditation teacher Thich Nhat Hanh proposes a way to delight in relationships: "When you hold a child in your arms, or hug your mother, or your husband, or your friend, breathe in and out three times and your happiness will be multiplied by at least tenfold. And when you look at someone, really look at them with mindfulness, and practice conscious breathing."

As you allow yourself "free fall" into your present experience—without trying to do anything or control anyone—you become more relaxed in your relationships. For example, rather than reach for words to fill an awkward lull in the conversation, you can use moments of quiet to stay present with yourself, until something arises that you want to say. As your comfort with silence grows, your capacity for intimacy expands.

By connecting with yourself through meditation, you backpedal from the temptation to "ride" on the energy of others; you avoid unhealthy clinging. Relationships enhance the love and connection you're finding within yourself. This isn't to suggest that you transcend your needs but that you reach out in a more warm and trusting way as you soothe and connect with yourself. You can take more risks to be yourself as you feel stronger within yourself. You're less anxious about losing others' love when you've found your own.

The art of meditation is best learned in a retreat setting, apart from the usual distractions and routines of your lives. A weekend training is often a good way to start. The Guide to Resources at the back of this book offers information about retreats and support groups.

There are many ways to calm and focus your attention; being consistent is most important. When combined with gentle attention to your universe of feelings, meditation can calm the chatter of your fabricated self long enough to hear the quieter music of who you really are.

Soothe Yourself

1. What activities help you relax and connect with yourself? Do you take time alone during the week? Do you have ways that you regularly connect with yourself?

(Find time each week—or preferably, each day—to connect with yourself. Experiment with what works for you.)

2. Do you spend time with nature each week, perhaps by taking walks, hiking, biking, or gardening?

(Being in nature is an important way to renew yourself. Being indoors or working in a building with no windows may prevent you from getting the natural light you need. Try spending at least twenty minutes outdoors every day. Of course, don't shame yourself if you're not able to get outside as much as you'd like.)

3. Do you take time to meditate, or have you considered learning meditation?

(Various forms of meditation may help you discover a new peace and vitality within yourself.)

4. Can you allow yourself to be comforted by other people? Can you let in caring or do you have blocks to receiving it?

(The combination of soothing yourself and allowing others to comfort you is most beneficial. Be flexible in your life. Know when you need a supportive hug, words of encouragement, or a friend's warm and attentive presence. Learn to ask for what you want.)

5. Are there ways you comfort and connect with yourself physically, such as through exercise, massage, or warm baths?

(Take advantage of simple things you can do for yourself.)

∞০∞

Respect Others through Kind Conversation

I fall *far* short of achieving real communication—person to person—all the time, but moving in this direction makes life for me a warm, exciting, upsetting, troubling, satisfying, enriching, and above all a worthwhile venture.

— CARL ROGERS

Gentle Honesty

Only radical conversation, the full sharing of what it is like to be me while hearing what it is really like to be you, can fulfill the promise of an intimate relationship.

—James Hollis

∾o∾

After college during my early twenties, I traveled. Fortuitously, I ended up living in a Catholic archbishop's residence. This affable and visionary archbishop wanted to create a community. Other residents of this palatial home were two retired priests, a cook, a housekeeper, and another young spiritual seeker like myself.

Every evening, three or four of us would arrive for dinner, gathering around a table built for ten (the cook and the housekeeper ate separately). Silence mostly prevailed, except for the predictable complaints of the seventy-eight-year-old priest: "Why does she serve the same meal over and over? Every night, it's the same thing: meat, mashed potatoes, string beans, and corn. Can't she make anything else?"

Having studied some psychology, I offered what I thought was a brilliant solution. "Why don't you talk to her about it? Tell her what you want." But my brave attempt at peacemaking fell flat: "Oh, she'll never change, that's just the way she is!"

Not ready to give up, I approached this gentle woman and asked if she'd consider more variety in her otherwise wonderful meals. Without hesitation she replied, "The Fathers don't like anything else I make. That's all they'll eat! They'll never change; that's just the way they are!" Somewhat amused, but also saddened, I concluded that there was quite a communication problem here!

The Tapestry of Your Feelings

Conversation is the vehicle for setting boundaries and allowing your authentic heart to be seen. It conveys the landscape of your inner life—your feelings, wants, and musings. The commitment to open, honest, kind communication forges a foundation that nurtures love; it builds a bridge of intimacy between two worlds. Conflicts can be resolved and closeness deepened by contacting and speaking from your authentic heart.

Children expect adults to anticipate their needs and wants. Parents are frustrated when their kids whine or cry for no apparent reason, finally asking in utter exasperation, "What's going on? Tell me what you want!"

As adults, we have similar difficulty finding the right words to convey the rich, complex tapestry of our feeling life. Of course, words can never say it all. And much is communicated through silence. A tender glance, gentle touch, or warm hug conveys more than words could ever say.

Much of the pain and isolation of our younger years probably resulted from poorly communicating what was happening in our inner world, whether it was our fears, our hurts, or our appreciation.

Psychologist Daniel Wile offers a helpful suggestion for keeping your relationships on track: "Whenever you find yourself feeling less satisfied with, less in love with, less turned on by, more walled off from, more disgruntled with, or more bored with your partner, look for feelings, wishes, worries, or complaints that you are not telling him/her and that he/she is not telling you—and see if you can talk to your partner about them. People start acting in crazy, confused, offensive, and desperate ways when they are unable to say important things that they need to say."

Communication Busters

Psychologist John Gottman spent over twenty years researching what creates happy marriages. He concluded that there are four types of interactions that sabotage your attempts to communicate with a partner. He calls these the "Four Horsemen of the Apocalypse" because of their cataclysmic effect on relationships. The four communication styles that are predictably destructive are:

1. Criticism
2. Contempt
3. Defensiveness
4. Stonewalling

In his book *The Seven Principles for Making Marriage Work*, Gottman concludes, "As these behaviors become more and more entrenched, husband and wife focus increasingly on the escalating sense of negativity and tension in their marriage. Eventually, they may become deaf to each other's attempts at peacemaking."

By becoming aware of your awesome power to injure love through what you say and don't say, you discover the value of communicating respectfully, kindly, and clearly. You can learn to be authentic without the attacks and unkind cuts that destroy love.

Five Blocks to Communication

Even as people discover what destroys communication, they often still have difficulty changing old patterns. What drives people to communicate in such destructive ways?

I've observed five blocks to effective, kindhearted communication.

1. A Lack of Awareness of What Is Happening inside You

You may not communicate effectively because you aren't aware of your inner world. You aren't connected to the various aspects of your authentic self from moment to moment. You don't know what you're feeling or what you think or want. Instead of communicating your felt experience, you may act it out in hurtful ways.

2. A Lack of Skills to Express What Is Happening inside You

You may know what you're feeling and wanting but not have the skills to express it effectively. You might blurt out your feelings in a contemptuous, hostile way. You may not know how to converse in ways that nurture trust and connection, such as by using "I" statements. You may tend to communicate by blaming and criticizing. Tragically, your relationships may flounder not due to bad faith or hostile intentions, but because of an inability to contact and convey your inner experience.

3. A Desire to Protect Others

You may hold back because you don't want to hurt or offend people. However, by not expressing difficult feelings, you may hurt people more in the long run because they don't know what you're experiencing. You may give messages that are confusing, such as ending a date with a promise to call without really being interested. Or you may withdraw from a relationship instead of talking about a hurtful comment that alienated you. You may stonewall or become defensive to avoid an unpleasant scene.

4. A Desire to Protect Yourself from a Painful Outcome

Due to a Fear of Rejection or Criticism

You may have the awareness and skills but be afraid to reveal your authentic heart. It takes courage to show your vulnerable self. Although you may think you're being noble by protecting others, being inauthentic or deceptive is mostly about protecting yourself. You may withdraw defensively to shield yourself from:

- Dealing with the other's hurt (you may not know how to respond or help).
- Facing your own feelings of hurt, rejection, or embarrassment (you may want to protect yourself from the possible effects of the other's anger or disapproval).
- Seeing yourself as someone who has the power to hurt people (acknowledging that you've hurt someone might conflict with your self-image of being a caring person).

5. A Lapse of Listening

You may be good at asserting yourself but not be a skilled listener. Communication isn't just about expressing yourself; it's also about knowing when to be quiet and receptive. Perhaps you're filled with opinions or insecurities that interfere with your hearing openly. You might avoid conversations because you don't want to know that someone is unhappy with you. You might become easily distracted, or rehearse your response, rather than listen. You might not know how to enjoy the contact that comes with being vulnerable.

EXERCISE:

> As you look over the five blocks to communication, do certain ones stand out for you? These may be the areas to pay attention to in your life.
>
> Is it difficult to communicate because you're not sure what you're feeling, or do you know what you feel but are reluctant to reveal it?
>
> (It's not always easy to know what you're feeling. Give yourself a little time to go inside yourself and sense what's really going on. Once you know, it takes courage to be emotionally honest with others—sharing your true feelings and wants.)

Our Sensitive Heart

By midlife, you've probably been hurt enough times to know that you're a sensitive human being—and perhaps more vulnerable than you'd like to admit. Stripped of defenses, the human heart is raw and tender. Midlife is a time to convey yourself not only clearly but also kindly. By approaching people gently, you provide an ambience for them to soften their defenses and be honest with you. When you're blaming and critical, you provoke shame and fear in others, which generates self-protectiveness and communication meltdown.

Many people communicate by attacking and blaming and haven't a clue why they don't get a rapt reception. Assertiveness is more effective when balanced with gentleness.

The Power of Gentle Honesty

Some people pride themselves on being blunt and direct. "I tell it like it is! I never hold back. I'm very direct." Communication is more effective when you're gently honest rather than brutally honest.

In a massive international study on mate choice, both men and women in thirty-two of thirty-seven cultures rated kindness as one of the three top qualities in a mate. It's no wonder that an unkind communication style, so common during the impetuosity of youth, destroys the love we seek. Anaïs Nin expresses the wisdom of kind-hearted honesty: "Respect for the vulnerability of human beings is a necessary part of telling the truth, because no truth will be wrested from a callous vision or callous handling."

When people feel attacked or treated harshly, they tend to close their heart. If you want to create a safer climate for authenticity and connection, then you need to notice the effects created by your manner of communicating, even if you feel wronged.

While boundaries safeguard you from others' intrusions, kind communication ensures that you don't intrude upon others. Boundaries protect you from being shamed; kindhearted conversation prevents you from shaming others.

Through respectful communication, you reveal what's happening within the boundaries of your own skin without criticizing or manipulating people. Boundary invasions promote defensiveness and undermine self-esteem; they disrupt trust and love.

Some people object to being careful about expressing themselves. Not wanting to "soft-pedal" their opinions or be "overprotective," they proudly declare, "I'm not responsible for other people! I call a spade a spade. People need to take care of themselves!"

Of course, you're free to blame and shame people. The catch is that you must deal with the consequences.

Insisting that you have no responsibility for others' feelings can be taken to an extreme, as happened in the Gestalt therapy movement in the 1970s and in other therapies that emphasize self-expression. You may then justify "self-empowering" words and actions that help *you* feel good without inconveniencing yourself by noticing the effect you're having on people you claim to love.

Denying any responsibility for the effects you create can legitimize abusive behavior. If people object, you can smugly reply, "Hey, that's your problem; I'm not responsible for you!" The message you really deliver is, "I don't care enough about you to find a more loving way to communicate," or, "I don't want to make any effort to create a more trusting relationship," or, "I'd rather remain narcissistically self-absorbed than realize how I'm affecting you."

Soften Your Approach

People who communicate harshly have hardened against their own tenderness. Not having learned to soothe themselves when they're hurting, they unwittingly transfer their pain to others. They may have been so hurt—and so self-protectively numbing of any pain—that they don't even notice when they're being destructive.

I often urge couples to experiment with putting safety ahead of self-expression in order to rebuild trust. Harsh and reckless communication doesn't respect the tenderness of each other's hearts; communication gets blocked. As people speak more gently with each other their defenses can relax, and they grow closer.

Relationships may deepen when you learn to use language that reflects the deeper strata of your feeling life while respecting the other's boundaries. By expressing your feelings and wants openly but kindly, you can maintain trust.

Through repeated impasses, many couples stumble upon the need for what Gottman calls a "soft-startup." This means raising touchy issues in a gentle way—without criticism, contempt, or sarcasm, which prevent you from being heard. As Gottman puts it, "If you start an argument harshly—meaning you attack your spouse verbally—you'll end up with at least as much tension as you began. But if you use a softened startup—meaning you complain but don't criticize or otherwise attack your spouse—the discussion is likely to be productive. And if most of your arguments start softly, your marriage is likely to be stable and happy."

A complaint is more benign than a crticism in that you are limiting your comments to a particular behavior, action, or communication that troubles or disturbs you. A criticism is more global, heaping on blame and character assassination, which is destructive to relationships. It carries the subtext "What's wrong with you?" For example:

COMPLAINT: I don't like when you come home late.

CRITICISM: You're always late! Why can't you ever keep your agreements? You're married to your work!

From observing videotaped couples in his "love lab," Gottman made the startling discovery that "96% of the time you can predict the outcome of a conversation based on the *first three minutes* of the fifteen minute interaction! A harsh startup simply dooms you to failure."

This isn't to preach perfection. Inevitably, you'll use accusatory "you" statements. That is sometimes better than not making any statements at all! At least you're announcing—albeit crudely—that there's a problem and that you're unhappy. Noticing your partner's defensive or pained reaction, you can:

- Become aware that you're being critical.
- Back off, take a deep breath, and practice self-soothing.
- Make an "I" statement that reflects your deeper feelings and wants without blaming.

Complaining is better than criticizing. But I believe that communicating from the depths of your felt experience is even better, which I'll explain in the next chapter.

How we treat others affects how they treat us. Our actions generate rippling effects that return to nourish or haunt us. Just as we need to respect the needs of our environment if we want it to support us, we need to communicate respectfully if we want to be esteemed and appreciated.

Rights and responsibilities go hand in hand, lest you spend a lifetime like the young Narcissus, preoccupied with your own reflection. But even if your interest is self-serving, you benefit from kind communication by creating a climate that invites love and intimacy to deepen.

Self-aware, kind conversation may feel cumbersome at first. But with practice it can become a natural expression of what's stirring within your authentic heart.

Express Appreciation

Some people are skilled at expressing their feelings and wants but are not aware that relationships need appreciation to thrive. A healing balm for the shame and insecurities of our past is to know we're loved, cared about, and appreciated. Even a small expression of gratitude can go a long way toward building safety and comfort into a relationship.

Everyone's needs are different, but verbalizing your love and appreciation for your partner at least several times a week can help create a climate of trust and connection.

EXERCISE:

When is the last time you expressed appreciation to your partner or to a friend? As you bring someone to mind whom you're close to, what would you like to say to him or her?

1 2

Speak and Connect from Your Authentic Heart

Disclosure is the breath of the self. It is your essence being breathed out into the world where those who are in your atmosphere can gradually begin to perceive who you are.
—Daphne Rose Kingma

∞

From my work observing what helps couples connect, I've distilled *four phases of communication* that nurture love and intimacy.

1. Get connected to your true feelings.
2. Hold your feelings in a self-soothing way.
3. Express feelings from your heart.
4. Open to the felt connection that comes through dialogue.

Get Connected to Your True Feelings

During younger years that were perhaps more impulsive, you may have confused *communicating* with *dumping* your feelings. You may

192

have expressed hurt and resentment through sarcastic remarks and vented frustrations by bullying people while claiming virtue for yourself. There may still be times when you hurt people through hostile words, gestures, or tone of voice.

Not surprisingly, venting frustrations by hurling verbal "smart bombs" on people doesn't resolve problems and create closeness. It only fuels the cycle of mistrust. It delivers your discomfort onto others, which prods them to withdraw or attack.

At times, you may have no idea what you're feeling. You're unhappy but don't know what's bugging you or how to talk about it. It's no wonder! Our education system prepared you to succeed in the marketplace, not the home place. You learned the three Rs, but the fourth R of relationships was left out. You took driving lessons for a driver's license, but there was no training required for a marriage license. Incalculable damage is done to your partnership, children, and society—not to mention yourself—when you don't have the skills to steer your marriage onto a safe path.

Communication forever rests on knowing what's really going on inside you. *Before finding the words to convey your experience truthfully, you need to know what that experience actually is.* Relationship impasses persist when you don't get to deeper layers of what you're experiencing. No matter how hard you work on problems, or communication, little will be resolved until you contact and speak from the depths of what's really happening inside you.

Focusing is one helpful way to contact deeper feelings, thoughts, and wants. Taking a walk, writing in a journal, or meditating before raising a tricky issue may also help. Sorting things out with a friend or therapist may also ease your way forward. The clearer you are about what's really going on, the further along you are in your attempts to communicate.

Hold Your Feelings in a Self-Soothing Way

The next step in communication is to become more spacious in relation to your feelings. That is, you need to embrace your feelings with care before letting them loose. Cultivating a caring, gentle presence toward your feelings allows them to be less volatile and overwhelming; you can then express them with greater clarity and kindness.

By developing a larger container for discomforting emotions, you develop a mature relationship with them. You're less driven to vent emotions that stir within you as you hold them warmly. You can then communicate them with greater ease and accuracy. Your feelings are less likely to burst or leak out destructively as you become friendly toward them. Instead of flooring the accelerator, you can proceed with caution.

The biggest obstacle to embracing feelings is the belief that something is wrong with you for having them, along with the fear that something bad will happen if you express them. You need to notice the self-critical voices that would shame and scare you and replace them with kinder self-talk.

The ground is then set for practices such as meditation and Focusing, which help cultivate a caring attitude toward the full range of your authentic experience. By developing self-awareness and communication skills, you're prepared to do battle in the lion's den of relationships. Of course, the main battle is with the dragons within yourself—the shame, fear, and pain that blunt awareness of what's really going on inside you. Midlife love blossoms as you cultivate a loving relationship with yourself.

Melt Defensiveness Gradually

Coming home from work and seeing a pile of dishes in the sink, David shouts at his partner, Kelly, "I've never known anyone so messy! You're totally inconsiderate and self-centered! I thought you agreed to clean up after yourself!" Hearing this hostile comment, Kelly becomes disheartened. Succumbing to shame, her inner critic muses, "Gee, am I really inconsiderate? Am I a selfish, worthless piece of trash? If so, this would confirm my worst fears." Stewing in self-doubts, she makes a quick U-turn and declares, "*You're* incurably compulsive! Why don't you just relax!"

We all carry self-doubts, as well as anxiety about our security in life. David's hostile communication has poked a raw nerve connected to Kelly's identity and safety. Unless she has the equanimity of the Buddha, she may alternate between feeling bad about herself and condemning David in an attempt to prop up her sagging self-worth.

Overwhelmed and wounded, Kelly is disabled from extending

herself into his world. Hearing his feelings, needs, and viewpoints is nearly impossible while she's scrambling to recover her dignity. Communication sputters into a power struggle.

One reason that kind, respectful communication isn't easy is that we're wired with a survival instinct for dealing with threats. Equipped with the "fight or flight" response, our hominid ancestors were prepared to run or attack when chased by toothy creatures. But in the relationship jungle things get more interesting. Your fighting or fleeing must be modulated to ensure your safety. Full-blown fighting might mean jail time; full-fledged fleeing might mean losing the relationship. So you may fight through verbal sparring—or withdraw to your big-screen television. These strategies provide some measure of relief, but much of your energy stays stuck.

From conversations with Peter Levine, a medical biophysicist, I've concluded that during interpersonal conflicts a lesser known instinctual reaction often operates. Physiologists call this the "immobility" or "freezing" response. Not seeing an easy exit when your partner is upset with you, your emotional energy gets stuck in flypaper. You don't know where to go, what to say, or how to respond. This is especially true if a current event is triggering a past trauma. As Peter Levine explains in his book *Waking the Tiger*, you may carry a "frozen residue of energy that has not been resolved and discharged; this residue remains trapped in the nervous system where it can wreak havoc on our bodies and spirits."

If you've been physically or emotionally abused or neglected as a child, you may experience yourself shutting down at the slightest hint of anger or disapproval from your beloved. If a parent or former spouse had affairs that created heartache, you might be flooded by old trauma when your partner looks at another man or woman. If you were yelled at in hurtful, unpredictable ways, you may by restimulated when your mate complains about dirty socks on the floor.

To protect yourself from being physiologically overwhelmed, you instinctually freeze up inside, just as you did when your irate parent skewered you with shaming words or punishments. As you close down emotionally to protect yourself from pain and anxiety, you distance yourself from your partner; you disappear. You're no longer in the present moment. You're relating to a ghost from the past, not your partner.

The reaction of freezing up often plays together with an attack reaction. As Levine puts it, "The more desperate attacks often come out of the feeling state of helplessness."

It doesn't take much to freeze up inside. Even if you suffered no obvious past trauma, you may have experienced developmental trauma when your needs for safety and connection were shattered by repeated shaming and ridicule. Consequently, you may react instinctively when you're afraid that someone will be disappointed with you. Perhaps you're reminded of the shame and pain of a father's constant criticism or disapproval. Maybe you feared that love would be withheld if you weren't a caretaker for your overwhelmed mother. You may have rushed in as the peacekeeper to save a parent from distress, or to save yourself from a tongue lashing.

A parent's anger, punishments, or constant irritability are experienced as a threat to your safety because of your small size and helplessness. In present time, the old instinct of self-protection may kick in at the slightest threat of discord, disconnection, or rejection. Instead of being in present time, you're triggered into "trauma time." You freeze up when your partner is angry or critical; you forget that you're now an adult who's capable of surviving without your partner's approval.

These are the very moments you need to practice self-soothing; otherwise, communication is impossible. You need to remember that your partner's occasional anger or inattention doesn't mean you'll die or dissolve. Your survival doesn't depend on another person's mood.

The Anatomy of Defensiveness

The freeze response helps explain why you become defensive and/or stonewall (Gottman's third and fourth horsemen) if your partner is upset or disappointed with you. Having been triggered, you freeze up and disappear emotionally. Your partner may react to your pulling away by becoming even more critical and contemptuous. Thus, Gottman's first and second horsemen come galloping out, which prompts you to freeze up and withdraw even more.

Unless you do inner work to change these patterns, it's difficult to hear people nondefensively. And it's easy to succumb to a "pursuerdistancer" cycle, where the more your partner pursues conversation and contact, the more you become cold and distant. The more you retreat into frosty immobility, the more he or she pursues you.

When you feel attacked or condemned, the common response is to become emotionally flooded and physiologically distressed. Your heart beats faster, breathing constricts, blood pressure rises, and stress hormones rush into your bloodstream, leaving you rattled or ready to explode. Interpersonal trust and connection are broken during these perilous moments.

The first step out of this common impasse is to learn how to soothe yourself so that you calm down and reconnect with yourself. You can then more easily access and express what you're really feeling. And you're more willing to trust that things could go well.

Practice Self-Soothing before Speaking

Self-soothing is a helpful practice prior to raising a concern. The conversation is likely to go better if you *slowly* tap the accelerator. You can then look around to make sure you haven't run over any bodies. If you have, you can do some psychological CPR: communication process repair. You can level off, back up, check in with the other person, check in with yourself, or start over with a softer approach. Or you can return to the conversation at some designated hour, after you've both taken time for self-soothing (research shows it can take at least twenty minutes to calm down). Raising issues in a gentle, respectful manner rather than in an acrimonious way helps safeguard your partner from being flooded and thereby withdrawing, attacking, or becoming immobilized.

If someone raises a concern with you in an inelegant way, self-soothing will help you maintain your self-worth, thereby minimizing defensiveness. You know this is *your partner's* concern or experience, without assuming you're to blame; you can then "talk down" your excitable inner critic. If you feel hurt or anxious, you can hold yourself gently as you listen to your partner's feelings or complaint. If you're being verbally attacked or abused, you can stop the conversation. Otherwise, you can hear your partner out, knowing you'll get your turn to respond. You're less likely to avoid issues if you are confident that you have options for taking care of yourself.

Express Feelings from Your Heart

It is only by becoming gentle toward your feelings through self-soothing that you have the presence of mind to convey yourself in a kinder way. The communication technique of "I" statements, where you share your feelings rather than judge and blame others, is effective only to the extent that you uncover and warmly embrace your genuine felt experience. When your feelings press heavily inside you—when they make you squirm or burn up inside—you try to whisk them away through a barrage of "you" statements that assault and accuse. As author Gabriele Rico puts it: "Blame is clever at finding logical reasons for our nameless sadness."

As you become calmer, you can speak more clearly and kindly. Free of pretensions, you can share your most private feelings and thoughts, even painful or difficult ones. You can experiment with finding your authentic voice, which resonates with your heartfelt experience.

Uncover Deeper Feelings and Needs

As David acknowledges the disrespectful nature of his words and tone of voice about their messy kitchen, he tries a new approach. He realizes that Kelly is likely to get defensive if he attacks her. So instead of making an accusatory statement ("You're totally inconsiderate and self-centered!") he explores what's happening within the confines of his *own* being. He knows he's angry and frustrated about their messy kitchen; that's abundantly clear. But as he gently attends to his frustration, he notices he feels hurt. He imagines that a messy kitchen means that she doesn't care about him. He's surprised and interested to notice that he's feeling not cared for.

Being more in touch with himself now, he's more able to speak from the gentle depths of his heart, and in a concise way that doesn't barrage her with words: "When you don't do the dishes, I feel hurt and I imagine you don't care about me." After revealing these tender feelings, he pauses to hear her response rather than search his mind for more arguments. She reassures him that she does care about him, yet wonders why a full sink bothers him so much. David responds that it's cumbersome to wash his dishes when the sink's full—it feels like another unwieldy chore in his life!

As he embraces his hurt in a self-soothing way, something even deeper emerges: the dishes are merely one instance of experiencing lack of control in his life, especially in his work environment, where he feel unappreciated. He begins to see how work stress and feeling unappreciated are spilling into his relationship.

As he identifies and communicates what's happening within the depths of his inner world, his partner becomes more willing to wash her dishes, knowing that doing so will alleviate some stress in his life. But more important, they've entered a dialogue where they're no longer in a power struggle. David is letting her in on his deeper life that until now hasn't even been clear to him! They both now understand how other stresses in David's life are affecting him—and affecting them as a couple.

Kelly had sensed that something was troubling him, but David couldn't get to what it was. Having finally seen and expressed what's been upsetting him, he feels relieved and is grateful that she understands him better. Now they can shift the conversation to something more meaningful than the kitchen sink, namely, David's sense of powerlessness and his need for appreciation. Uncovering what's truly going on inside him, they can now really talk. And they're happily poised to slide into the fourth step of communication, which is to really connect.

The Process beneath the Content

If your priority is to nurture love and trust during the second half of life, then it behooves you to notice *how* you talk to others—the process beneath the content. As you become more conscious of the process, rather than rushing to fix the problem, you may communicate with more compassion. As a foundation of safety and connection strengthens, you weave the tiny threads of trust that connect you more deeply. Your relationships can then accommodate conflict without being ripped apart.

To the degree that you neglect to embrace the fears and vulnerabilities that arise in every relationship, you'll resort to combative communication that pushes people away:

- What's wrong with you?
- You'll never get it!
- When will you finally stop being a jerk?

As you become kinder toward yourself, you invite contact by showing your vulnerability. Instead of blaming, you might instead use an "I" statement:

- I'm sad to feel disconnected from you.
- I'm afraid we're drifting apart.
- I'm feeling lonely for you.

A Secret to Intimacy

These kinder, self-disclosing statements reflect inner experience, not outer judgments. They reveal your soulful longings. They tell your partner how *you* are being affected by his or her behavior, or they reveal what's getting triggered in you.

By investigating and disclosing what's happening in your own world rather than speculating on what's happening in your partner's, you discover a secret to deeper intimacy. By limiting communication to your own felt experience, you extend an invitation to understand you rather than promote a power struggle.

The difference between feeling battered by someone's judgments and hearing their heartfelt communication is explained by Laura, a fifty-four-year-old client who was raised on a steady diet of criticism. "It makes a huge difference when he tells me what he's feeling, instead of vilifying me with cutting comments. I've had so much criticism and harshness growing up—I don't want it anymore. It makes me freeze up. I want to feel safe with my partner. I want to feel his heart. When he tells me he's afraid or sad, it's easier to hear. I melt inside. Then we both soften and feel closer." Becoming more intimate through respectful conversation takes repeated efforts and the patience to tolerate backsliding.

Apologizing

You're bound to be imperfect because you're human. There will be times when you blame, withdraw, or stonewall. But as self-awareness grows, you can catch yourself and later come back to apologize. For example, you might say, "I realized I was blaming you. I'm sorry. I don't want to do that." Or, "I know I withdrew from you yesterday when you wanted to talk. I feel bad about doing that. I was just feeling overwhelmed and needed time to sort things out." By finding the strength to admit mistakes, apologize from your heart, and make amends, you keep love and trust alive.

Open to the Felt Connection That Comes through Dialogue

Many people have conversations but no real connection; they don't avail themselves of the lushness of relating. Eager to make points and win points, they're not really present. They don't listen from their hearts. They're "in their heads" rather than comfortably at home in their feelings and bodies.

Others have interesting talks about their relationship or other topics but don't allow themselves to relish the warm feelings and closeness that come from really engaging. They're not fully present with each other. They've prepared a sumptuous meal, but they don't savor the feast of speaking and listening from their authentic hearts.

As you attend to how you converse with people, notice how you feel *being in* the conversation. The richness of communication lies only partly in conveying information (your viewpoints, feelings, wants, etc.). It's also about sharing a connection that's encoded in the information. Are you merely conveying your needs, news, or knowledge, or are you amplifying and celebrating the experience of being together and learning about each other? Are you really present with each other? Is your breathing relaxed and easy, or are you tightening up inside?

Sharing your feelings, history, or other information can deepen empathy and connection—but only if you're available to *experience* the connection. If you're distracted, defensive, or planning your response, you're not emotionally available. Whatever is shared goes into a black hole, not into each other's hearts.

Some couples who want a deeper connection don't know how to promote it, or don't know what to do when it presents itself. They say they want open communication, but they recoil when they get it.

Tom, a fifty-year-old financial planner, grew up in a family where feelings were taboo, and he now had difficulty expressing himself in his marriage. "I never knew what feelings were. I go along with what Cindy wants without telling her how I feel or what I want; I don't make waves. It's like I don't really exist in this relationship."

Tom's wife, Cindy, a forty-eight-year-old designer, implored him to share his feelings more openly instead of being so tight-lipped. But when he did, he was met with a cold shoulder. She had particular difficulty hearing his anger, even when it was expressed in a non-blaming way. Anger was associated with a "rage-aholic" father who exploded unpredictably. Any feelings that resembled her father's rage caused her to shut down. Cindy also couldn't hear Tom's fears about his job because she had anxiety about survival. So instead of hearing him openly, she'd change the subject or offer empty reassurances, such as, "Let's not worry about it."

Cindy's lack of responsiveness confused Tom. She was imploring him to express his feelings, then she didn't welcome the ones he expressed! This placed him in an impossible double bind. If he presented a self that made her feel safe, he'd be showing a false self, which she didn't want. If he was authentic, she'd withdraw.

Since Tom's efforts to share his authentic heart weren't being supported, he reverted to his usual style of staying hidden; the relationship deteriorated.

The discrepancy between what you *think* you want and what you're *emotionally* prepared to accept is common. As one partner changes, the other fears the unknown effects of this change. As Shakespeare knew, we often prefer to "bear those ills we have than fly to others that we know not of." Moving toward a deeper sharing of hearts may require that you risk disturbing the equilibrium to which you've grown accustomed.

After exploring her resistance to acknowledging her own fears and pain, Cindy was gradually able to be less defensive: "Now when he expresses feelings, I'm more there to listen, instead of pushing him back into his shell by being critical or offering trite reassurances. He needs to feel safe with me. It's becoming easier for him to open up now, and we're *both* feeling closer."

Sharing your deeper experience is no guarantee that you'll be heard. But you increase your chances of resolving conflicts and growing closer if you're committed to sharing your inwardly felt world as clearly as you know it.

EXERCISE:

The next time you're in a conversation, notice if you're mainly involved in exchanging ideas or experiencing connection and caring. Can you find a balance between speaking and experiencing the contact? Notice what's happening with your breath. Is it shallow and constricted? Is your stomach tight? Repeatedly practice noticing your breath and allowing your stomach to soften and your body to relax.

(Many people talk without any felt connection with the other person. Experiment with feeling the connection with people, whether you are speaking or silent. You may then enjoy people more.)

Use Freedom Responsibly

When I was a kid growing up in Brooklyn we'd often say mean things to each other: "Your mother dresses you funny! Your mother wears combat boots!" When someone protested, we'd say: "It's a free country. I can say whatever I want!"

Thankfully, we have freedom of speech. But the way you use your freedom makes the crucial difference between whether you create love or distance. You're free to communicate your complaints and wants. Your partner is free to respond or not. If she compromises too much, she might sacrifice her own freedom and well-being, thereby betraying herself. If she keeps altering herself to meet your needs, then she may hate herself and resent you—which might doom the relationship. But if she's impervious to your needs and longings, then she'll alienate you, and your relationship may be doomed for a different reason.

Freedom cuts both ways. She's free to continue her current habits. You're free to end the relationship if it causes too much pain. It's important to choose wisely, as you're responsible for dealing with the consequences of your actions.

Trust and love grow as you care enough to listen and willingly change some behaviors because you love your partner and don't want to hurt him or her. Such freely chosen change is more enduring and likely to build intimacy than change driven by pressure, guilt, or obligation. By listening to each other's authentic hearts, you may break through an impasse by seeing your beloved's pain and needs more clearly.

Two Hearts Touching

If you want genuine relationships, you're responsible for finding the strength to be gently honest. *In your honesty lies a realness, an intimacy.* When you have this honesty, two lives can touch each other with integrity—naked of deadening defenses and awkward attempts to protect each other from authentic feelings and wants.

It's tragic to slide through life without being and showing yourself. By fully experiencing and honoring your fears, hurts, passions, and longings, and sharing them selectively with people you trust, you can move into a midlife that brings abundant love, joy, and connection.

Improve Your Communication

1. When you're with people, do you listen openly and empathetically, or are you planning your response?

(Listening is an essential part of communication. Simply being present for someone is an act of love.)

2. Is it okay to reveal to yourself what you're actually feeling and experiencing?

(You may find that you hide the truth from yourself. It takes strength to be emotionally honest with yourself and to face your true feelings.)

3. Do you take some time to consider *how* you want to say something, or do you just blurt it out? Are you so cautious about what you want to say that you don't say anything?

(There's a fine line between being reckless and being too cautious. If you're insensitive to how you're received, you might intrude on a person's boundaries. If you're overly concerned about others' feelings, you might withhold important truths. Finding a balance is essential.)

4. Can xyou affirm your right to express your feelings and wants while maintaining respect for others? Can you assert yourself while giving the other person an opportunity to express his or her feelings and wants?

(Healthy relationships require a balance between expressing yourself and being receptive to hearing the other person. Communication is all about being affected by each other, not dominating and winning.)

5. Can you be direct *and* kindhearted, assertive *and* tender? When you raise touchy issues, can you do so in a gentle way?

(You must integrate different aspects of yourself to have mature relationships. Assertiveness is more powerful when it's gentle. Kindness is more real and potent when you have a clear, strong sense of yourself.)

6. Can you soothe yourself rather than get defensive when others express anger or displeasure to you?

(Staying connected to yourself creates a grounding that enables you to hear people without getting so defensive.)

7. How approachable are you? Do you think people feel safe expressing their feelings to you?

(It isn't easy to see oneself clearly. You may want to get feedback from your partner or a trusted person to understand how you come across.)

∞∞∞

Build Trust through a Process Commitment

Many legally married couples have
yet to be married emotionally.
—DAVID SCHNARCH

Being Committed
to the Process

I think that people normally talk about marriage as an institution, or they think of marriage as a structure, and it's not, *it's a process*. It's a *set of processes* which people engage in and you never know where they're going to go.

—Carl Rogers

❦

R omantic notions about love have generated confusion around the meaning of marriage and commitment. In young love, the goal is to nail down a marriage—fulfilling your dream of marital bliss. But as you've probably discovered, marriage alone doesn't deliver happiness.

All too often, marriage is an attempted external solution for an internal predicament—a rescue mission to soothe insecurities rather than a confirmation of an evolving love and trust. Marriage vows may exteriorize these silent pleas:

- Take care of me!
- Rescue me from life!
- Protect me forevermore!

A true marriage is a joyful celebration of a *preexisting engagement* of two authentic hearts.

Sincere marital vows may offer a tangible measure of safety and solace, but a deeper challenge is to understand how to nurture connection and happiness in the marriage. As psychotherapist Carl Rogers puts it, "No matter how intensely a couple mean such vows, they cannot hold to them unless the marriage is satisfying. If it is not, they either demean or destroy themselves or each other, or they break the bonds—and sometimes they do all these things."

Joanne and Howard thought they had the perfect union. They were high school sweethearts and got married several years after graduation when Joanne became pregnant. They were excited to be parents, but soon after the baby was born, things changed. Howard resented all the time his wife lavished on the baby. Joanne felt neglected when Howard took a second job to pay their mounting bills. Frustrations and resentment often grew to a boiling point, and their small apartment made it difficult for them to take time apart.

Joanne was left heartbroken during those times Howard walked out when she wanted to talk, especially when he came back home intoxicated. She finally couldn't take it anymore, and filed for divorce.

Like many young couples, Joanne and Howard weren't ready for marriage or parenthood. They didn't really know themselves. They never learned how to communicate, and they didn't have the skills to resolve conflicts. They hadn't grown enough to establish a solid trust that could sustain their love through the vicissitudes of marriage and family life. Their marital vows weren't informed by the knowledge of what it really takes to make a marriage work.

The infrastructure that supports love is a "process commitment." This bespeaks a commitment to the *process* of creating conditions under which love, trust, and intimacy are most likely to flourish. Such a process requires a growing wisdom about how to create a sound foundation for love. It humbly recognizes that you can't maintain love through willpower or a mental decision, and that the only control you have is relating to your partner in a way that builds trust, which in turn sustains love.

What Really Nurtures Trust?

"We're soul mates. We'll stick together in good times and bad. We're committed to making our marriage work!"

These popular declarations are meaningless unless you know *how* to nurture a lasting connection. The deeper challenge of love is knowing how to create and sustain emotional trust, which nurtures a rich and meaningful union. By trusting each other's commitment to the tasks of personal development that are essential supports for love, you're creating an environment in which you're likely to *want* to stay together.

As you relish a growing mutual trust, you nurture a sacred bond of love. You then remain together because you're happily involved with each other rather than confined by responsibility alone. *A demand for commitment is actually a plea for involvement.* The important thing is the felt connection, not just having a body around who can pay the bills, do chores, and protect you from feeling alone. Involvement is what really keeps a couple together. The eightfold path I've been outlining is a formula for deeper involvement.

Gone are the days when marriages were held together by duty, obligation, and long-suffering. People want and deserve something more—the richness, joy, and meaning that are the promise of love. Midlife is often an era of reevaluation, of pursuing your soul's longing and "following your bliss," as mythologist Joseph Campbell put it.

Shifting your understanding of commitment from a duty-based guarantee of permanence to nourishing a sacred bond of trust has profound implications for the way you pursue the promise of love. Most important, it makes you accountable for how you conduct yourself in relationships. *Your marital security then rests upon a commitment to various aspects of personal growth*, such as your commitment to knowing yourself, being authentic, setting boundaries, and communicating with more vulnerability and less blame. There are no free rides. You need to work on being and becoming the healthy, self-aware partner that you're looking for.

The commitment to personal growth not only serves you; it's the best gift you can give your partner—far more long-lasting than flowers or candies. This commitment to mature love creates a larger container for resolving conflicts and facing the challenges that await you in later years.

Seemingly noble commitments may be by-products of deeply held fears of abandonment, loss, or loneliness. Such fears are especially common if you haven't learned to embrace them through self-soothing. You then expect others to embrace fears you refuse to face. You rely on others as your source of happiness rather than finding a wellspring within yourself.

This is not to suggest that you must fully embrace your fears and hurts *before* entering a relationship. That's too perfectionistic. It is *through* a partnership that you may become aware of old wounds, which are more apt to heal within the vessel of a sacred love relationship. By disclosing your fears, hopes, and sorrows, you invite others to respond caringly. But you must then pick up the slack by using their love as an inspiration to love and affirm yourself, rather than as a substitute for self-love and self-soothing. Love relationships support you to grow, they don't do the growing for you.

Although lifelong marital vows are intended to protect you, they might later be experienced as a life sentence. What if your mate treats you disrespectfully, or steadfastly refuses to look within himself or herself for the source of marital problems? Even worse, what if you are physically or emotionally abused? If you forever renounce the sad option to exit an unworkable marriage, you may condemn yourself to lifelong misery.

I've often been saddened to hear people express some version of the following:

- I thought love meant sticking it out no matter how much I was suffering!
- Staying in a miserable marriage proves how loving I am!
- Who said you're supposed to be happy in a marriage?

These negative attitudes reflect confusion about love.

Some people stay in agonizing marriages because of religious teachings against divorce. But would a compassionate God want you to suffer needlessly and sacrifice your life to be a caretaker for someone who damages you? Or is a loving God understanding and forgiving?

Another pitfall of traditional commitments is that you may become mentally and emotionally lazy. Feeling "safely" married, you may have less incentive to approach your partner with the same respect that existed prior to marriage. You may slip into a perilous comfort zone of being casually contemptuous, since your spouse is now "stuck" with you. If he or she wants to escape mistreatment, you can attack with the guilt-provoking accusation: "You're not committed to your vows. You don't love me!"

A lavish wedding may put you at risk of reverting back to the romantic images of marriage brewed in your fantasy world. When I visited my old friend Vivian in New York, she told me that she finally married her live-in partner. As she explained: "We were happily living together for years. Then putting a ring on my finger turned me into his mother. He wanted me to cook his meals, clean the house, care for the kids, and work, too!" Fortunately, her husband realized that his outdated model for marriage was what he saw between his parents and that his unrealistic expectations had almost derailed his relationship with Vivian.

Marriage vows can convey your purehearted intention to work through difficulties on your lifelong journey of loving and learning. But the dark side of your vows is believing that your mate is now responsible for your well-being. If you become overly dependent, you may be less motivated to pursue your own growth. You might abandon other friendships, neglect your spiritual path, or become lax about proper eating and exercise (many people gain weight after marriage).

As your life begins to feel empty, you may pin your dissatisfactions on your partner, whom you accuse of slacking off on his or her job as caretaker. Midlife is a time to become more realistic about what marriage can and cannot provide. The relationship can thrive if you hold realistic expectations of marriage (not too high or too low) and connect with the vitality of your own soul.

Another's heart is not yours to own, but it is yours to share for as long as it's given freely. As psychologist and Catholic priest Eugene Kennedy sees it, "At the heart of love there is a deep but simple secret: the lover lets the beloved be free. What he would like to possess totally, he must allow to have a life separate from, although shared with, his. This is the gift which lovers work at giving to each other all through their lives."

When Parting Is Wiser

Sadly, you may need to separate from a person who is unable or unwilling to make the midlife passage to a more mature view of love and marriage. It could be a tormenting self-abandonment to remain with a partner who clings to old models based on unrealistic expectations, enmeshment, and loss of identity.

James Hollis states convincingly why separation is a viable option when one person refuses to grow.

> When one spouse continues to block change, be assured that he or she is still controlled by anxiety and invested in the projections of the first adulthood. Quite possibly, the recalcitrant spouse will forever resist taking on the necessary responsibility; if so he or she thereby forfeits the right of veto over anyone else's life. No one has the right to block the development of another; that is a spiritual crime.

Rather than drown in a sea of disjointed communication and disconnection, you may need to "save yourself" while trusting that your partner will be extended a life preserver by a power greater than anything you can offer. Removing the props upon which your partner's fantasy world has been erected may, in a peculiar way, be his or her best hope for unraveling the truth and pursuing midlife growth. Sadly, it sometimes takes a crisis to pinpoint a vital choice: grow or languish.

Pain is sometimes a bitter but effective pill for people whose narcissism prevents them from seeing how they're affecting others. These young souls are known in Jungian psychology as the *puer aeternus* (eternal boy) or *puella aeterna* (eternal girl). They have a low tolerance for frustration, perhaps because they were so frustrated as children that they have difficulty bearing more. Or perhaps they were so gratified that they keep expecting their environment to soothe them; they didn't have an appropriate amount of frustration to prompt a turning within so they could learn to soothe themselves.

If these individuals can learn to embrace sorrow and other feelings that accompany frustration and loss, they may mature. Harsh lessons are sometimes a gift of tough love that nudges people toward growth. As the poet Goethe put it: "With apprehensive, holy dread the better soul in us awakes."

Commit to Conditions That Nurture Love

By now, you may think I'm antimarriage. Not at all! Midlife marriages can be more rewarding because there are fewer illusions. I'm simply suggesting that marriage cannot substitute for the personal development necessary to nourish and sustain love.

Meaningful vows can strengthen a healthy commitment between people who are growing toward wholeness within themselves. A marriage ceremony can be a jubilant celebration of a special union, as long as you don't delude yourself by thinking marriage will somehow rescue you. Whether you're married or not, you're faced with the lifelong challenge of:

- Soothing and staying connected to your authentic self.
- Communicating more authentically and effectively.
- Dealing with existential issues such as death, loss, and meaning.

Your commitment is most viable when you're dedicated to nurturing a vital, growing relationship. Aiming for stability rather than authenticity can ruin a relationship. Instead of expressing yourself and facing conflicts, you may placate your partner to "save" the relationship. Sadly, you save the marital form but remain intimate strangers because you've ignored the marital process.

However hard your ego might try, you cannot control or force love. Kenny and Julia Loggins, authors of a lovely book about their marriage, entered this sacred relationship with their eyes open: "In the old form of marriage, people promise each other, 'I will never leave.' Although we all would love to believe we can make that promise, I don't see 'forever' as fully within the realm of what we have control over."

You have no ultimate dominion over the course of marriage. But the good news is that you can create conditions under which love and trust are *more likely* to prosper. By being committed to bringing forth your genuine hearts, you nurture a connection that is real and alive. This mature commitment improves prospects for creating a satisfying, enduring alliance.

Release Each Other with Love

By leaving a relationship too early, you may keep repeating the same tired patterns. The midlife recognition that you won't live forever brings added motivation to invest time, energy, and perhaps money (to see a counselor or attend workshops) into learning how to nurture trust and connection.

Although maturity prods you to work things through whenever possible, love doesn't oblige you to remain in a partnership that is harming you. At some point, you may need to let go of a relationship before you damage each other—and harm any children who may suffer collateral damage from the bombs you drop on each other.

The willingness to release each other due to unacceptable differences can be one of the purest expressions of love and acceptance. This explains why some couples on the verge of parting decide to stay together. Their honesty and caring, in addition to a willingness to let go rather than splatter each other against the wall, may open an unexpected doorway to new love. As one woman in midlife recounted, "At first, he didn't want to hear about separation, but something shifted and he became okay with it. There was a softness and sensitivity that I hadn't seen for a long time. He started to hear my feelings more. Then I wondered, 'Do I really want to give up a man like this?' Our love deepened by going through this crisis together."

There are no easy answers to the complex issues involved when needs and wants differ, or when one or both of you stray from the narrow path of growth. Formulating proper questions may help you discover your wisest course:

- Can you accept and love your partner as he or she is?
- Are you expecting too much or too little from your beloved?
- Are you living your lives *through* each other to an unhealthy degree while neglecting other relationships?
- Do your dissatisfactions stem from failing to discover a source of love and nurturing within yourself?
- Do you have a shared vision and co-creative purpose that's larger than the partnership?
- Do you know why you're together?
- Are you creatively engaged in life, or are your needs and passions focused too much on each other?

The most responsible commitment you can make to another person is to your own continuing growth. By renewing the connection with your own authentic heart you repeatedly bring the best of yourself to the relationship. As you become more present and genuine, you create a stronger foundation for trust and love.

1 4

The Key
Ingredients of Trust

At no moment is love separate from the stage of growth we have reached.

—Eugene Kennedy

∽o∾

The human heart is sensitive and vulnerable. Although it makes you susceptible to hurt, it also allows for sweet, tender union. These warm connections can be formed, preserved, and deepened by maintaining a sacred trust.

Trust is nurtured as we consistently embody three essential qualities:

1. Emotional honesty
2. Respect
3. Sensitivity

Emotional Honesty

One way to understand how to build trusting relationships is to ask yourself, "What do I need from people in order to trust them?" Your first response might be that you need honesty. You want people to be straight with you, not deceptive or manipulative. When you catch people in a lie or deception, your trust is shaken. Your sense of that person is altered; your sense of reality is turned upside down. Trust requires truth.

But telling the truth isn't easy. Most people lie to one degree or another, especially about their feelings. You may share information truthfully, honor your vows of sexual fidelity, and be honest on your taxes. But you may be deceptive in a deeper way: through emotional dishonesty. You may fail to recognize the little betrayals of trust that can destroy a relationship.

- Do you ever feel sad but smile sheepishly?
- Do you sometimes feel angry or irritable but refuse to acknowledge these feelings?
- Do you withhold your genuine feelings because you're afraid of being laughed at or rejected?
- Do you see yourself as someone who's never angry or sad, perhaps because you don't want to be labeled "rude" or a "sad sack"?

Emotional honesty means revealing where you are emotionally—letting people know your true feelings, wants, and needs. Emotional dishonesty is a self-betrayal that keeps you from healing emotional wounds and experiencing the inner peace of self-acceptance. Without this honesty, there can be no emotional connection, depth, or trust. The experience of connection is nourished by authenticity, not mere promises. If you don't share your authentic fears, hurts, joys, and sorrows, as well as express your anger in a responsible manner, people don't get a sense of how they're affecting you—or how life is touching you. Unexpressed feelings may then leak out indirectly, perhaps through a snide comment, a careless act, or an irritable tone of voice. These indirect communications generate distance and distrust.

Talk to Me!

Henry, a fifty-two-year-old artist, was afraid of failing at work and felt insecure about being a parent. Instead of revealing these natural feelings, he kept quiet much of the time and wouldn't respond to the requests of his wife, Susan, to talk about what was going on. "Everything is just fine," he'd tell her. As often happens, Susan assumed that his silence meant that he was angry with her. Eventually, she learned to keep her distance. Trust and closeness were far away.

Over time, Henry realized how hard it was to be honest with himself about what he was feeling: "I'm ripping *myself* off by keeping everything inside. And I'm hurting my wife by withholding my real feelings. She can sense something is off, but I show myself as having everything under control." When Henry finally took the risk of divulging his fears and insecurities, a new closeness emerged with his partner.

It can be frustrating, if not infuriating, when your beloved withholds his or her feelings. At times, you may want to shake your partner to their core: "Talk to me! What's going on with you? You seem aloof and distant!" These passionate pleas occasionally work, but they're more likely to be felt as pressure, which pushes your mate further away.

When you don't let people into your emotional world, they feel distant from you. They feel disconnected, even if they can't quite put their feelings into words. They have to guess about how you're feeling. Oftentimes, they imagine the worst, which further erodes trust and closeness.

You don't come across clearly when your words aren't congruent with your true feelings. The mismatch between your body language and your words often damages trust more than a direct expression of authentic feelings. When your emotions leak out indirectly, whether through an irritable comment, a cranky voice, or rolled eyes, you confuse and distance people.

Integrity in Self-Honesty

One reason it's difficult to communicate with others is because you must first be emotionally honest with yourself. If your feelings weren't accepted and mirrored back to you as a child, you didn't get to know and affirm your real emotions. Although you may have glimmerings of fear, sorrow, or anger, you're reluctant to acknowledge them. You may fear being criticized or rejected if this is what happened earlier in life when you were vulnerable. So you become proficient in hiding your feelings not only from others but also from yourself! A self-critical structure in your psyche solidifies, which keeps you in line.

Authenticity is a central part of integrity. People mistrust you when they think you're being insincere or indirect. As you come to live with integrity, you'll see how emotional honesty serves everyone in the long run, even if it sometimes creates short-term discomfort.

When Dennis was in his early thirties he moved in with Sandra despite serious reservations. "She insisted on it, so I figured, 'Why not?' But I wasn't ready. I just went along with what she wanted. I don't like disappointing anyone. So I go along with the program, never show my feelings, and end up disappointing myself and everyone else. Years later during an argument I told her I never wanted to live together. She was furious. I wish I'd had the courage to say it at that time. The truth has a way of coming out sooner or later. As I've gotten into my forties I realize I need to be honest even if I don't like the immediate consequences." As Dennis discovered, trust is compromised when truth is withheld.

Heal the Split Within Self and Society

As we've seen, society encourages you to fashion a fabricated self rather than to know and show your authentic self. Becoming aware of your true self isn't part of the social curriculum, though it's an essential part of the life curriculum. The values of succeeding, achieving, and competing overshadow the values and skills necessary to create loving partnerships, healthy families, and peaceful communities.

When our training in scientific and technical intelligence isn't balanced with emotional intelligence, our psyche becomes split. We become proficient in knowing facts but deficient in knowing ourselves—our feelings, needs, and longings, and how to communicate them. Consequently, our society has succeeded in becoming an economic giant while many of its citizens remain emotional infants, tragically ignorant about how to build a foundation for trust and love. Through a commitment to become emotionally honest with ourselves and others, we take a step toward healing the fragmentation that exists within ourselves, our relationships, and our society.

Respect

It is not enough simply to trust a person's honesty; you also need to feel respected by that person in order to trust. Respect derives from the Latin term *respicere*, which means "to look at." You want to be seen as a good, honorable person. It's hard to trust someone who:

- Sees you with eyes of suspicion, blame, or contempt.
- Judges, attacks, or criticizes your character.
- Ignores or invalidates your feelings, needs, and wants.
- Doesn't listen to you.
- Communicates in an accusatory, shaming, insensitive way.

You're likely to feel guarded with a person who doesn't respect you—hardening into a defensive stance, rather than softening into closeness.

It takes self-respect to not tolerate others' disrespect. Some people remain in abusive relationships, hoping that if they're a little more loving, understanding, or patient, they'll someday be respected. But that day may never come. Midlife is a time to safeguard your well-being and allow self-worth to derive from how you see yourself, not how others treat you.

One person told me tearfully, "My husband makes fun of my weight at parties. It's so humiliating. When I tell him this hurts me, he says, 'Don't be so sensitive.'" This woman loved her husband, and he claimed to love her. But these put-downs were destroying trust and closeness.

You can't trust someone while bracing for the next verbal assault. Trusting means feeling safe with a person, letting down your guard as you relax into being together.

You can't expect to *get* respect unless you *give* respect, which implies a relationship of mutual sensitivity among equals. Giving respect means honoring the uniqueness and dignity of each person. It means being present and interested in seeing things from the other person's viewpoint. There is no greater measure of respect than your readiness to listen with a receptive heart. The insightful book *Wisdom Circles* says it well: "Listening from the heart means you give a 'Welcome' sign to the speaker, who's wondering whether to trust you with his or her thoughts and feelings. Through your respectful silence, eye contact, body posture, and attentiveness, you signal that you are listening with empathy."

Disrespect may derive from your own fear, insecurity, or ignorance. You may feel threatened by a differing viewpoint or be envious of others' successes or positive qualities. Or you may simply not realize how respect is an essential part of loving.

One fifty-six-year-old client, Blair, grew up believing that a man's job was to make his partner feel good. So whenever his wife, Shelley, was upset, as she was when she worried about her ailing mother, he felt responsible to turn it around for her. He'd say things that his parents frequently said to him: "Crying won't do you any good," or, "You worry too much! Don't think about it so much!" These suggestions came from a well-intended place, but they were making Shelley feel worse. Seeing this, Blair finally got it: "Her feelings are legitimate just because they exist. I don't need to talk her out of them, or make her justify them, or try to fix her. I just need to respect her feelings, even if I don't always understand them. I also need to accept my own feelings more."

Sensitivity

Through your own sensitivity, you become receptive to other people's worlds:

- You are touched by their sorrows and delight in their joys.
- You are aware of what makes a person happy, sad, or fearful.
- You allow yourself to be affected by their feelings and wants.

Such sensitivity toward other people's inner worlds goes a long way toward building trust.

Trust grows as you share your thoughts without coming across as being superior. You express your needs and wants without making others obligated to satisfy them. You honor your own experience while allowing others the right to have theirs. Sensitivity and respect toward others' boundaries helps them feel safe with you.

Sensitivity means remembering important details about people who are close to you. For example do you know:

- How they grew up?
- What experiences shaped who they are today?
- Whether their history created special sensitivities you want to understand so that you don't throw salt on an old wound (like being teased about weight or looks)?
- What was disappointing about their earlier relationships and what they are seeking now?
- What vision they have for their life and for your life together?

Being sensitive toward a partner or friend's history, sore spots, and yearnings helps that person trust that you're attuned to the unique person he or she is.

Being sensitive means being attentive to your partner's everyday life. This includes hearing how your partner's day went, how you might share chores, or what he or she wants in order to make life easier.

You nurture trust by listening with a quiet heart and an open mind. This means suspending biases, extending your warm presence, and making eye contact with receptive and responsive eyes. Rather than offer advice, you offer yourself—your caring ear and heart.

It is interesting that "heart" begins with the letters H-E-A-R. To truly hear means to listen not just with your mind but, more important, with your heart, which hears in a different way than the analyzing mind.

You Get Points for Trying

Even if you cannot fully understand a person's feelings, needs, or beliefs, you engender trust through a sincere intention and effort to understand. People want to be heard—they want you to "get" their heart—just as you want others to appreciate you. You don't have to agree or comply. You have a right to differing needs or viewpoints. But by addressing differences with an attitude of respect and sensitivity, you can preserve—and often deepen—trust.

Sensitivity doesn't mean syrupy affection, feigning sweetness, or being compliant. Nor does it mean neglecting yourself and surrendering your reality to fit into another's world. It simply means knowing that tender hearts are easily broken and treating people with the same sensibilities with which you want to be treated.

Some people, especially men, dismiss the need for sensitivity or even denigrate it as "touchy-feely stuff." The "sensitive New Age guy" is a stereotype that has become the butt of jokes in sitcoms and steak houses. Even Robert Bly, a leader of the men's movement, warns men not to become "soft males." Sadly, this advice may send waves of shame through men who are already embarrassed to show their tender side.

Many men who have been fearful of their mother's wrath allow themselves to be controlled in their relationships. But that's a problem of passivity, not sensitivity. The difficulty isn't with being soft, but with being lost. Such men don't have access to the full range of their humanness. Sensitivity is suspect when it's out of balance with potency and assertiveness.

Healthy people can bring forward their tenderness and their strength. Maturity means feeling the strength in your tenderness and the tenderness in your strength.

Viewing sensitivity as a weakness overlooks the courage required to open yourself to another person. It takes strength to risk being shamed and rejected for showing your authentic heart. It takes knowing and affirming yourself to accept differences, respect other viewpoints, and keep your heart open. It takes a mature kind of virility to stay connected to yourself while generously extending yourself toward another's world. Without sensitivity, you'll never invite the warm, loving connections you want.

Byron Brown wisely points out the true meaning of strength: "It is difficult to feel strong and fluid, strong and open, or strong and vulnerable at the same time. . . . True strength is not about being massive and muscular and intimidating. Strength arises out of your very aliveness, the dynamic flow of your soul. It is an expression of the vital, juicy, dynamic quality of being a living, growing organism."

The most sensitive people are usually those who deny how sensitive they really are! The people who are the most easily angered, quick to end relationships, opinionated, contentious, and controlling are those who are the most vigilant in protecting their sensitive heart from potential hurt. However, their reactivity reflects a disembodied sensitivity. Having cut themselves off from their vulnerable core, they're at the mercy of it. That's why they react so strongly and defensively when anyone gets close to poking their sensitive spots.

The more you love yourself, the less you need to armor your heart to protect against the loss of others' love. Developing a stronger connection with your authentic self allows you to be more open and vulnerable.

The commitment to be honest, respectful, and sensitive ensures that your midlife journey toward love and intimacy is not a narcissistic one. Personal growth means balancing a commitment to yourself with a responsiveness to the well-being of others.

Deepen Trust and Clarify Your Commitment

1. What does marriage mean to you? What are you committed to in your marriage or partnership?

(Many people don't realize what they're committing themselves to. They simplistically equate commitment with staying together no matter what. Doing the work required to have a healthy relationship multiplies the likelihood that trust and intimacy will endure.)

2. Do you understand the difference between being *responsible for* your partner and being *responsive to* your partner? Do you understand the difference between your partner being *responsible for* you and being *responsive to* you?

(Being responsible for your partner may lead you to lose yourself in the relationship. Being responsive recognizes that two mature people are allowing themselves to be affected by each other.)

3. How emotionally honest are you in your close relationships? Do you let people see your true feelings or do you withhold them?

(Emotional honesty means taking the risk to reveal your true self. Building trust is a gradual process. As you're treated with respect and sensitivity, you feel safer showing your authentic heart to trusted people.)

4. Do you show respect for people's feelings, views, and wants? Can you allow yourself to be sensitive to others' feelings and needs?

(The best way to get respect is to give respect. People appreciate being treated in an authentic and sensitive way and are likely to reciprocate.)

5. Are you willing to risk trusting again, even though you've been hurt in past relationships?

(Old hurts and fears may be holding you back. You need to hold these hurts in a self-soothing way in order to risk loving again. If you don't take wise risks to trust again, you risk being alone.)

6. What do you need in order to trust someone?

(Understanding your needs for honesty, respect, sensitivity, and so on will steer you toward people you can learn to trust. If you don't get these things in your current partnership, you may need to be more assertive, be more expressive of your hurt, or insist on seeing a couples therapist to rebuild trust.)

∾⧉∾

Deepen Your Understanding of Love and Sexuality

The moment you have in your heart this extraordinary thing called love and feel the depth, the delight, the ecstasy of it, you will discover that for you the world is transformed.

—J. Krishnamurti

15

The Ingredients
of Love

I believe it will become clear that not only do self-love and love of others go hand in hand but that ultimately they are indistinguishable.

—M. Scott Peck

∽⚬∾

We're now ready to deepen our understanding of what it really means to love. However, talking about love is rather pretentious. As the popular Taoist saying warns: "Those who know do not speak; those who speak do not know." Yet there's such massive confusion around love that if we don't become clearer, our naive notions will prevail. Love will always be a matter of the heart, but our mind needs to understand what love requires of us—and how to stay on track.

It's easier to say what love is not than to consider what it actually is. Claiming to comprehend this riddle is like presuming we know the meaning of life itself. As soon as we say "This is love," its meaning slides away, like sand slipping out of our grasping hand. And how fortunate we are to have a word that points beyond words toward the sublime mystery of human existence! With this caution in mind, we can point *toward* love. If we can glimpse its rough outlines, we can deepen our understanding while remaining awed by love's everlasting mystery.

EXERCISE:

What does love mean to you? What does it really mean to love another person? Write down what comes to mind. See if what you wrote down corresponds with the discussion that follows. Perhaps you have some unique, creative ways of understanding love.

Aspects of Love

1. Don't hurt people.
2. Extend caring and empathy.
3. Let in caring.
4. Express your affection.
5. See people as they are.
6. Maintain mutuality.
7. Embody your love.

Don't Hurt People

Perhaps the first step toward love is knowing how *not* to treat people. Confucius's golden rule of reciprocity advises, "Do not do unto others what you would not want others to do unto you." Similarly, the Dalai Lama defines compassion as "A state of mind that is non-violent, non-harming, and non-aggressive."

There's good reason why spiritual traditions urge us to avoid behaviors that wound people. Under the name of "morality" or "ethics," these values include not killing, not stealing, not lying, not earning a livelihood in ways that cause harm, and not hurting people through unwise sexual contact.

Of course, being in relationships means you'll get hurt or hurt others sometimes, even if there's no intention to harm. For example, while setting a self-respecting boundary, you might ruffle someone's feathers. Or you may need to separate from an unworkable relationship rather than prolong your suffering.

Not harming others requires a sturdy sense of self that doesn't react hurtfully if we feel offended or mistreated. A self that is easily fragmented or shattered is a danger to others.

If we don't have the strength to tolerate a little shame or defeat—if we don't have the internal boundaries to affirm our worth and prevent others' perceptions from poisoning our self-perception—we may react viciously.

The Anatomy of Vengeance

Lacking a strong self, some people scramble to protect their self-image by being vengeful when things don't go their way. Just read the newspaper to see how many homicides and shootings are triggered by real or imagined rejection. Frivolous lawsuits are ways to wage war without weapons—retaliation for feeling wronged in some way.

Untrue child abuse charges toward an ex-spouse are a particularly vicious form of vengeance. Such an accusation not only damages one's former partner emotionally and financially, but the stray projectiles mangle the children's fragile hearts. Children need to have a loving relationship with both parents. Using a child to get back at an ex-partner, such as by turning a child against a parent or interfering with visitation rights, produces a heart-wrenching aftermath known as parent alienation syndrome.

The impulse to lash out is launched by the ignition of a tightly packaged bundle of pain and shame. Stored, unbefriended pain is a combustible disaster waiting to happen. Unable to soothe and validate yourself in healthy ways, you may implode through self-destructive behavior, depression, or physical symptoms—or explode through horrifying actions.

As your former lover is projected as the enemy, you may feel justified in destroying that enemy. Not having skills to soothe your hurt, fear, and shame, you may revert to the temper tantrum of a child.

When You Hurt Others You Hurt Yourself

Your growth isn't complete until you've recognized the major ways you've contributed to the pain of other human beings and accompanied that recognition with appropriate remorse. Hurting others hurts yourself. This is the deeper meaning of the Eastern concept of "karma," roughly translated as "actions." Karma is often understood to mean that hurting others will result in being hurt *by* others—what goes around comes around. A deeper meaning is that the very act of hurting a person immediately deepens a wound of separateness within yourself.

Much has been made of moralistic reasons to love. But there are also self-serving reasons for being kind. The defense mechanism that protects you from knowing how you've hurt people dulls your ability to be open, gentle, and loving. As a result of this emotional self-strangulation, your capacity for joy is diminished. As your personality hardens, your ability to love is impaired. Violating the code of your conscience is therefore self-destructive. Loving yourself is inconsistent with hurting others. By hurting people, you hurt yourself in a very real way—you limit your potential for serenity and happiness.

On a larger scale, our nation will not become compassionate until its citizens do the inner work necessary to provide the foundation for true compassion. As you embody greater awareness and sensitivity, you will recognize that your well-being is not antagonistic to the well-being of others; in fact, it depends upon it.

Awareness Exercise:

Visualize a time you felt hurt by a partner. How did you deal with it? Did you blame and attack? Did you retreat and not talk about it? These responses are natural when you feel hurt.

The next time you feel hurt, take some time to be gentle with your hurt before talking about it. See what words come as you speak from your feeling of hurt. Try to avoid blaming and criticizing.

Extend Caring and Empathy

When we are absorbed in our own need for love, it's difficult to see others clearly. Oftentimes, what we call caring is actually dependency, which may become apparent when our wants are frustrated.

Caring means being interested in others' well-being. When you really care, you take time to discover how people feel and what they need to be happy. Caring means being sensitive to how others experience the world; you allow yourself to be touched by their reality. What's important to them matters to you. When people sense that their concern is held close to your heart, trust and closeness grow. The flowering of such caring is a sweet blossom of midlife growth.

Empathy provides the grounding for caring. To be empathic means that you feel what others feel; you have some experience of what they're experiencing. If they feel hurt, you not only *know* they're hurt, you *feel* it along with them, at least to some degree. If they're angry, embarrassed, or afraid, you sense these same feelings within yourself—perhaps not with the same intensity, but you catch the flavor of their pain or upset. As you hear their hopes, dreams, or excitement, you feel moved to offer support.

Psychologist Carl Rogers explains one reason empathy is difficult: "If I am truly open to the way life is experienced by another person—if I can take his world into mine—then I run the risk of seeing life in his way, of being changed myself, and we all resist change. So we tend to view this other person's world only in our terms, not in his."

Empathy enables you to move beyond the projections and desires colored by your longings and expectations. It offers the gift of seeing people as they are, which provides the only doorway into mature love.

Awareness Exercise:

When you see your partner after work or call a friend, do you immediately describe how your day went or talk about your concerns? Or do you first ask how the other person is doing? If you frequently seek attention, you may want to experiment with inquiring more about others. If you're more comfortable when others talk, you may want to explore bringing forth your authentic self.

Presence: The Ultimate Gift of Love

With the perspective of midlife, you've probably discovered that sex alone doesn't furnish the intimacy you want. Nor can your children offer the lasting magic to keep your partnership together. It is empathic presence that provides the basis for love and intimacy. Knowing how it feels to walk in the shoes of the other nourishes connection.

Vietnamese Buddhist monk Thich Nhat Hanh teaches that "The most precious gift we can offer others is our presence." Similarly, psychologist and Zen teacher John Tarrant states, "Attention is the most basic form of love: through it we bless and are blessed."

When you care for a person, you're present for him or her. Conversely, when you're really present, you can't help but care. Your heart is touched and your experience of the moment is transformed:

- You hear people's concerns and longings.
- You see their vulnerability.
- You're moved by concern for their well-being.
- You want to meet their needs as best you can.
- You want them to be happy.

Your capacity for caring presence can become more palpable in midlife because your wider range of experience invites greater empathy for what people have been through. The word "care" derives from the word meaning "sorrow." You can embody deeper levels of empathy to the degree that you've embraced human suffering and are willing to be present for others' pain. Knowing life's sorrow deepens compassion.

Empathic Resonance

Empathy not only enables you to be compassionate when people are hurting, it also enables you to take delight in their joy. The ability to be present extends to people in their sorrow *and* happiness.

There's no finer art than empathic resonance with the life outside yourself. This growth beyond narcissism requires that you live with eyes and heart opened toward yourself and others. *If you ignore your own tender feelings or are disgusted by them, you'll overlook the ones you encounter in others.* Living an armored life, you'll be confined to the prison within your own skin. But as you gently embrace a full range of feelings within yourself, your heart is prepared to extend itself toward others' feelings and concerns.

For example, as you know the sorrow of losing a loved one, you can draw upon your experience of loss when you are with friends who are grieving. If you've tasted the pain of separation, your heart goes out to those facing similar anguish. Having been hurt by the loss of love, you know from the inside how this feels—some deep part of you resonates with their experience.

Empathy deepens intimacy with loved ones and creates connection with those you're dating. Sharing your disappointments and hurts from previous relationships (though not on the first date!) can build trust and understanding with someone mature enough to appreciate your openness. By midlife, people are more prone to appreciate expressions of realness.

Appropriate empathy doesn't compel you to "take on" people's pain and be stuck with it. As you develop a sense of boundaries and a capacity for self-soothing, you acquire the strength to be present without getting lost in others' emotions. You can find a rhythm of "touching in" with their pain and then returning to yourself—hopeful that your caring has made a difference.

Empathy helps you get close enough to others' experience to be touched by it. However, you'll never know exactly what it's like to be them. I've often seen clients who expect their partner to know *exactly* how they feel about everything, including all the ways they've been hurt by their partner.

By being without boundaries in your sorrow, such as when you've been hurt by a partner's behavior, you may continue punishing that partner—trying to get him or her to feel the hurt you feel. This subtle vengeance only adds fuel to the fire. You need to learn how to communicate your feelings appropriately.

Reconciliation is expedited when the person who hurt you takes responsibility for his or her actions. It may be unwise to trust again unless you can first trust that your partner "gets it"—that that person recognizes how he or she has injured you and understands what prompted that behavior.

However, there will always be some portion of your sorrow that only you will experience, and that you must be willing to embrace in your solitude—and perhaps resolve with a trusted therapist. You may then heal hurts so that you can reopen your heart to a current or future partner.

Let In Caring

Many people are adept at extending empathy but have difficulty *receiving* it. You may take care of others but neglect yourself. Perhaps you've sacrificed your own needs—or aren't sure what they are. Midlife is a time to realize that it takes strength to reach out for the love and contact you need; it's a time to find a balance between giving and receiving.

Sacred Gratitude

Midlife wisdom and humility means acknowledging your longing for love and connection, free of any pretensions that you've transcended human needs. If you ignore your whispering heart, it may get your attention through a load roar—perhaps through physical symptoms or even a heart attack.

As you overcome the shame of having needs and wants, you can express them clearly. For example, you might say, "I'd really like to cuddle with you tonight," instead of, "You never spend time with me!" The next challenge is to receive love when it comes your way.

Conventional ways of receiving gifts or compliments cut off a precious moment of vulnerability between giver and receiver. Sadly, you may not avail yourself of the joy, excitement, intimacy, or gentle tears that might flow if you surrendered control and opened to the simple pleasure of receiving.

Your heart's capacity to experience gratitude is a sacred gift and wonderful feeling. Thanking people for their generosity, thoughtfulness, or caring moves you beyond self-centered entitlement and toward an appreciation of life's blessings.

EXERCISE:

> Think about a person close to you. What do you appreciate about him or her? How has that person touched your heart or improved the quality of your life? Notice if you feel moved to send a card expressing your sentiments. Or you may want to express your appreciation when you meet or speak next. You may do this with as many people as you like.

It Is Harder to Receive Than to Give

By observing myself and others, I've concluded that most of us have more difficulty receiving than giving. When giving, we're "in control" in a certain way. Our actions are deliberate and willful. When receiving, *we must surrender control and open to the feelings that are awakened in us by the giver.* We may feel awkward, embarrassed, or even ashamed if we feel unworthy of the gift. We might divert our eyes or change the subject rather than open our arms—and our heart—to receiving.

Many of us have become so afraid or embarrassed to receive love that we're not emotionally available to allow it to seep into our bones. When old hurts, shame, and fear have contaminated our natural sensitivity and innocence, we have difficulty tolerating the direct experience of love and intimacy. We feel clumsy and uncomfortable, perhaps because we've had poor role models for learning how to enjoy tender contact. Or we may have been criticized for being selfish and impolite if we didn't immediately offer a syrupy, even if insincere, thanks. Midlife is a time to allow giving and receiving to flow equally.

By evaluating "giving" as morally superior to receiving, we overlook the fact that giving and receiving are two sides of the same coin of shared love. If everyone specialized in giving, then who'd be available to receive? Giving has more meaning when the receiver has the strength to be receptive. The art of receiving is itself a form of giving.

It's a precious gift to the giver to be visibly touched by the gift. Sensing the recipient's gratitude feels nourishing to the giver and bestows meaning to the gift-giving. If the recipient feels appreciative, then both the giver and the recipient may be transformed through this precious exchange.

It saddens me to see how we miss sweet moments of contact, where our hearts can touch each other in their splendid delicacy. During the deepest moments of intimacy and love—when two people are the most vulnerable and open—how can we distinguish giver from receiver? Each is giving in his or her own tender way.

AWARENESS EXERCISE:

- The next time someone compliments you, notice how you respond. Does your stomach tighten or breath constrict, or can you relax and receive the compliment? Do you thank them mechanically? Do you think "Thank you" in your head, or feel gratitude in your heart?

- When a friend offers a gift, do you insist, "You shouldn't have done it," or do you receive it graciously? How does it feel to receive it? Do you feel shy or vulnerable? Can you allow those feelings to be?

Blocks to Giving and Receiving

As much as you may value empathy and compassion, you cannot embody these qualities if you resist the flow of feelings within yourself. If you're not committed to self-awareness, you won't live at the level of depth necessary to respond to people with loving empathy. You won't know the flavor of their fear or the depth of their hurt. For example, you can't respond as compassionately to a friend's divorce if you haven't embraced your own fears and tears when facing loss or separation. If you don't know how to grieve and let go, you may even encourage a friend to attack a former partner. You might inject your own unresolved acrimony into his or her situation if you've never known the relief of softening into your underlying hurt.

If you internally collapse when confronted with painful feelings, you'll never develop the gentle strength to offer people who are hurting. Rather than offer deeply felt empathy, you may encourage people to bypass feelings by extending superficial reassurances such as, "Everything will be fine," or, "Don't let it get you down," or, "Don't worry, God loves you." If you could find words to respond to these well-intended but superficial remarks, you might say, "But I *do* feel down; is something wrong with me because of that?" Or, "I know God loves me. I want to feel that *you* love me! I need to feel a connection with my fellow humans." People want to be loved, not fixed.

Don't Avoid Feelings through Religion

Many religious leaders value compassion but aren't skilled at helping people develop it. Some authoritarian preachers even condemn people who embrace their feelings as being self-absorbed. Human emotions are often messy and don't lend themselves to the certainty demanded by those who crave control. Warmly welcoming your authentic feelings adds richness to relationships and creates a spirituality rooted in the depth of your heart rather than in the shallowness of your head.

Midlife is a time to realize that feelings such as hurt, fear, and embarrassment aren't your enemy. The real tragedy is when you neglect to establish a caring relationship with these feelings. Difficult feelings don't mean you're a failure, or that something is wrong with you, or that you're self-centered. What generates suffering and self-absorption is your:

- Aversion to your feelings (not being comfortable with them).
- False interpretation of your feelings (thinking that your feelings mean that something is wrong with you).
- Attempt to bypass feelings (trying to push them away).

As the saying goes, "What you resist will persist!"

You can't offer mature love and support when you haven't embraced your own deeper feelings. Instead, you'll aid and abet people to overpower their feelings with ideas, judgments, and other diversions, just as you do.

Loving empathy cannot be forced or faked; it is a by-product of your personal growth. When you're consistently present for yourself, it's a short step to "be there" for others. People can often sense when you're there for them—when your understanding is grounded in your own life experience. Caring and empathy are precious gems created in the sacred chamber of your own befriended feelings.

As you become friendly and loving toward your inner world, you become less fearful of life. Living with greater openness, freedom, and trust, you're more readily touched by others' pains, fears, and joys. Becoming a seasoned lover of life, you can enter your later years building a community of people who truly care about each other—where love and sensitivity replace the competitiveness and posturing of younger years. Even if you're not in a partnership, life becomes richer as you develop a loving friendship with yourself and others.

Self-Love or Self-Pity?

Many people wonder why they should welcome feelings that may be painful. I'm often asked, "Isn't that feeling sorry for yourself, isn't that wallowing, isn't that masochistic?" There's a vast difference between indulging in sorrow ("Woe is me") and gently embracing sorrow. It's the difference between unproductive sulking and warmly tending to yourself—sinking into self-pity versus loving yourself by soothing your sorrow.

Warmly embracing pain leads to a release of that pain. As the spiritual teacher Krishnamurti puts it, "If you begin to understand what you are without trying to change it, then what you are undergoes a transformation." Carl Rogers, a founder of Humanistic Psychology, makes the same point from a psychological perspective: "The curious paradox is that when I accept myself just as I am, then I can change."

As you become committed to embracing, or at least accepting, feelings that you normally resist, you demonstrate a mature commitment to loving relationships. This art of loving is not eagerly practiced today. Opening to authentic feelings is scary if the conditions of childhood required you to subdue yourself. But continuing to avoid feelings and squelch your soul requires a tiresome vigilance, a diverting of attention from the very place inside yourself where love is felt.

The art of befriending a full range of feelings leads to a quiet strength that provides a stable foundation for love and intimacy. As you trust yourself to deal with the spectrum of feelings that life brings, you release the tension that results from avoiding them. As one married man in his fifties put it, "I'm starting to trust that it's okay to let my feelings be as they are—instead of trying to change them into something else. When I'm easy with myself, it's easier to listen to my partner, instead of being defensive. It's easier to care and feel close."

As you become friendlier toward your feelings, it becomes apparent that loving yourself and loving others are inseparable. Buddha taught, "You can search throughout the entire universe for someone who is more deserving of your love and affection than you are yourself, and that person is not to be found anywhere. You yourself, as much as anybody in the entire universe, deserve your love and affection."

LOVING-KINDNESS EXERCISE: Allow ten minutes.

This meditation from the Buddhist tradition is intended to help you experience love, affection, and respect for yourself and others.

Sit comfortably with your eyes closed. Take a few moments to connect with yourself by allowing your attention to rest with your breath. Now take a few minutes to repeat the following phrases to yourself in a heartfelt way:

- May I be healthy and free of danger.
- May I be peaceful.
- May I be happy.

Just as you want these blessings for yourself, others want them also. As you are filled with love and good wishes for yourself, visualize a person you love and extend loving-kindness toward him or her. Repeat the following phrases from your heart.

- May (say his or her name) be healthy and free of danger.
- May ——— be peaceful.
- May ——— be happy.

Continue in this manner with as many people as you like. This meditation traditionally includes people with whom you are having difficulty. If you feel comfortable experimenting with this, visualize one such person and include him or her in the meditation.

If you like, you may end with the following affirmation:

- May all beings be free of suffering.
- May all beings be peaceful.
- May all beings be happy.

Feel free to design phrases that resonate with the wishes and longings of your own heart. This meditation is intended to purify and open your heart and expand your capacity to love.

Express Your Affection

The capacity to feel affection toward people is another facet of mature love. As you rest within your authentic heart, you're more available to touch and be touched. Love is not something you give, *it is something you are*. It's a nectar that oozes naturally from your depths as you become more open, compassionate, and discerning.

Focusing teachers Edwin McMahon and Peter Campbell describe affection as "a body-response of surrender, of letting go, of openness and vulnerability to being inwardly changed. . . . Our body-presence allows the other to bring tears to our eyes, caring to our touch, warmth to our embrace, gentleness to our voice, patience to our restless need always to be 'doing.' Through affection, we become more inclined to allow the object of affection simply to 'be.'"

When you experience affection, you feel warmly toward people; you allow them to be just as they are. Such warmth and acceptance flow from being open and accepting toward yourself and life. If your mind is busy finding fault or comparing yourself with others, you're far from beaming affection toward people.

By cultivating an attitude of gentleness toward yourself, you tend an inner flame that radiates the light of affectionate love. Feeling safer within yourself, you can loosen your boundaries beyond the exclusive love of "me against the world" to include all of humanity and the other creatures with whom you share this fragile planet.

Affection implies:

- Warmth in your heart.
- Gentleness in your eyes.
- Openness and receptivity to the other person.

See People as They Are

The authentic heart sees and appreciates people as they are, not as you want them to be. When love is your guiding light, your intention is to honor what is meaningful to others, not impose what *you* think should be important to them. Trust grows when people sense that their inner world is recognized and validated.

You can see others clearly to the degree that your perception is unclouded by your own needs and expectations. For example, if you want to make love, you may not recognize that he isn't in the mood. If you want validation, you may not see that she also needs to be appreciated. If you want to be liked, you may neglect to ask yourself, "Do I like him?" You may win a woman's heart, but more important, will you still want her once you have her?

According to psychologist Abraham Maslow, the degree to which you're motivated by your own deficiencies prevents you from seeing people "as wholes, as complicated, unique individuals, but rather from the point of view of usefulness. What in them is not related to the perceiver's needs is either overlooked altogether, or else bores, irritates, or threatens." It takes much growth and maturity to truly respond to the "other-ness of the other," as the philosophers of love put it.

A Native American saying advises: "Do not glimpse with the same eyes a person you have not seen for three days." Relinquishing rigid perceptions of people gives them a chance to change and grow. It's annoying to be told, "I know you!" Pinning our narrow definitions on people leaves them feeling trapped and shamed—and pushes them away. Seeing a person with fresh eyes, you may relish the delight of mutual presence—the joyful dance of two authentic hearts.

Glimpse People's Beauty

Past disappointments leave many people reluctant to let themselves be seen. Understanding how tender the human heart is, we can understand why people hold back. By knowing sorrow and disillusionment, we can exhibit more sensitivity toward others' unexpressed hurts and fears. As Plato reminds us, "Be kind, my friends, for everyone you meet is fighting a hard battle."

As you become more loving toward yourself and accepting of personal shortcomings, you can allow people to be themselves—without binding them with controlling perceptions. Seeing more clearly, you can appreciate people's beauty and preciousness. *The more you love people as they are, the more they're freed to become all they are.* The safer they feel to be themselves with you, the more they may show you the love and passion residing in their tender heart.

Maintain Mutuality

It is rewarding to love without expectations or payback, such as the way a parent loves a child. But mature relationships cannot thrive unless they're mutual; there must be a flow of giving and receiving. Midlife love implies a shared, respectful, two-way love.

Mutuality is necessary to maintain vitality and richness in relationships. Although you might believe you're unconditionally loving, your inner resources will dry up if you don't receive love and respect in return. If a partner is abusive or dependent on drugs or alcohol, it may not be realistic to expect yourself to be unconditionally loving and accepting. You need a grown-up partner who's your equal—and on a path where he or she can meet you.

Mutual love involves a nurturing give and take—a flow of affection, caring, and understanding that feels mutually satisfying. This involves a relatively even exchange of giving and receiving, but without keeping score. During any particular moment, one person may have more to offer. But if a mismatched capacity to love persists, there may develop an inequality that undermines the relationship.

Mutual love also breaks down if you're afraid of allowing yourself to need someone. This situation may lead to a "hostile dependency," characterized by a conflict between needing a person and the fear of losing yourself. Fearing fusion or being ashamed of needing anyone, you may bolt or sabotage the relationship. Or you may become resentful for having normal human needs.

Love implies mutual respect. You deeply value and honor each other and pay attention to the effects of your words and behavior. There's a balance between "me" and "you."

Embody Your Love

Authentic love cannot be reduced to a philosophical concept, a romantic ideal, or an ethical principle. Experiencing the richness of love means feeling it within your bodily depths.

Enjoying a bodily felt love doesn't refer to its sexual aspect, although sexual feelings are more compelling when they arise from love; indeed, love is the best aphrodisiac. The bodily felt component of love may be described by words such as warmth, delight, pleasure, lightness, joy, and ecstasy. When love is present, you are bodily alive in the moment.

When you experience a bodily felt love, you're not mentally preoccupied. You're not thinking, planning, judging, or performing, nor are you haunted by the shadow of an awkward self-consciousness. You enjoy a richness, fullness, and presence as your body is relaxed and receptive.

When love is mutually felt, there's a lovely openness between two people—the sharing of an aliveness that's part of the energy of life itself. Such rejuvenating love has the power to heal you. Within the refuge of this nurturing love, you feel safe to release subtle tensions and anxieties that stem from separateness.

Your muscles, tissues, and internal organs absorb emotional tension, whether from rejection, worldly demands, or dealings with difficult people. You may not be aware of how this stress accumulates in your body—until you suddenly relax. Experiencing another's love has the power to touch and comfort you in a deeply felt way.

Feeling loved and accepted, you may become aware of stored pain, shame, or loneliness inside you. This explains the mystery of why you may cry upon feeling loved. Newly connected with your heart, you may suddenly notice the pain of *not having been loved*, and the sadness of missing out on the beauty and delight of a deeply felt connection.

You may quickly apologize when you "break down" and show tears. You might say, "I'm sorry," or, "I lost it." In reality you didn't lose it. You found it! You found a precious part of yourself that you had split off and can now reintegrate into yourself. Suppressing this natural sorrow obstructs a love and joy longing to be born.

Have you ever found yourself wanting to separate shortly after experiencing love more deeply? The "unprocessed" pain of life comes up most acutely within a context of suddenly feeling loved, just as dark colors stand out in a light background. If you fail to comprehend what's happening, you might be scared by the intensity of your feelings and push your partner—and love—away.

It is most vital at this juncture to work skillfully with your feelings so that you can continue to stay open to both yourself and your partner. Rapid healing and growth can occur during this fertile time. Love has the power to heal you if you courageously open to its mystery and magic. This is also a time to practice self-soothing so that you don't misguidedly attack or alienate your partner, like a wild, wary cat scratching a person who is offering a handful of food.

Within the trusting environment of mutual love, you're on the verge of being transformed, but only if you can trust that it's safe to let in love. This situation presents a blessing and a threat. The blessing is that the rare elixir you've long awaited is close at hand. But you cannot fully receive this nourishment unless you trust the wisdom of your body.

Herein lies the conundrum. You can't let love into the "marrow of your bones" until you release the accumulated tensions, hurts, and fears that get in the way. When your cup is full of inadequacies, cynicism, or anger, you can't receive anything new.

Heal Pain through Feeling It

In order to release the "stuff" that obstructs the nourishing energy of love, you must be willing to feel some portion of the stored hurts brought suddenly to life by a newly found love. It is only when you allow yourself to feel this pain in a self-soothing way that it can finally begin to release. Psychiatrist Alexander Lowen explains it well:

> We cannot recover the capacity for joy without re-experiencing our sorrow. And we cannot feel pleasure without going through the pain of rebirth. And we are reborn again when we have the courage to face the pains of our lives without recourse to illusion. There is a dual aspect to pain. Although it is a danger signal and represents a threat to the integrity of the organism, it also represents the body's attempt to repair the effect of an injury and to restore the integrity of the organism. . . . If we are afraid of pain, we will be afraid of pleasure.

In order to open your heart to love, you need to cooperate with your body's attempt to release the pain that's reawakened in its presence. Gently embracing old heartache creates a healing pathway through which it can release. By refusing to face uncomfortable feelings, you react once again by closing down—constricting your breathing and subtly squeezing yourself more tightly in order to cut off pain and, as a sad consequence, the opportunity for love.

AWARENESS EXERCISE:

> Have you ever felt on the verge of tears when lovemaking or when with your partner? Did you allow yourself to cry or did you hold back? What was the outcome?
>
> If you're currently in a partnership, do you feel safe to show sadness when it comes up? If not, do you need something from your partner or something from yourself to feel safer?

Trust Your Heart's Wisdom

We need people who can relate to our pain with kindness and caring. One client, Amy, aged forty-six, began crying during a tender exchange of love. Her critical mind judged herself to be ridiculous for feeling this "inappropriate, unexplainable" emotion. Then she remembered the famous words of the philosopher Pascal, "The heart has reasons which reason knows nothing of." Realizing that her sorrow had its own wisdom, she allowed her tears to come.

Her partner, Jim, was familiar with the unpredictable ways of love. By being warm and caring toward Amy, he helped her release her pain through sobbing, which led to a new sense of lightness in her body and a deeper closeness with Jim. As she put it, "My tears were about not having felt loved this way before. I couldn't hold back the pain anymore. It was a risk to let it out, but we had built trust through our commitment to be real with each other." As she allowed herself to feel her sorrow and understand its meaning, it released even more. By emptying old pain, she received new love.

As you feel more relaxed and open in your body, you enjoy a greater depth of intimacy with people equally capable of relishing the energetic charge that is part of intimacy. Sexual attraction resulting from shared emotional intimacy is infinitely more fulfilling than pure physical attraction. As one man in his fifties knew, "In my twenties, I used to jump into bed on the first date. It was physically satisfying but emotionally empty. It's much richer to have sex after getting to know a person. I go slower now. I give love a chance to grow."

Our society often equates sexual arousal with sexual fantasies and images. Some sex therapists encourage this trend by teaching people to enact their fantasies as a primary way to overcome sexual dysfunction. This view overlooks the pivotal role of emotional intimacy in achieving sexual fulfillment.

Tend the Flame Within to Stay in Love

When you meet someone who awakens your heart, life opens up in a sparkling way. The source of love must then be tended to within yourself, lest you mistakenly look to the other as the source of your newfound aliveness. By nurturing a gentle presence toward yourself, you create conditions that support the gift of shared love. By culti-vating an internal state of love, you connect with people who are also cultivating this loving presence toward themselves.

Not realizing that the wisest way to maintain love is to nurture its source within, you may lean too heavily on your partner. You may even punish him or her in creative ways for not giving you what you feel entitled to. If your pressure succeeds, obligation replaces free-dom; the responsibility to be loving replaces the spontaneous delight in loving. Consequently, the free flow of love is inhibited. As the relationship becomes a chore for your partner, the seeds of separa-tion are sown.

Love might be preserved as you take responsibility to manage your own life apart from the relationship. The original joy of being in love is more likely to endure when you maintain an appropriate degree of autonomy—that is, when you create a satisfying life out-side of the relationship. Then, if your partner is temporarily unavail-able, you have other sources of nurturing, such as close friendships, creative art, or silent meditation.

As your partner feels less pressured and more accepted, he or she is freed to respond to you based upon love, not duty. As the story goes, if you free your horse and it's really yours, it'll return to you—as long as you keep the gate open.

Sustaining love requires becoming large enough to embrace whatever arises during the course of being together. Conflicts are opportunities to bring focus to areas within you needing further attention so that you might become more aware, more integrated, and more loving.

Be in Love with Life

You cannot expect to stay in love unless you are in love with life itself—delighting in what the French call joie de vivre (the joy of life). Loving yourself, loving others, and loving life become inseparably linked in the more mature stages of growth. The more you live, breathe, and experience your being "in love," the more your heart is available to touch and be touched.

The experience of loving comes more readily to people who know that love is not a commodity. It is a state of being. It's an orientation of openness and caring toward the world and other people.

Psychoanalyst Erich Fromm expresses clearly this multidimensional nature of love:

> Love is not primarily a relationship to a specific person; it is an *attitude*, an *orientation* of character which determines the relatedness of a person to the world as a whole, not toward one "object" of love. If a person loves only one other person and is indifferent to the rest of his fellow men, his love is not love but a symbiotic attachment, or an enlarged egotism. . . . If I truly love one person I love all persons, I love the world, I love life. If I can say to somebody else "I love you," I must be able to say, "I love in you everybody, I love through you the world, I love in you also myself."

Love is a state of being—a disposition of openness and caring toward people and nature. Love may explode into birth through a special connection with your beloved, but the deeper source is a mystery. Some call it God, a Higher Power, or any one of a thousand other names. I prefer to call it Life.

Love as a Way of Life

The skills that empower your journey into midlife love become more than mere skills. They become a way of being and a way of life. As you learn what it takes to love yourself, your partner, and your friends, you're cultivating an attitude and awareness that move you beyond your small circle. As you develop empathy and caring, your embodied love extends to the needs of all beings with whom you share the planet. As you learn to see your partner more clearly, how can you not simultaneously see and feel the needs of those who are homeless and those not getting the medical care they need? As Sam Keen envisions it in *To Love and Be Loved,*

> Once I begin to be moved by compassion, I will inevitably become concerned with the welfare of an ever widening circle of fellow-creatures. In this way love may give our lives an increasing richness of meaning . . . but it does not leave us content, satisfied, and secure. If we are not troubled by what is happening to our kindred on the mean streets of Nigeria, Nicaragua, and New York, it is only because we refuse to allow our compassion to expand beyond that range of our potency.

Although your journey toward love begins by wanting something for yourself, it inevitably leads beyond yourself. Since the nature of love is expansive, it cannot be corralled and tied down. It involves letting go, not holding on.

Love is the temptress that lures you through your longing into its abode. Then, instead of gratifying your craving for more and more, love, the divine trickster, awakens your realization that the love you seek exists within yourself. Love never fully satisfies; it transforms. You gradually discover that love isn't something you've been looking for; *love is a way of looking.*

The Church of Love

Rather than fulfill the young quest to expand the "I," love gives you eyes to expand your vision. Seeing more clearly, you realize you cannot be wholeheartedly happy as you behold those who are deprived and desperate. As you taste the delectable joy of what's possible, you're moved by love to extend yourself to ease others' burdens and discomfort. Serving others is a true joy. In Hinduism, karma yoga is a path of action that brings a person closer to God.

Instead of being driven to consume more for ourselves, we're inspired by a vision of spreading the love we know into the hearts of others. We're stirred to make some small contribution to fulfilling the deeper meaning of the word "Church," which is to bring people together into the larger cathedral of love. In a world where doctrines and dogma threaten to divide and destroy, love is the one uniting force that can dismantle our inner and outer armoring, bring us to our senses, and remind us that we have far more in common than we have differences.

A Deepening Sexuality

At one level marriage is about relationship, but at another it is the creation of a vessel in which soul-making can be accomplished.

—Thomas Moore

❧

Relationships of depth aren't necessarily sexual ones. Being sexual is only one aspect of being intimate. For some people in midlife, family life and nonsexual friendships are thoroughly satisfying, and a sexual partnership isn't a priority. Others are committed to learning more about themselves before dating again. Some have felt so wounded in sexual relationships or so violated by rape or abuse that they're taking a sabbatical from sexual love. Other people in midlife are refocusing on their careers or engaging in creative projects and are temporarily unavailable for a committed partnership. A sexual liaison isn't required for a meaningful life. But it can add depth and richness when circumstances are suitable.

Can romantic euphoria be explained by brain chemistry? Some scientists think so. As they explain it, when you meet someone you find desirable, an amphetamine-like neurotransmitter known as PEA (phenylethylamine), along with other neurotransmitters such as dopamine, bathe your brain in a "love cocktail." This leads to the feeling of being in love, which is deliciously compelling but which can also override good judgment and accurate perception.

The effects of this chemical feast appear to diminish after eighteen to thirty-six months, leaving you with the unsavory choice of either breaking up ("I guess it wasn't love after all!") or developing a mature partnership without supercharged chemical assistance. As Pat Love, author of *Hot Monogamy*, puts it, "All of us have experienced this downshift in desire—slowly but predictably, euphoria sneaks out the back door while reality, that perpetually unwelcome houseguest, makes its sullen appearance."

Whatever the ultimate outcome of research on love's chemistry, it's safe to assume that we'll still maintain a mind and free will; biology is not destiny. But by understanding that biological forces are yanking at us, we realize that instant attraction can be hazardous to our health. Midlife experience tells us that there's more to consider; for example, who is this person I'm inviting into my heart and bed? Rather than get lost in chemical nirvana while singing the praises of love, we can consult with our wisdom about what's best for us.

Personalize Sexual Love

The inner work of awakening your authentic heart prepares you for the delights of midlife lovemaking. As hormones subside over time, you're less driven by the biology of instinct and more animated by the psychology and spirituality of connection. As midlife wisdom opens your eyes and heart, you become responsive to the actual person before you. Instead of being a slave to hormones, you allow sex to become an expression of an ever-deepening personal love. Rather than drown in a chemical flood of impersonal passion, you swim vulnerably to the heart of the other person, where you delight in touching his or her essence.

One midlife man expressed the difference between sex based on blind passion versus mature love: "I was so driven by desire that I didn't see who she was. The sex was exciting, but I felt emotionally empty. I overlooked a lot. We didn't really talk. Our values and visions were totally different. I go more slowly now. I wait till there's a feeling of emotional intimacy and love before expressing it sexually. Then sex feels more whole and satisfying." As you create a climate for love and trust, sex becomes a coronation of your love—a celebration of the gift that life has given you.

Midlife lovemaking can be infinitely richer because you have more of yourself to offer and are more adept at the art of giving and receiving. The wounds that deepen your compassion, the sorrows that heighten your joy, the losses that enlarge your heart's capacity to love, the trials that strengthen you—all of this creates the groundwork for a rich midlife sexuality.

You need to *have* a self before you can offer it to another person. Developing a stronger, nonrigid sense of self affords you the luxury to merge in rapturous union with your beloved, knowing you can safely let go because you have a self to return to. Entering the sweet garden of mature lovemaking, you can leave your mind and self-consciousness behind and bask in the delectable pleasure of sensual surrender.

Many young people and those in early midlife hold the dreary assumption that aging means erotic dehydration. But the good news is that more people than you may realize are having great sex right through their sixties, seventies, and beyond! In a 1998 study by The National Council on the Aging, 48 percent of Americans sixty years and older are sexually active (defined as engaging in some form of sex at least monthly for the past year). Among respondents with sexual partners, 80 percent are sexually active. Half of all respondents over sixty said the emotional satisfaction of their sex lives is more or equal to what it was in their forties.

The reasons given for greater satisfaction include:

- A new marriage or partnership.
- Being more in touch with each other.
- No children to disturb them.
- More time to enjoy sex.
- Less stress.

Reasons given by the 26 percent of respondents who reported less emotional satisfaction included:

- Less physical desire.
- A medical condition that prevents them from having sex.

- Medications that reduce desire.
- Having a partner who has less desire due to a medical condition or other reasons.

Perhaps most encouraging of all, when sexually active people over sixty were asked about the emotional satisfaction of their sex life, 74 percent of men and 70 percent of women said they are as satisfied or more satisfied than they were in their forties.

The Biology of Attraction

I've seen many people entering their forties, fifties, and sixties who've given up having a rich sexual partnership. This is understandable. The rejections and betrayals of younger years, coupled with mind-numbing exposure to the profit-driven media hype that promotes the beauty of youth, can be discouraging. As you internalize the values and views of our culture, it's no wonder you'd want to throw in the towel. That's all the more reason to do your midlife homework of becoming more inner-directed rather than allowing your mood and manner to be outer-directed—shaped and swayed by the craziness around you.

The field of evolutionary psychology offers sobering clues about society's love affair with youth and beauty. Based on research from international studies on mate selection, David Buss, professor of psychology at the University of Michigan, concluded that men in particular "place a premium on physical appearance because of the abundance of reliable cues it provides to the reproductive potential of a potential mate." He goes on to suggest that physical features such as "full lips, clear skin, smooth skin, clear eyes, lustrous hair, and good muscle tone [reflect] physical cues to health and youth, and hence to reproductive capacity. . . . Men who failed to prefer qualities that signal high reproductive value . . . would have left fewer offspring, and their line would have died out."

In each of the thirty-seven societies studied, men prefer wives younger than themselves (2.5 years on average). This research suggests that men's attraction to younger women shouldn't automatically earn them a diagnosis of being immature or vain. There's an evolutionary origin to dating behavior that goes back millions of years. The wired-in biological drive to reproduce is a compelling explanation of the biological aspect of male motivation.

But wait. Although standards of beauty may not be arbitrary, but rather reflect reproductive appeal, those standards are massively exploited by the advertising industry and media. When these images get fanned throughout society, they lead to distorted perceptions, unnatural standards of attractiveness, and colossal efforts among women to embody the images they see. Buss explains that the one airbrushed photograph selected as the *Playboy* centerfold or magazine cover girl is the most appealing of hundreds or thousands of shots taken. And the chosen model is perhaps one of hundreds or thousands of applicants.

In short, women don't look this way in the real world! According to Buss, these images "exploit men's existing evolved standards of beauty and women's competitive mating mechanisms on an unprecedented and unhealthy scale." Women who buy into this hype and compare themselves to these images (which is easy to do!) are likely to feel shamed, inadequate, and depressed.

Evolutionary psychology is illuminating, even if it doesn't paint a pretty picture. But it's not the whole picture. The hopeful news is that we're not just biological beings enslaved to genetic programming. Human beings are complex creatures. Biology has a place, but so does human psychology and spirituality.

Transform Attraction

Existential and other philosophers believe that your tastes and attractions are loose-wired, not hard-wired. We are born with predispositions, but thanks to our free will, intelligence, and creativity they are not written in stone. As men mature, they can see the actual person before them, which can have a transforming effect on their attractions. Likewise, as women grow into their own economic and personal strength, they're no longer destined to pursue men who have economic resources and power, which is *their* loose-wired genetic programming—the female equivalent of men seeking younger women.

The sobering truth for both men and women is that as you approach sixty, you cannot compete in looks with a thirty-five-year-old model. But as your muscle tone declines and skin sags, your spirit doesn't have to droop as well. What you may lack in physicality you can more than make up for in your psychospiritual development.

If you feel compelled to compete with the exaggerated media images of beauty, you're lost. If you succumb to the belief that aging means you're no longer desirable, that conviction will shape how you feel. How you see yourself influences how you're perceived, thereby helping create the very reality you fear. A sagging spirit reduces the prospects for attracting a mate.

EXERCISE:

> The next time you look in the mirror after taking a shower, notice what you see. Do you notice your graying hair, balding head, wrinkles, sagging stomach, or other imperfections? Can you appreciate anything you like about your body?
>
> Now give your body some appreciation. This is the body that processes the food and fluids that keep you alive, gets you around, expresses your love, and is the temple of your soul. Recognize the growing maturity and wisdom represented by your wrinkles and other signs of aging. Give thanks to your body for all it does for you. If you feel inclined to do more for it, such as getting more exercise or eating differently, you're free to do so.

Affirm Inner Beauty

One challenge of midlife growth is knowing and affirming yourself apart from how others may try to define you. Setting an internal boundary with a society that worships external beauty enables you to maintain self-respect and integrity.

As you walk the path suggested in this book—accepting and loving yourself as you are—you can relax enough to realize that there's an abundance of beauty inside you. Although you have a body and must care for it, you are not your body. You're much more than your physical form. Every spiritual tradition acclaims your essential inner beauty. If you can recognize that there's a beauty in you that's soul-deep—discovering what Buddhists call your Buddha nature or what Christians call the Christ within or what Hindus call the Atman—

you will become radiantly attractive to others. What would your life look like if you really believed that your soul's beauty is relevant not only to inner peace but also to attracting and creating loving relationships?

Fulfilling sex isn't so much a function of having a hot body but of having a sizzling consciousness in that body. After many years of pursuing his own emotional and spiritual growth, a friend in his sixties described the exquisite connection he was experiencing with his partner, a woman in her late fifties. "I've never tasted anything so wonderful. The emotional honesty and risk taking leads to great sex. Her inner beauty radiates through her physical form and the voltage that comes from just touching her or looking into her eyes is like an adolescent voltage. I've never had such exhilarating sex before!" The emotional development of this couple allowed for a depth of connection rarely experienced by the young.

A woman in her mid-forties described the joy of her sexual connection with a man in his sixties. "The emotional contact is just outrageously exquisite. We have such a deep feeling of love and friendship. We can surrender to each other and joke around in a way that reflects our trust and intimacy. That kind of play and surrender isn't as easy with someone whose identity is still forming. It's easier to hit buttons in younger people because they're more self-conscious and insecure."

Another man who just reached fifty found himself sexually attracted to an older woman. "I never would have thought it possible. At first, I wasn't drawn to her physically at all. But as I'm getting to know her, I feel this wild attraction! When I express feelings she listens attentively and sensitively. I've shown her my vulnerable side and she doesn't pounce on me. And she knows she can talk to me and I won't react negatively. I can't stop thinking about her now!"

Attain Wise Innocence

Realizing that there are people out there who will be attracted to you can free you to relax and be yourself. You need not shame yourself by comparing yourself to others, although you can make reasonable efforts to look your best.

The more comfortable you are being yourself, the more you can meet people in a manner that is simultaneously wise and innocent. When the blessing of wise innocence informs your sexuality, you offer other people a healing and rejuvenating gift—a delicious benediction that awaits you for having done your midlife homework.

As two authentic hearts meet, a new kind of passion is born—an eroticism born of tender souls entwining. This mature intimacy may alternate between the hot passion of wild desire and the cool passion of a slowly building ecstatic communion, as in Tantric approaches to sex. These further reaches of your sexual potential are not a function of fancy techniques. They're a product of your personal growth— the afterglow of walking the path to love.

Personal Development Means Extraordinary Sex

David Schnarch, a sex therapist and author of *Passionate Marriage*, has good news for midlife lovers: "Aging is not the inevitable downward spiral you have learned to expect with dread. Many aspects of your feelings and thoughts can more than offset declining hormonal drive and reflexive responses. . . . The deeper and more meaningful the level of connection—and the more emotional energy you bring to your encounter—the greater the contribution to total stimulation."

The path to love and intimacy I've been describing can simultaneously lead to the best sex of your life! As you become less defensive and more relaxed, you're no longer fearful or ashamed to reveal yourself. You can open your eyes and heart when making love. When you allow yourself to see and be seen—opening the windows to your soul—the electric energy of connection can delight you in a manner unknown to the inexperienced.

Making love transports you to a new level of exquisitely tender contact when you're connecting with your partner heart to heart, being to being. No lovemaking techniques can substitute for the erotic charge that flows when lovers approach each other with engaging, receptive eyes, and the simple trust of being unguarded and vulnerable together. Dropping your facade and insincerity, you can allow your sexuality to transport you toward a blissful and nourishing communion of souls.

Through midlife growth, the excruciating longing to connect transforms into the satisfaction of actually connecting. Being together and returning to the refuge within yourself becomes a natural rhythm of life.

Come Home to Yourself

Extraordinary sex can become more ordinary in the fullness of time, as you create a sound foundation. As Schnarch knows, "Reaching your sexual potential doesn't occur until late in life because it takes time to work on the many elements that contribute to your total level of stimulation. It also takes a great deal of personal development."

Psychotherapists refer to the process of personal growth that leads to flourishing relationships as "differentiation." Carl Jung called it "individuation." Others call it "autonomy." These terms point to a journey of wholeness that involves knowing, being, and affirming your authentic self ever more fully. Coming home to yourself makes you attractive in a way that's more compelling than physical appearance.

The challenge of loving relationships is to differentiate yourself in ways that open your heart to connection. That's what the eight-fold path to midlife love—or love at any age—is all about. You can move toward people, and you can return to home base. You can be authentic, set boundaries when necessary, soothe yourself, and communicate in ways that support love and intimacy. You can connect deeply, but without losing yourself in the fusion of young love. Being less shame-bound, you can also laugh at yourself, accept your foibles, and find humor in life. These tasks of personal growth prepare you for an interpersonal union far richer than what you might attain through pure biological drive. Being grounded in yourself, you can surf on the connection you feel with your beloved, allowing it to guide you into the ever deeper mystery and miracle of being alive.

The Autonomy/Intimacy Dance

You thrive neither in isolation nor in fusion. Through the wisdom of midlife experience, you learn to balance autonomy with intimacy; in fact, autonomy and intimacy can't exist without each other. Sam Keen expresses well this dance between your solitude and togetherness: "You move from solitude toward another, lose yourself in ecstatic union, and swim back to the island of the self. . . . Love is solitary communion, being alone together. . . . To keep it alive, you must maintain boundaries."

Like the pulsating dance of protons and electrons, autonomy and intimacy need each other to work together smoothly. The famous remark of Rabbi Hillel encapsulated this autonomy/intimacy dance long before the field of psychology was born: "If I am not for myself, who will be for me? If I am only for myself, what am I?"

Deepen Your Experience of Love and Sexuality

1. The next time you're appreciated for giving a gift or doing someone a favor, notice how you feel when you hear that appreciation.

(Do you quickly reply, "It was nothing, no problem," or do you let in their gratitude? You may feel vulnerable when you let in people's appreciation, but if you can open yourself to it, you might enjoy a wonderful moment of contact.)

2. Are there ways you extend your love beyond your family?

(People with families often have limited time, but it can be fulfilling to extend your love toward a wider humanity. Giving love away is the best way to keep it. Having a larger vision of the purpose of a loving partnership can add meaning to your life.)

3. Are you able to extend empathy to people or do you find yourself quick to give advice and solutions?

(People usually need our nonjudgmental attention more than they need our advice. If this is difficult, experiment with simply listening to people. Hear their feelings and let them see that you care and understand.)

4. Do you ever feel more sexual after a heart-to-heart conversation with your partner? Do you understand how a mutual showing of vulnerability and sharing of authentic feelings can enhance the sexual charge and aliveness in a partnership?

(Sex is often more passionate and heartfelt as you *see* your partner's heart, that is, as you become present for his or her feelings, longings, and needs.)

5. Do you look into your partner's eyes when you're making love? Do you take time to feel present with each other?

(Notice how the quality of the connection might deepen as you allow your mind to become quiet and connect with the being who is before you.)

Toward a Mature Spirituality

To be enlightened is to be intimate with all things.
—Zen Master Dogen

❧

A s your understanding of love deepens, so does your appreciation of what it means to be spiritual. Residing deep within you lies an intelligence that draws you toward a larger sense of who you are—toward a greater presence to yourself, other people, and the natural environment of which you're part. You may be unaware of the quiet workings of this guiding force that invites you toward life.

For some people, long walks, gardening, camping, or art evoke deeper contact with something essential within themselves. Others discover their inner depths through some form of physical relaxation, such as yoga, tai chi, or massage. Lovemaking, communication, or meditation are also pathways to yourself.

The sense of being inwardly drawn toward something larger than your normal sense of self reflects a profound spiritual yearning. Like a plant irresistibly drawn toward light, a stirring within *you* calls you toward the center of your being, if not toward the center of Being itself. As you follow the path toward love, you may notice an inexplicable urge that invites you in some mysterious way into more direct and immediate contact with life.

Trust Your Experience

Although a sizable majority of us embrace the concept of God, many people's understanding of spirituality never develops beyond their grade school comprehension.

Within each of us lies a "holy discontent" that keeps us quietly groping for a greater sense of love, joy, peace, aliveness, compassion, and other qualities that we refer to as spiritual. As we bring greater awareness to our faint strivings for spiritual well-being, we can proceed on this journey with greater wisdom and precision during midlife.

The meaning of religion is often limited to ritualistic practices and supernatural beliefs far removed from what you can feel, sense, and comprehend for yourself. You're exhorted to "have faith" in religious texts, which often contain contradictory passages and swirl in controversy around which sections are authentic and which ones have been altered by scribes. Since it's impossible to really know, it's questionable to place your trust in beliefs that you can't verify through personal experience.

For example, one passage in the New Testament exhorts you to "Turn the other cheek," while another suggests, "Be angry, but do not sin," which implies that it's okay to stand up for yourself. It's vital to understand your own experience of anger so that you can make an intelligent decision about whether, when, and how to express anger. Interpreting religious texts with an eye to your experience in the twenty-first century makes spirituality more relevant.

If your religion teaches you to distrust your experience, it removes you from life; it disrupts the natural learning that leads to an internalized morality and spirituality. Also, to whatever extent the threat of punishment or dire consequences is instilled, religion promotes fear and shame, not love. In order to protect yourself from the pain of criticism, rejection, or isolation, you may create a spiritualized self-image. True spirituality incubates in a climate where you feel safe to be your true self. If you're busy trying to be someone you're not, you become numb to your heart's simple moment-to-moment experience of life. These feelings pressure you to supplant your authentic self with a fabricated, spiritualized self.

Become a Saint by Being Yourself

By perpetuating simplistic notions of life and love, religion often fuels the idealized strivings that hijack you from yourself, and thereby from an authentic path of love and spirituality. As Christian monk Thomas Merton observed, "For me to be a saint means to be myself. Therefore the problem of sanctity and salvation is the problem of finding out who I am and of discovering my true self."

A story from Zen Buddhism illustrates how spiritual enlightenment doesn't mean bypassing human emotions. We may deepen our joy, love, and wisdom, but feelings such as fear, sorrow, and anger do not disappear.

One day it was announced by Master Joshu that the young monk Kyogen had reached an enlightened state. Much impressed by this news, several of his peers went to speak with him. "We have heard that you are enlightened. Is this true?" his fellow students inquired. "It is," Kyogen answered. "Tell us," said a friend, "how do you feel?" "As miserable as ever," replied the enlightened Kyogen.

You harm yourself when your comprehension of spirituality doesn't mature, or when blind faith numbs you to your world of feelings. You may then deny yourself the very experiences you need to grow toward a mature, midlife spirituality. By trying to fit yourself into some snarled image of how a spiritual person is supposed to feel, think, and act, you move away from the inherent love and spirituality that flows from discovering your authentic heart.

The Spirituality of Feelings

Feelings are signals that are essential guides for your life. If you're numb to your universe of feelings, your personal development is arrested. You might even invite danger. Disconnected from fear, you might ignore early warning signs that are telling you to avoid a dangerous person. Disconnected from anger, you might cut off a source of vitality needed to set boundaries. If you're shameless, you might hurt others without having guilt to alert you to your hurtful behavior, such as the man who accused me of arousing his guilt for betraying women. If you regard sorrow and misfortune as weakness, as apparently did Ronald Reagan (according to his biographer, Edmund Morris), how can you develop compassion for the homeless or empathy for others' sorrows and losses?

"Who am I?" has been a fundamental question from Buddha (religion) to Socrates (philosophy) to Freud (psychology). Who you are isn't confined to your identity as a successful executive, a parent whose child excels in school, the clubs you join, or the cars you drive. Beyond these status symbols and images a deeper question lies: who are you really?

The answer, of course, lies beyond definition. But you can point toward a direction that spiritual traditions have variously called the Soul, the Higher Self, the God within, or the Ultimate Reality, and that psychospiritual teachings refer to as your essential nature, true nature, or true self. These terms bespeak a place inside you that is tender, sweet, compassionate, loving, and expansive. As you remove the veil of your fabricated self and all of its idealizations, you come directly in touch with something larger than your usual, confined sense of self.

Your authentic heart consists of various qualities of being, just as the color spectrum consists of different qualities of color. These various shadings of your true self include love, compassion, freedom, strength, intelligence, lightheartedness, aliveness, joy, fulfillment, curiosity, worth and value, and the capacity for intimacy. The more you heal your shame and become grounded in your true nature, the more these essential qualities blossom in a full and felt way. The more these soulful qualities develop and dovetail with one another, the more you become a whole, integrated, radiant being. The more the various facets of the diamond shine through the right kind of polishing, the more luminous you become. This vibrant, contactable being is who you really are, beyond limited identities driven by the shame of inadequacy, the fear of failure, and the hurt of rejection.

An atmosphere of love brings out the authentic heart. When children are valued, loved, and supported to follow their natural curiosity, they blossom. When being loved and accepted depends on their achievements or approved behaviors, children are pushed and prodded to fabricate a self that will be acceptable. Their hearts go into hiding.

Love provides a climate where you are supported to blossom into your fullness. Midlife love relationships hold the promise of helping you feel so accepted and loved that you're safe to experience and show the full range of who you are. The freedom to feel and reveal your genuine feelings, thoughts, and wants liberates you from the tyranny of internalized "shoulds" and rules that restrict your soul.

What Is Most Personal Becomes Transpersonal

The freedom to be yourself eases your way toward genuine spiritual development. Spiritual teacher A. H. Almaas describes it well: "You cannot make yourself grow; you can only cease to interfere. You cannot make yourself happy; you can only stop judgments. Growth and expansion are natural; they are the life force itself." The more you become attuned and connected to your true nature, the more you naturally grow toward the further reaches of your spiritual potential.

The paradox of personal and spiritual growth (or psychospiritual development) is that the more you become an individual, the more you feel your interconnectedness with others and with life. The more individuated you become—the more you disengage from internal and external critical voices in favor of trusting your authentic self—the larger your capacity for vibrant love and connection. What is most personal leads toward what is most transpersonal and spiritual. You evolve by embodying your humanity, not by transcending or bypassing it. As you discover and expand your authentic heart, the life energy of love naturally extends itself toward the life outside of you.

Let Your Feelings Be a Bridge to Your Soul

Beyond their guiding function, feelings are the raw material for developing essential qualities of your authentic heart. Since these aspects of your essential being are *qualities*, not *ideas*, they must mature through your felt experience of life. You don't get in touch with them by taking courses or reading books (though these can certainly help) but by butting heads with the world. Your experience of success and failure, joy and sorrow, breakdowns and breakthroughs means wrestling with a full range of human emotions.

For example, anger contains a power and potency that is the raw material for developing your sense of strength. This doesn't mean you act out anger. As you experience the strength contained in anger, you become an assertive, not aggressive, person. You use its energy to state limits or express outrage toward abuse, injustice, and unfairness.

You may also find strength by opening to vulnerable feelings you may label as negative, such as your weakness, emptiness, loneliness, or grief. By embracing authentic feelings that don't fit your idealized image of yourself, you dissolve blocks to accepting and loving yourself as you are. You can tap new inner resources by grappling with difficult feelings. For example, you may find true strength by experiencing the utter collapse of what you've defined as strength: tightening your gut, locking your jaw (keeping a stiff upper lip), and being vigilant.

The quality of your heart known as courage develops by wrestling with your fears. You don't become courageous by obliterating fear but by acting in the face of it. Being a heartful warrior means feeling your fear and riding your anxiety and adrenaline right into the heart of a necessary action!

Embracing sadness and hurt in a caring way helps you develop self-compassion, which provides a basis for feeling compassion toward others. The experience of guilt and shame can transform from neurotic self-denigration into a vibrant sense of conscience. As you become guided by an intrinsic conscience and conscientiousness, you can disengage from the critical, shaming voices inside and outside yourself.

Feelings don't happen randomly. They arise from a wider ground of being. They make sense even if you're not sure how. They contain a wisdom that calls for attention.

The notion of trusting the wisdom of your feelings may be foreign to you. And indeed, listening to your feelings is something akin to learning a foreign language. Connecting with your felt sense of different situations or people means noticing the more subtle sensations coursing through your body. Making space for such experience makes a good deal of sense, quite literally. For most of us, this more sensible approach to life means getting out of our heady analysis and learning to honor the wisdom inherent in our authentic, felt experience rather than the habitual voice of our thoughts and inner critic.

Trusting and honoring your feelings doesn't mean acting impulsively or never consulting with your thoughts and values. Rather, it means allowing a deeper source of intelligence and wisdom to unfold, which embodies an intrinsic set of values that all people of good faith hold dear, such as sincerity, kindness, and not harming people.

Feelings are a vital link to life, but clear thinking is also necessary. Understanding is a key to wisdom. The point is to *integrate* your thinking with the wisdom of your feelings and senses rather than force your experience to fit neatly into preconceived conclusions. As Zen master Suzuki Roshi reminds us, the "beginner's mind" allows many possibilities to open. If you become an "expert," you lose your sense of wonder and openness.

When your attempt to grow spiritually takes place from the outside in, it becomes mechanical religion. You're led to believe that the right rules, rituals, and beliefs will lead to the promised land. Midlife commitment is a time when spirituality can grow from the inside out, building on a base of self-awareness, self-embracing, and self-integration that informs how you relate to people and the world.

Viewed from the perspective of an embodied spirituality, many people who don't identify themselves as "spiritual" are actually more spiritual than self-proclaimed believers. The cruel behavior of many self-identified religious people betrays the fact that their spirituality is only skin-deep. In contrast, many people who don't consider themselves religious are kind, loving people. As the Dalai Lama explains, "religious belief is no guarantee of moral integrity. Looking at the history of our species, we see that among the major troublemakers— those who visited violence, brutality, and destruction on their fellow human beings—there have been many who professed religious faith, often loudly."

Spirituality isn't about your self-image; it's about the peace and love in your heart. As Thomas Merton knew, "As long as you have to defend the imaginary self that you think is important, you lose your peace of heart."

Unfortunately, the way religion is commonly taught affords few opportunities to pursue a psychologically sound approach to spirituality. Rather than guiding you toward the living spirit within you, authoritarian religions often promise "easy salvation" through dependence upon rigid beliefs and behaviors. These outer-directed approaches have taken many people on a long, barren journey away from their authentic heart. There are now Twelve-Step programs for people recovering from religious addiction. Religion, like any powerful drug, can sedate people from feeling pain and anxiety, which may explain why fundamentalism is especially rampant in countries where there is little hope of living a happy life.

Sterile Beliefs versus Lived Experience

Those having difficulty distinguishing bodily lived experience from beliefs make the mistake of substituting words for experience. People who are more comfortable with thinking than feeling are easily seduced by appealing ideologies. The anxiety that accompanies life's complexities is managed by following simplistic formulas for living.

For example, religious teachings commonly implore us to love and forgive. Most would agree: these are noble ideals. But how useful are these notions if you're not simultaneously taught how to love yourself so that love may naturally flow toward others? And how can you truly forgive without denying your real feelings?

Words such as "love" and "faith" mean different things to different people, based upon personal history. If "love" means being smothered and controlled, then loving others means violating their boundaries by imposing your viewpoints "for their own good." If "faith" means believing what people or books (including this book!) tell you without consulting your own experience, then it can create a society of followers who pledge allegiance to silver-tongued demagogues offering empty promises. If "loyalty" means remaining committed no matter what, then you lose your autonomy in favor of the collective. Authoritarian governments, such as Nazi Germany, thrive on insecure people who seek certainty, and therefore place their trust in some larger power to provide safety, meaning, and direction.

People become dangerous to themselves and others when they think they understand something when they really don't. Truly loving others is a far more complex task than the simple-sounding admonition to love makes it seem. You cannot do justice to love unless you can *feel* that love in your heart, which first means healing the hurts and fears that have been contaminating your heart. You cannot deeply touch another person unless you've communed with the tender depths of your own soul. You cannot embrace others until you've softly embraced your own hurts and fears. You cannot accept others' humanity until you've acknowledged your own foibles and forgiven yourself for personal shortcomings.

Approach Love as a Developmental Process

If you "try" to love prematurely, or if you hasten to view yourself as a loving person, you skip crucial steps—bypassing territory that needs patient exploration so that you may authentically love yourself and others. When love remains an ideal, you mouth the words, but you don't sing the song. You mimic behaviors that you think are loving, but you don't embody authentic love.

Authentic love arises when you're in touch with your inner feelings apart from your beliefs of who you think you are—or should be. By identifying with your ideas and ideals, you build a sheltered nest in a secluded corner of your mind. You're then far away from your lived experience. Life is more fluid and unpredictable than the ideas you can muster about it.

Whenever we point confidently to what we believe is true, life has a way of surprising us with exceptions to our rule. Every time we think that we understand something, life reminds us of the limits to our knowledge. As an old Sufi saying reminds us, "Whatever perspective you arrive at, there is always one beyond it."

Wisdom Begins with Ignorance

The wiser you become, the more you realize how much you don't know. The more you lay claim to certainty, the more you miss life's subtleties. Truth that arises from your quiet depths requires no defense. You can relax with the truth of your current felt experience while knowing that an ever deeper understanding awaits you.

When you have the wisdom to live with a healthy degree of insecurity, life's secrets open, petal by petal. As you empty yourself of the presumption of knowledge, life gradually reveals its truths. By being supple and flexible, you learn and grow. Brittle with presumed self-knowledge, you're headed for a midlife crisis or late-life predicament when reality turns out to be quite different from your well-ordered ideas about it, such as when you face divorce, disability, or some other loss.

The more you create a spiritualized self-image, the further removed you become from the experience of love and truth as described by the great spiritual teachers. The more you harden into haughtiness and self-righteousness, the more you distance yourself from the living truth. Reality is far more vast than what you think it is; there are always nuances you miss. Spiritual growth invites you to continually shatter the false idols created by the mind's anxious search for security and open to the life that exists beyond the known.

Adhering to comforting religious beliefs and rituals can provide a convenient escape from living your life, making your own mistakes, and discovering truth grounded in personal experience. The spiritual emptiness that is rampant today may be temporarily relieved by joining a religious fellowship that claims to have all the answers.

Those with tendencies toward unhealthy dependency are easy prey for self-assured though arrogant evangelists who exude an air of authority. Governor Jesse Ventura's crass comment that religion is for "weak-minded people" contains a kernel of truth: many religiously minded people don't think and feel for themselves. Their unmet need for acceptance and belonging make them targets for opportunistic religions. The smug certainty that manifests itself as intolerance toward others spreads shame and hurt, not love. Rather than nurture connection and community, these religious groups breed divisiveness.

Religion becomes dysfunctional and irrelevant when it degenerates into a simplistic set of beliefs far removed from the original inspiration that created them. Religions develop around leaders, such as Jesus or Buddha, who spread a message of love and enlightenment. They embody a radiant compassion and invite people to embrace love, peace, and joy.

Religious organizations were established to give form to this passionate vision of uncovering the love that lies within us. Many churches do a good job of bringing out the best in us. But sadly, participating in organized religion often deteriorates into yet another way to gain control over something whose very nature eludes control. Religions that offer simplistic formulas for "salvation" trivialize the complexity of life and miss what is required for genuine spiritual development. A spirituality of control smothers the spirit, which has

prompted many people to search for the living spirit outside of organized religion.

Sound Spirituality

Healthy spirituality involves resting in the palpable love and trust
that reflect your true nature. Mature love and trust grow through
repeated experiences of facing your authentic fears and hurts and
coming through the other side feeling stronger, wiser, and more
whole. Having faced life's little crucifixions in a bodily lived way, you
become more trusting that you will survive—and be "resurrected"
with an ever greater love, compassion, and awareness.

Love is a river that flows deeply within us. Beliefs are a shallow
stream destined to dry up in the eventual light of truth. Through
trust and faith, you learn to surrender to the ever-changing flow of
life, though not without periods of pain and trepidation.

Healthy spirituality recognizes a power, presence, or intelligence
in the universe greater than what our small minds can comprehend.
Yet the reality we call "God" is not something that exists outside of
ourselves. If there is any way to understand this awesome mystery it
is by understanding what it means to love and be loved. As St. John
tells us, "God is love."

The soulful qualities we need to move toward mature love are
the very ones that gently guide us toward a palpable spirituality—
one that brings us ever closer to ourselves, others, our environment,
and the quiet pulse of life itself. Just as we'll never fully understand
the nature of God, we can never fully grasp the depth and meaning
of love. Yet our lives remain empty and meaningless unless we align
our human passion with its true source—the eternal yearning to live,
move, and have our being in love.

The term "spiritual" derives from the Latin word *spiritus*, which
translates as "breath, courage, vigor, the soul, life." Such words refer
to something vital and alive in us, in contrast to the drier word "religion," which *Webster's Dictionary* defines as "any system of belief, worship, conduct, etc., often involving a code of ethics and a philosophy."

Being spiritual means being in touch with your inner life and
inner depths, as well as living and loving from these depths. A commitment to spiritual development means being committed to facing
the truth, discovering who you really are, and treating each person as

a precious human being worthy of love and respect. Spiritual growth brings you ever closer to the radiant splendor of your authentic heart, prompting you to treat all life with sensitivity and reverence.

Embrace Yourself

The journey toward midlife love leads to a spiritual way of life. As you discover a refuge within your heart, you find a source of strength and peace that simultaneously nourishes you and radiates toward others. As you become more gentle with yourself, you become kinder toward people and other creatures. As you accept your own limits, you're more tolerant of others' flaws and foibles. As you connect more with the fullness of who you are, you're less driven to fill an inner void by preying on people or accumulating possessions. As you perceive with eyes of love, you act more generously toward your neighbor. As you feel gratitude for who you are and what you have, you're more disposed to perceiving and responding to the needs of the larger human family and the natural environment.

You move in this direction not because you "should" (moral obligation), but because you want to. It's an effortless delight to love when you're at home with yourself. Since love is at the very core of who you are, being yourself and being loving are ultimately inseparable. Your loving presence becomes a natural expression of your connection with life. Like your breath and heartbeat, loving is the life pulse that flows through you.

As you cultivate a loving climate within yourself, you may begin to understand sacred teachings in a new, experiential light. For example, the concept of grace takes on fresh meaning when—through Focusing, meditation, or a reflective walk—a tight, painful place within you suddenly shifts, and you experience a quiet rush of aliveness and openness. It is not through a controlling act of will that such transformation occurs; it is by consistently and caringly embracing yourself that you may be "graced" with a resolution.

Similarly, loving your neighbor becomes a natural expression of living from your authentic heart. As you feel more connected with yourself, others, and life, you no longer need to protect yourself by insisting that you're right. You don't need to bolster your self-worth by blaming and shaming people—or proving your superiority. As you feel your inherent worth, you're less prone to compare yourself or feel envious. You can find delight in others' joy and success and wish them well without feeling threatened or inferior.

Spiritual virtues such as loving-kindness, fellowship, goodwill, tolerance, patience, and discernment develop as you pursue midlife growth. As you heal your hurts, befriend your feelings, and accept yourself as you are, you're less stingy with your love and affection. Through your commitment to the lifelong process of learning, deepening, and connecting, you become more spiritually alive and generously present.

Our Shared Reality

Beyond your ordinary sense of self lies a vast terrain of which you remain mostly unaware. Being preoccupied with survival and security keeps you functioning within a narrow band of possibilities. As you attend to these limited though important tasks, another self lies dormant, as if waiting for the weather to clear before coming out to play.

Environmental conditions hostile to the emergence of a tender, sturdy spirituality have endured throughout the centuries. Only during brief "golden ages" in history have conditions supported the flourishing of a deep inner life.

Political and economic conditions are rapidly changing throughout the world. The global trend toward democracy creates a climate of opportunity for people to pursue personal and spiritual development. It is now incumbent upon us to create conditions that facilitate the growth of secure, healthy human beings living in harmony with their communities and natural environment so that these democracies will teem with healthy, whole people who learn to love, not hate. The institution of democracy itself depends upon the personal growth of its citizens, so they will act responsibly, vote wisely, and grow in ways that prompt them to live ethically because they *want* to (the law of inner development), not because they *have* to (the law of the state).

Honor Our Interconnectedness

It is increasingly obvious how interdependent we are on the global level of economics, financial markets, and environmental health. Clearly, the well-being of one nation affects the welfare of all. What may not be as obvious is how interconnected we are on an emotional and psychological level.

As you become more loving with yourself, you become more awake to life; your eyes open. You become affected by the emotional waves emanating from people who are struggling and hurting in some way. How can you not see and feel people's pain when your heart is open? How can you not hear and respond to the silent cries of other living creatures whose lives and habitats are being destroyed by the relentless sprawl of humanity? How can you not live with sacred awe and wonder toward magnificent redwood groves and miraculous natural settings that took eons to form—but that developers would ravish in an instant? The more you shed defenses and allow yourself to be touched by life, the more vividly you experience how the world touches you and how you touch the world.

Those who believe they can corral happiness for themselves alone (or solely for their families) while remaining unresponsive to the larger community are living an illusion. As my bumper sticker says, "Everyone does better when everyone does better." Loving well and wisely means opening ourselves to the wide spectrum of life, which, as John Lennon put it, flows within us and without us.

Happiness will remain elusive if we pursue individual freedom alone. Deeper peace and fulfillment are the culmination of transforming our world—making it a healthier, safer, and better place to live and raise our families.

Serve Others and Create a Climate of Freedom

As the world becomes a friendlier place—as the pain and suffering around us subside through social and political evolution, cooperation, and psychological growth—we'll be less encumbered by the defensive need to numb ourselves to our collective pain. We can live with more freedom and openness—and less fear and guardedness—as others achieve economic security, physical health, and emotional and spiritual well-being. As our community members and global neighbors become healthier and happier, *our* potential for happiness and freedom grows.

My hope is that as we grow wiser, we'll mainly face the *natural pain* that accompanies life, such as natural disasters, sickness, loss, and growing pains, rather than be deluged by the additional torment we cause each other due to fear, greed, and ignorance, including the belief that we can meet our needs only by depriving others of theirs or by bending nature to our will. We may never create an ideal society, yet the strength of our collective vision born of midlife wisdom—one that embraces unity and diversity, individuality and community—can move us toward the more loving world that every child can envision.

On the subtle level of our interconnectedness, we participate in something much larger than our narrow sense of self. As we respond to people with warmth and caring, we create a climate where love can evolve. As people with midlife wisdom increasingly assume positions of power in society, we can create environments of trust, where people are free to grow into their radiant selves.

Growing in this spiritual direction doesn't happen through good intentions alone, but rather through the inner work that can especially flourish during the middle years. As Gandhi put it, you must *be* the change you want to see in others. This means finding a path— one that helps you become more whole and connected with yourself. It must be a path that makes sense to *you*. It might be the path of Focusing or meditation—or some spiritual practice or spiritually oriented psychotherapy. It could be psychological counseling with someone who's kind and insightful. Or, perhaps most effectively, it may be some sound blend of these practices. But it must be a path that connects you with the depth and breadth of your authentic heart.

Midlife is a time to fulfill the potential that is your birthright. It's a time to relish the pleasant rewards that come through courageously wrestling with the manifold dragons on the path toward becoming a whole person.

The eightfold path I've outlined is a comprehensive path toward love, connection, and joy. It is not the only path. There may be other paths and practices that will help you grow toward mature love. But any genuine path takes work, or better said, requires "right effort," as Buddha put it. By becoming passionate about developing yourself and understanding what it takes to love and be loved, you'll gradually embody the gift of love.

My hope is that you will practice these steps and invest in whatever support you need to keep you focused and motivated on this path toward yourself. Consider these steps "experiments in living," as Gandhi phrased it. See whether they move you toward a greater integrity, freedom, empowerment, and happiness. If not, make whatever adjustments you feel are necessary to move you forward. Trust your own experience and learn from it.

As you stay committed to a path that guides and supports you to live from your authentic heart, a new dimension of life and love opens. You find a source of strength that nourishes you and allows you to love more freely and deeply. You discover the beauty and bounty of who you really are and who others are. Your growing wisdom helps you understand yourself and others more fully and enables you to let go of futile attempts to understand and control everything.

May you become more and more comfortable with yourself and more present to the richness of life. May you enjoy gratifying, loving connections that touch your heart and nourish your soul.

References

Introduction

Hesse, Hermann. *Demian*. New York: Bantam Books, 1969.

Safransky, Sy. *Sunbeams: A Book of Quotations*. Berkeley: North Atlantic Books, 1990.

Sheehy, Gail. *New Passages*. New York: Random House, 1995.

———. *Understanding Men's Passages*. New York: Ballantine Books, 1998.

The First Step

Fields, Rick. *Chop Wood, Carry Water*. Los Angeles: J. P. Tarcher, 1985.

Hollis, James. *The Middle Passage*. Toronto: Inner City Books, 1993.

Hopkins, Andrea. *The Book of Courtly Love*. San Francisco: HarperCollins, 1994.

Keen, Sam. *To Love and Be Loved*. New York: Bantam Books, 1997.

May, R., E. Angel, and H. Ellenberger, eds. *Existence*. New York: Basic Books, 1958.

Moore, Thomas. *Soul Mates*. New York: HarperCollins, 1994.

Ortega y Gasset, José. *On Love*. New York: World Publishing Company, 1957.

The Oxford Dictionary of Quotations. New York: Oxford University Press, 1979.

Rilke, Rainer Maria. *Letters to a Young Poet*. Translated by M. D. Herter Norton. New York: W. W. Norton & Company, 1934, 1954, renewed 1962, 1982, by M. D. Herter Norton.

Safransky, Sy. *Sunbeams: A Book of Quotations*. Berkeley: North Atlantic Books, 1990.

The Second Step

Amodeo, John. *Love & Betrayal.* New York: Ballantine Books, 1994.

Barrett, William, ed. *Zen Buddhism: Selected Writing of D. T. Suzuki.* Garden City, N.Y.: Doubleday, 1956.

Bradshaw, John. *Healing the Shame That Binds You.* Deerfield Beach, Fla.: Health Communications, 1988.

Brill, Ronald. *Emotional Honesty & Self-Acceptance.* Philadelphia: Xlibris, 2000.

Brown, Byron. *Soul without Shame.* Boston: Shambhala, 1999.

Buber, Martin. *The Knowledge of Man.* New York: Harper & Row, 1965.

Faludi, Susan. *Stiffed.* New York: William Morrow & Company, 1999.

Kaufman, Gershen. *Shame.* Rochester, Vt.: Schenkman Books, 1985.

Kennedy, Eugene. *In the Spirit, in the Flesh.* Garden City, N.Y.: Doubleday, 1972.

Mason, Marilyn, and Merle Fossum. *Facing Shame.* New York: W. W. Norton & Company, 1986.

Miller, Alice. *The Drama of the Gifted Child.* New York: Basic Books, 1981.

Murphy Paul, Annie. "Born to Be Good?" *USA Weekend,* July 23–25, 1999.

Nicholson, William. *Shadowlands.* New York: Plume, 1991.

Ornish, Dean. *Love & Survival.* New York: HarperCollins, 1997.

Perls, Fritz. *In and Out the Garbage Pail.* New York: Bantam Books, 1972.

The Portable Blake. New York: Viking Press, 1968.

Sartre, J.-P. *Being and Nothingness.* New York: Philosophical Library, 1956.

Satir, Virginia. *Peoplemaking.* Palo Alto, Calif.: Science and Behavior Books, 1972.

Shah, Idries. *Caravan of Dreams.* Baltimore: Penguin Books, 1974.

Sullivan, Patrick. "Man Trouble: Author Susan Faludi Says American Men Are an Endangered Species." *The Sonoma County Independent,* October 7–13, 1999.

The Third Step

Richard Bach quoted in Borysenko, Joan. *Fire in the Soul.* New York: Warner Books, 1993.

Casteneda, Carlos. *Journey to Ixtlan.* New York: Washington Square Press, 1992.

Hendricks, Gay, and Kathlyn Hendricks. *Conscious Loving.* New York: Bantam Books, 1990.

Kingma, Daphne Rose. *Finding True Love.* Berkeley: Conari Press, 1996.

Kritsberg, Wayne, John Lee, and Shepherd Bliss, with foreword by Thomas Moore. *A Quiet Strength.* New York: Bantam Books, 1994.

Maslow, Abraham. *Toward a Psychology of Being*. New York: D. Van Nostrand Company, 1962.

Mitchell, Stephen. *Tao Te Ching*. New York: Harper & Row, 1988.

Ornish, Dean. *Love & Survival*. New York: HarperCollins, 1997.

Dr. James Pennebaker research quoted in Ornish, Dean. *Love and Survival*. New York: HarperCollins, 1997.

Paul, Jordan, and Margaret Paul. *Do I Have to Give Up Me to Be Loved By You?* Minneapolis: CompCare Publishers, 1983.

Rilke, Rainer Maria. *Letters to a Young Poet*. Translated by M. D. Herter Norton. New York: W. W. Norton & Company, 1934.

Safransky, Sy. *Sunbeams: A Book of Quotations*. Berkeley: North Atlantic Books, 1990.

Sheehy, Gail. *Understanding Men's Passages*. New York: Ballantine Books, 1998.

Sherven, Judith, and James Sniechowski. *The New Intimacy*. Deerfield Beach, Fla.: Health Communications, 1997.

UCLA study by Margaret Kemeny from Sheehy, Gail. *Understanding Men's Passages*. New York: Ballantine Books, 1998.

The Fourth Step

Amodeo, John. *Love & Betrayal*. New York: Ballantine Books, 1994.

Evans, Christine B. *Breaking Free of the Shame Trap*. New York: Ballantine Books, 1994.

Fossum, Merle, and Marilyn Mason. *Facing Shame*. New York: W. W. Norton & Company, 1986.

Gibran, Kahlil. *The Prophet*. New York: Alfred A. Knopf, 1972.

Hollis, James. *The Middle Passage*. Toronto: Inner City Books, 1993.

Human Touch studies quoted in Ornish, Dean. *Love and Survival*. New York: HarperCollins, 1997.

The New Testament. Translated by George M. Lamsa. Philadelphia: A. J. Holman Company, 1940.

Whitfield, C. *Boundaries and Relationships*. Deerfield Beach, Fla.: Health Communications, 1993.

The Fifth Step

Beck, Aaron. *Love Is Never Enough*. New York: Harper & Row, 1988.

Campbell, Peter, and Edwin McMahon. *Bio-Spirituality: Focusing as a Way to Grow*. Chicago: Loyola Press, 1985.

Chödrön, Pema. *When Things Fall Apart*. Boston: Shambhala, 1997.

Cornell, Ann Weiser. *The Power of Focusing*. Oakland: New Harbinger Publications, 1996.

Deikman, Arthur. "Experimental Meditation." *Journal of Nervous and Mental Disease* (1963), 136, 329–343.

Dreaver, Jim. *The Way of Harmony*. New York: Avon Books, 1999.

Gendlin, Eugene. *Focusing*. New York: Bantam Books, 1981.

Gibran, Kahlil. *The Prophet*. New York: Alfred A. Knopf, 1972.

Kaufman, Gershen. *Shame*. Rochester, Vt.: Schenkman Books, 1985.

Levine, Stephen, and Ondrea Levine. *Embracing the Beloved*. New York: Doubleday, 1995.

May, Rollo. *Man's Search for Himself*. New York: New American Library, 1967.

Rexroth, Kenneth. *Love and the Turning Year: One Hundred More Poems from the Chinese*. New York: New Directions, 1970.

Small, Jacquelyn. *Awakening in Time*. New York: Bantam Books, 1991.

Suzuki, Shunryu. *Zen Mind, Beginner's Mind*. New York: Weatherhill, 1973.

Walsh, Roger. "Meditation Research: An Introduction and Review." *Journal of Transpersonal Psychology* 2 (1979).

Whitfield, Charles. *Co-Dependence: Healing the Human Condition*. Deerfield Beach, Fla.: Health Communications, 1991.

Yeats, W. B. *Collected Poems*. New York: Macmillan Publishing, 1950.

The Sixth Step

Amodeo, John, and Kris Wentworth. *Being Intimate*. London: Penguin Books, 1986.

Buss, David M. *The Evolution of Desire*. New York: HarperCollins, 1994.

Garfield, C., C. Spring, and S. Cahill. *Wisdom Circles*. New York: Hyperion, 1998.

Gordon, Thomas. *Parent Effectiveness Training*. New York: New American Library, 1975.

Gottman, John. *Why Marriages Succeed or Fail*. New York: Fireside, 1994.

Gottman, John, and Nan Silver. *The Seven Principles for Making Marriage Work*. New York: Crown Publishers, 1999.

Hollis, James. *The Middle Passage*. Toronto: Inner City Books, 1993.

Kingma, Daphne Rose. *Finding True Love*. Berkeley: Conari Press, 1996.

Levine, Peter. *Waking the Tiger—Healing Trauma*. Berkeley: North Atlantic Books, 1997.

Remen, Rachel Naomi. *Kitchen Table Wisdom*. New York: Riverhead Books, 1996.

Rico, Gabriele. *Pain and Possibility*. Los Angeles: J. P. Tarcher, 1991.

Rogers, Carl. *Person to Person*. Lafayette, Calif.: Real People Press, 1967.

Safransky, Sy. *Sunbeams: A Book of Quotations*. Berkeley: North Atlantic Books, 1990.

Wile, Daniel. *After the Fight*. New York: John Wiley & Sons, 1988.

The Seventh Step

Amodeo, John. *Love & Betrayal*. New York: Ballantine Books, 1994.

Amodeo, John, and Kris Wentworth. *Being Intimate*. London: Penguin Books, 1986.

Brown, Byron. *Soul without Shame*. Boston: Shambhala, 1999.

Hollis, James. *The Middle Passage*. Toronto: Inner City Books, 1993.

Kaufmann, Walter, ed. *Goethe's Faust*. Garden City, N.Y.: Doubleday, 1961.

Kennedy, Eugene. *In the Spirit, in the Flesh*. Garden City, N.Y.: Doubleday, 1972.

Loggins, K., and J. Loggins. *The Unimaginable Life*. New York: Avon Books, 1997.

Rogers, Carl. *Becoming Partners*. New York: Dell Publishing Company, 1972.

Schnarch, David. *Passionate Marriage*. New York: Henry Holt and Company, 1997.

The Eighth Step

Buss, David M. *The Evolution of Desire*. New York: HarperCollins, 1994.

Campbell, Peter, and Edwin McMahon. *Bio-Spirituality: Focusing as a Way to Grow*. Chicago: Loyola Press, 1985.

Dalai Lama. *The Art of Happiness*. New York: Penguin Putnam, 1998.

Fromm, Erich. *The Art of Loving*. New York: Harper & Row, 1956.

Garrity, Carla, and Mitchell Baris. *Caught in the Middle: Protecting the Children of High Conflict Divorce*. New York: Jossey-Bass, 1997.

"Healthy Sexuality and Vital Aging." Executive Summary, a study by the National Council on the Aging. Survey conducted by Roper Starch Worldwide. Released September 1998.

Keen, Sam. *To Love and Be Loved*. New York: Bantam Books, 1997.

Krishnamurti, J. *Think on These Things*. New York: Harper & Row, 1970.

Love, Pat. "What Is This Thing Called Love?" *Family Therapy Networker* (March/April 1999).

Love, Patricia, and Jo Robinson. *Hot Monogamy*. New York: Plume, 1999.

Lowen, Alexander. *Pleasure*. New York: Penguin, 1970.

McMahon, Edwin, and Peter Campbell. "A Bio-Spiritual Approach to Spirituality: Healing a Spirituality of Control." Pamphlet series.

Moore, Thomas. *Soul Mates*. New York: HarperCollins, 1994.

Peck, M. Scott. *The Road Less Traveled.* New York: Simon and Schuster, 1978.

Rogers, Carl. *Person to Person.* Lafayette, Calif.: Real People Press, 1967.

Safransky, Sy. *Sunbeams: A Book of Quotations.* Berkeley: North Atlantic Books, 1990.

Salzberg, Sharon. *Lovingkindness.* Boston: Shambhala, 1995.

Schnarch, David. *Passionate Marriage.* New York: Henry Holt and Company, 1997.

Tarrant, John. *The Light inside the Dark.* New York: Harperperennial Library, 1999.

Thich Nhat Hanh. *Living Buddha, Living Christ.* New York: Riverhead Books, 1995.

Williamson, Marianne. *A Return to Love.* New York: HarperCollins, 1992.

Conclusion

Almass, A. H. *Diamond Heart Book Two.* Berkeley: Diamond Books, 1990.

Campbell, Peter, and Edwin McMahon. *Bio-Spirituality: Focusing as a Way to Grow.* Chicago: Loyola Press, 1985.

Dalai Lama. *Ethics for the New Millennium.* New York: Penguin Putnam, 1999.

Goleman, Daniel. *Working with Emotional Intelligence.* New York: Bantam Books, 1998.

Hyams, Joe. *Zen in the Martial Arts.* New York: Bantam Books, 1982.

Kornfield, Jack. *A Path with Heart.* New York: Bantam Books, 1993.

McMahon, Edwin M. *Beyond the Myth of Dominance.* Kansas City, Mo.: Sheed & Ward, 1993.

Merton, Thomas, ed. *Gandhi on Non-Violence.* New York: New Directions, 1964.

Suzuki, Shunryu. *Zen Mind, Beginner's Mind.* New York: Weatherhill, 1973.

Walsh, Roger. *Essential Spirituality.* New York: John Wiley & Sons, 1999.

A Guide to Resources

❦

The personal growth necessary to live from your authentic heart isn't easy to achieve alone. You may benefit from finding a counselor or therapist who can help guide you on the path toward authentic love. I may be able to provide a referral to someone in your area if you send an e-mail or a stamped, self-addressed envelope to me:

John Amodeo, Ph.D.
P.O. Box 564
Graton, California 95444
e-mail: midlifelove@aol.com
(707) 829-8948 or (415) 681-1030
web site: www.johnamodeo.com

The Association of Humanistic Psychology (AHP) has a web site that includes psychotherapists, many of whom may help you embody the principles in this book. I do not personally know these individuals, so please check them out for yourself and work with them only if you feel comfortable doing so.

AHP web site: www.ahpweb.org

Focusing and Spirituality

Institute for BioSpiritual Research
P.O. Box 741137
Arvada, CO 80006-1137
tel/fax (303) 427-5311
web site: www.biospiritual.org
(For information about Focusing workshops and materials based on the work of Peter Campbell and Edwin McMahon)

Focusing

The Focusing Institute
34 East Lane
Spring Valley, New York 10977
(914) 362-5222
web site: www. focusing.org
(Membership information, workshops, and publications)

Focusing Resources
2625 Alcatraz Avenue #202
Berkeley, CA 94705
(510) 666-9948
web site: www.focusingresources.com
(Newsletter and information about Focusing)

Meditation Retreats and Classes

Spirit Rock Meditation Center
P.O. Box 169
Woodacre, CA 94973
(415) 488-0164
web site: www. spiritrock.org
(For information on meditation retreats and classes held in California
and throughout the country. I suggest you begin with a class or weekend
course.)

Insight Meditation Society
Pleasant Street
Barre, MA 01005
(978) 355-4378
web site: www.dharma.org
(For information on retreats, retreat centers, and classes)

Further Resources

For my column on spiritual relationships, visit the web site of Fearless
Books: www.fearlessbooks.com (click on Heart & Soul icon)

Emotional Health Education
web site: www.emotionalhonesty.com

Center for Studies of the Person
web site: www.centerfortheperson.org
(619) 459-3861
(Client-centered psychotherapy resources, conflict transformation)

Recommended Audiotapes

John Amodeo, Ph.D.
P.O. Box 564
Graton, California 95444
web site: www.johnamodeo.com

Charlie and Linda Bloom
P.O. Box 2187
Sonoma, CA 95476
(707) 939-1139

John Bradshaw Cassettes
P.O. Box 980547
Houston, TX 77098
web site: www.bradshawcassettes.com

Index